RADIO-CONTROLLED
MODEL AIRCRAFT

RADIO-CONTROLLED MODEL AIRCRAFT

DAVID BODDINGTON

THE CROWOOD PRESS

First published in 2004 by
The Crowood Press Ltd
Ramsbury, Marlborough
Wiltshire SN8 2HR

www.crowood.com

British Library Cataloguing-in-Publication Data
A catalogue record for this book is available from the British Library.

ISBN 1 86126 679 0

Photo previous page: For many radio-controlled model aircraft enthusiasts building and flying a scale model of a full-size aeroplane is the pinnacle of their ambitions. This North American P-51 D 'Mustang' is an accurate replica of the World War II fighter and will reproduce the flying characteristics of its larger counterpart.

Typeset and designed by D & N Publishing, Hungerford, Berkshire.

Printed and bound in Singapore by Craft Print International.

Contents

CHAPTER 1

Past Glories and Future Triumphs

Welcome to your new hobby/pastime/sport of radio-controlled model aircraft. There are some who consider it to be a hobby, some a sport (in fact, it is officially recognized as a sport); indeed, if I were to be pedantic I would probably consider the building aspects as a hobby and the more energetic outdoor activities as a sport. However, such debate is immaterial – it is all about involvement, satisfaction and enjoyment.

Nor is it a new activity – there have been electronically guided model aircraft for close on a century, the earliest examples being hydrogen-filled model airships that were flown as a music hall act around theatre auditoriums using a basic form of spark-emitted radio signal. During World War I the first radio-controlled

OPPOSITE PAGE:
Model aeroplane displays and exhibitions are held throughout the country; see the modelling magazines for details.

target aircraft were introduced, although they were far from reliable and were probably a greater danger to the operators than useful as targets for the guns. The Americans made greater strides in producing practical remote-piloted vehicles in the interwar period, and it was not until the 1930s that the British came up with the Queen Bee, a modified de Havilland Tiger Moth, and similar target aircraft. However, the radio systems on these were still very basic and unreliable, especially should it come to the aircraft having survived target practice and needing to be landed.

During World War II the German air force developed radio-controlled flying bombs in the form of gliders packed with explosives, which were controlled from the air by an operator in a twin-engined, manned bomber. This was a fairly basic form of control, but had some limited success.

However, great leaps forward have been made since those early days, and modern armies and air forces make

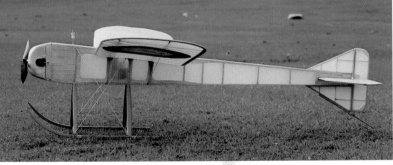

This model depicts the Aerial Projectile, designed in 1917 to carry an explosive charge and operated by a wireless-control mechanism.

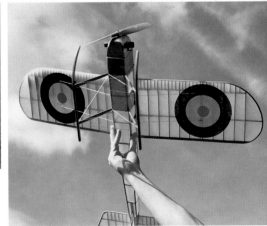

full use of remote-controlled flying vehicles for both surveillance purposes and attack with explosive warheads – not to mention biological and chemical warfare! While this may make for grim reading, there is a spin-off for modelling activities. The development of transistors, electronic chips, rechargeable batteries, and miniature and subminiature actuators and receivers has largely been possible through research and development in the military field. With ever increasing miniaturization being one of the aims of the military technicians, modellers will continue to benefit from their extensive and expensive development work.

Radio control in practical model aircraft terms can be traced back to America where, in the late 1930s, Walt Good and his brother successfully flew a series of models in which control was positive, rather than the occasional guidance of a free-flight model. Standards of control and the commercial availability of equipment continued to improve in the USA during World War II, but it was not until the post-war period that radio-control equipment became available in the UK. Gradually, commercial radio-control outfits came on to the market, where the purchaser had less to do to make the equipment ready to install in the model. There were many enthusiasts prepared to make their own radio gear, although many of these attempts were doomed to failure. Indeed, when watching these individuals, with their heavy ground-based transmitters and 'pear' switch for operating the rudder, it was difficult to know whether the cavortings of the model were due to a radio command, or simply the natural manoeuvres of the model.

From these early beginnings, radio-control equipment advanced and the 1960s brought forth transistorized systems of much lower weight. However, for the majority of modellers the single-channel, rudder-control only system was all that could be afforded, possibly with the refinement of an additional two-position engine throttle control. These controls were either fully on or off and non-proportional. The same applied to the more sophisticated multi-channel equipment, which, by incorporating a reed bank in the receiver, could operate up to twelve functions. This would give up elevator, down elevator, right aileron, left aileron, right rudder, left rudder, fully open throttle to low throttle and two channels for a trim control on one of the functions, or for undercarriage retracts and flaps. As stated, these were not proportional controls and the only way of achieving an intermediary control function was by blipping the transmitter switch, which was biased towards a central position.

ABOVE: Full-size Tiger Moth aircraft were converted to be radio-controlled and used for gunnery target practice.

American Walt Good and his brother were among the first to achieve successful radio-controlled model flying; this is his Rudder Bug design.

Before transistors, the receivers and transmitters used miniature valves and the escapements were rubber-driven. This is a 'hoax' system fitted to an electric-powered Super Sixty.

In spite of the on/off form of actuation the degree of control of the models was surprising. For instance, with a rudder-only control model it was possible to loop the model, by putting it into a spiral dive to build up speed and then centralizing the rudder so that the excess speed was converted into lift and the model would climb and go over the top into a loop. Similarly, a roll could be performed by commencing a loop and then, when the nose of the model was above the horizon, signal a rudder control. For the multi-channel fliers it was feasible to perform most types of aerobatics, even allowing for the fact that only two channels could be operated simultaneously. Although this was an electronic limitation, it was also a fact that the operator only had two thumbs to spare. Watching a master of reed equipment operating a transmitter during a full aerobatics schedule was a sight to behold. The thumbs would be dancing from one switch to the next, sometimes holding a full signal, but most of the time pulsing away to give an intermediate control-surface setting.

With the advent in the 1960s of proportional control, where the control surface moves in direct relation to the movement of the transmitter stick, radio-controlled flying became a much more civilized affair. Initially, it was very expensive, in real terms costing a couple of thousand pounds by today's values, but it gradually reduced in price as mass production, from

The Astro Hog was a very successful early multi-control aerobatic design, flown in its original form with non-proportional radio control.

Electric-powered airships are strictly for indoor exhibition flying – the normal wind conditions would be excessive for outdoor work.

the USA and Japan, took over. By modern standards the outfits were still very basic, having mostly only four functions (elevator, ailerons, rudder and engine throttle) and no servo reversing, but they were a great improvement on anything that had gone before.

Now, as we shall see, radio-control equipment is becoming ever more sophisticated and increasingly computerized. One of my colleagues realized that, given certain weather parameters, he could record a flight program, insert the tape in his computer transmitter then stand back and watch the model fly automatically through the pre-recorded program. He looked slightly hurt when I pointed out that the whole point of having radio control in the first place was so that *we* could control the model and make it follow the directions and manoeuvres that we were commanding!

IT TAKES MORE THAN TWO TO TANGO

To achieve successful radio-controlled flight you need three elements – the model, the radio-control equipment and the operator. With today's manufacturing standards we can be pretty sure of the first two elements, but what of the operator? Controlling a model in flight requires the operator to have reasonable eyesight, reasonable hand and eye co-ordination and a modicum of common sense. The younger generation often have the first two skills in abundance, but sometimes lack the last. More mature persons may not have the 20/20 vision they had in their youth and their reactions may have slowed a little, but this does not mean that they will be unable to learn to fly a model aeroplane; they may just have to work harder at it to conquer their limitations and achieve their goals. Give me a lad of twelve to sixteen years of age and I will be able to teach him to reach the solo stage of flying in a few weeks. For someone well past their flush of youth it is likely to take longer, but when success finally comes, it will be all the sweeter.

Video games have helped to develop hand and eye co-ordination, which is a vital skill when operating radio-control transmitters. However, it is often noticeable when a young video-game fanatic takes the transmitter that the control sticks tend to be pulsed, rather than moved smoothly and proportionally. Better as a training aid to learning to fly are the simulators for flying aircraft, in particular those dedicated specifically

to model aircraft. We will look into the value of these as a training aid later in the book.

But returning for a moment to hand/eye, or rather eye/brain/hand, co-ordination and the undeniable fact that this slows with the onset of age. What can be done for the mature potential radio-control flyer to enable him to compensate for deteriorating faculties? Sight is the main thing and it is vital for the mature flyer to get his sight checked and ensure that he is wearing glasses to the correct specification. It is amazing how many people try to fly – and drive a car – with defective eyesight and incorrect glasses, or even none at all. Even with the right glasses eyesight will be poorer with age, but this can be compensated for by having larger and more brightly coloured models. And slower reactions can be compensated for by not only having larger models but also by flying slower aeroplanes, which will allow

There are virtually no limits to the types of full-size aircraft that can be replicated as radio-controlled models. This is the famous 'Dambusters' Lancaster.

Helicopters are very popular, particularly with young aeromodellers. They are not the easiest of models to fly, but very rewarding.

We don't get anywhere near enough lady flyers in the hobby and yet there is no reason why they should not be every bit as good – or better – than men.

reason why women should not be as good in all aspects of aeromodelling, and probably better in some. Over the years I have tried to encourage more female participation, with a singular lack of success, though I remain hopeful that we can turn around this deplorable situation. One factor that would certainly help would be to have more family-friendly sites where the basic amenities are available. At present, only a handful of flying sites in the UK can boast any form of facilities. Fortunately, the USA, Australia, South Africa and many European countries are way ahead of Britain and, as a result, have enjoyable social gatherings.

Before we leave the ladies, just remember that even if they do not actually participate in the activities, we would not be able to continue our interests without their help and understanding. It can be a demanding and all-embracing interest, and we owe it to our families to keep both our activities and spending in proportion.

Aeromodelling combines many skills. If you build your models, you need to be a woodworker, a metalworker, a decorator with artistic skills, a little bit of an electronics buff (although not too much) and you have to understand internal combustion (IC) engines or their electric equivalents. Most of the modelling is done on a singular basis, in the comfort of your own

a little more time to make any corrective actions. This does not mean that the older modeller cannot fly a scale model of a four-engined Lancaster, or even a fast pylon racer; it does mean, however, that he will need to have had plenty of experience at flying radio-controlled model aeroplanes to make up for the other limitations. One of the most difficult subjects to master is the model helicopter. For this, the co-ordination on both of the transmitter sticks has to be first rate – someone once described flying a helicopter as being like balancing a pole on each hand, but with your arms crossed. Helicopter designs have improved over the years and the introduction of gyros and other computer transmitter aids have made life very much easier, but, even so, if you see an elderly person flying a helicopter with verve and a *joie de vivre*, the chances are that they have been flying their machines for quite a long time.

Without wishing to be sexist in any way, I will probably be referring to aeromodellers as 'he'; it is not because I have anything against the ladies, far from it, but the fact remains that the vast majority of active aeromodellers are men. This may be a sad reflection on the male-chauvinist attitude to our hobby, for there is no

Radio-control modelling and flying involves many skills and interests. It is partly solitary and partly a sociable group activity. It is suitable for all ages.

home, but this is followed by the social side where you meet fellow enthusiasts to fly your models. The choice of models is enormous – there are fixed-wing power models of trainer, sports, scale and racing types. You can have monoplanes, biplanes, triplanes, floatplanes, flying boats, ski-planes. There are gliders, of many and various types, autogyros and helicopters. Big ones, small ones, outdoor and indoor, I could go on, but I'm sure that you have got the idea by now. I'm hooked and have been for the past fifty years – I hope you will be, too.

If you decide to join our happy band I wish you every success and all the luck in the world. Ignore any facetious comments about 'Boys playing with toys'; such utterances will only come from ignoramuses who do nothing in their lives. Also, if you are told that flying model aeroplanes is simply a substitute for flying 'real' aircraft, tell them that there are many who fly both types and hold them in equal regard. I know of one famous aviator who refused to fly a full-sized Spitfire on a second occasion, simply so that he could get to fly his model aeroplane with some friends.

Record speed model, jet powered at 254mph. Richard Noble, left, was very impressed.

BELOW: *Sheer beauty. This near half-scale Bristol Bulldog is powered by a 450cc twin-cylinder engine and is magnificent in the air, a real crowd pleaser.*

CHAPTER 2

In the Beginning

Knowing where to start with a new hobby is always one of the most difficult decisions. It is all so interesting and exciting, there are so many possibilities and alternatives, and how do you know whether you will actually enjoy the hobby? There is no certain way to go, but common sense and a little advice should point you in the right direction. The first indications of

Everybody's favourite, the Supermarine Spitfire – this is the less well-known two-seat version. For RC enthusiasts the Spitfire is not a good first model.

what there is to offer with radio-controlled aeroplanes may come from a distributor's catalogue. These publications, often containing 200 or more pages, may only serve to confuse and unless they are also a guide, with articles specifically written for the beginner, they will consist of a pictorial list of highly desirable products of a bewildering variety. For instance, with radio-control equipment varying in prices from £40 to £1,000, how do you know which equipment to purchase? Hopefully, in the next few chapters, we will be able to lead you through the first faltering steps and on to a successful and rewarding time in the sport of radio-controlled model aircraft.

Early jet aircraft, such as the Gloster Meteor, are particularly suitable subjects for our first generation of model gas turbine engine, although ducted fan propulsion is also suitable.

TO BUY OR TO BUILD

At one time, if you wanted to learn to fly a radio-controlled (RC) model aeroplane, you had no option but to build the model yourself, learn to cover it, install the radio equipment and fit the engine. You would then either find some fellow aeromodellers to help you learn to fly it, or, usually with disastrous results, attempt to fly it on your own. Those days have long gone and now you have a wider choice to becoming proficient at flying a radio-controlled model. ARF or ARTF (almost ready to fly) model kits abound and most of them are constructed to good standards, probably better than your first efforts would be in building a model from a conventional kit, or from a plan. You may, if you talk to an experienced 'old-time' modeller, hear him say that this is not the way of true aeromodelling, and that building the model yourself is the only 'proper' way. However, this is rather a blinkered and negative viewpoint, and you should choose the way that suits you best.

Whether you opt for the ARTF approach, or the more traditional route, will depend on a number of factors. How much leisure time do you have? For a working man, or woman, time may be at a premium, with many other leisure pursuits and family commitments to take into consideration. If it comes down to a choice of being able to fly by following the quick, ARTF, route, or not flying because of not having time to build a traditional model, there is no argument,

you take to the air with an ARTF. Perhaps, though, you are retired and have more spare time at your disposal, or perhaps you are the sort of person who has always enjoyed making things and using tools. For such a person the actual building of the model may give as much pleasure, sometimes even more, than the flying. If you are in this position, then building the model yourself will be your route. There will be plenty of advice in this book to help you to get started.

However, before deciding to start building from scratch there are a few other factors to take into consideration. Do you have the availability of a workshop? If you are going to be working on the kitchen table you might be well advised to go for the ARTF route, as it takes less time and requires fewer tools. There are few things more frustrating than being halfway through the construction of a wing and being told that you must move 'your toy' because the dinner has got to be prepared. But if your work area is in the garage, will it be warm enough out there during the winter? Winter time is when most people want to do their building, with the remainder of the year generally being earmarked for flying and repairing. For the practical person, who likes to use his hands for making things, there are few greater rewards than building his own model and then seeing it in the air, under his own control.

Most of us have preconceived ideas of what we want to achieve with a hobby or pastime. For budding aeromodellers it often involves the flying of a Spitfire or a fast jet. These are worthy aims, but it is not where we start. For attaining success in our ultimate aims we must start at a more prosaic level, that is, with a simple basic trainer model. This may seem to be a little mundane, but I can assure you that the successful flying of a trainer, and in particular the first solo, will put you on a high that will stay with you for many a year. Successful flying with a trainer is your open sesame to the fascinating world of radio-controlled model aircraft of all types; failure, through trying to run before you can walk, will certainly bring disillusionment.

FIRST – JOIN A CLUB

Before going on to describe the selection of models available I will make a plea, which will oft be repeated, to locate your nearest model club, and (so long as there is one) join it and take all the assistance its members can offer. In these early stages some sage words of advice and practical help may make all the difference between success and failure. I had to learn the hard way, as there were no experienced radio-control modellers around when I started fifty years ago, but this is not a method that I

would advocate, nor does it have any special merit. Why do something the hard way when there is an easy way – and that is by accepting help where it is available. Being a member of a club also has the benefit that valuable help with the safety aspects of the sport will be given.

PLAN YOUR FUTURE

Irrespective of how much money you may have to spend, the fact remains that there is no 'perfect' trainer that will suit all persons in all situations. For instance, you may have a local model flying club which, because of the noise constraints of the internal combustion engine, especially two-strokes, is only allowed to fly gliders and electric powered models – it would be rather pointless recommending a 1,525mm (60in) wingspan '40' (0.40cu in engine) trainer for that situation. To purchase your first trainer and associated equipment is therefore very much a 'horses for courses' deal. You should first ask yourself a few questions and the answers, honest answers, should lead you in the right direction. So let's take a look at some of the factors you should be considering.

Radio-controlled model aeroplanes are now able to perform a greater variety of aerobatic manouevres than their full-size counterparts. This model is specifically designed for advanced '3-D' manouevres.

AGE AND ABILITY

Newcomers may be in awe as they watch experienced aeromodellers flying models at a public display. They may be flying large multi-engined scale models, highly aerobatic types, speed models, jets or helicopters. It all seems highly skilled and beyond the limitations of the viewer. In truth, over 90 per cent of people who take up RC model aircraft flying are capable of becoming sufficiently proficient to fly a model solo. That does not mean that all will become 'Aces', able to fly all models and perform a complex routine of aerobatic manoeuvres, but they will at least be able to pilot a sports-style model safely around the sky and bring it into a landing where nothing is broken. How long will it take you to learn to become a proficient RC model flyer? This will depend on many factors, such as how old you are, what sort of aptitude you have, how often you can go to training sessions if there are any available and how keen you are to learn to fly. Assuming that you are sound in mind, limb and eye, your co-ordination is reasonable, then there is no reason why learning to fly should not, with a little patience and perseverance, be possible. What is true is that a sixteen-year-old whizz-kid at computer games with 20/20 vision will learn a whole lot faster than someone of sixty, with slightly fading eyesight, hearing and reactions. For the latter, it is necessary to choose wisely, not to expect too rapid progress and to have patience – everything comes to he who waits!

The 'ideal' trainer for the senior figure is probably something that is a little slower and also larger than the average model. There have been many arguments in the past as to whether a trainer model should be controlled by three functions (rudder, elevator and throttle control) or four (the addition of ailerons, the movable control surface on the wing that controls roll); it is an argument that continues still. For the less young I would recommend the three-channel approach and a model of at least 1,525mm (60in) wingspan. Some of the Ben Buckle Vintage/Trainers kits, such as the Red Zephyr (1,830mm/72in wingspan) and Majestic Major (2,235mm/88in wingspan) will give much pleasure in the traditional methods of building; they also fly quite sedately, although they require reasonably calm weather conditions. There are other, smaller designs, such as the Junior '60' (made by Flair) and Super '60' which will be almost as suitable.

A perennial favourite, the Keil Kraft Junior '60' was designed for free flight, but has been adapted for radio control and still makes a good trainer for mature students.

Vintage radio control has a strong following, although mostly by modellers who remember the designs from the first time around. Climb and duration contests are regularly held.

FLYING AIDS

There are two flying aids that may help towards learning to fly. These are the simulator and the HAL 2100 Autopilot. Simulators, used in conjunction with a personal computer, are a good way of getting used to flight attitudes, the operation of the transmitter controls and the general feel of flying an RC model. Of course, this is not a substitute for flying an actual model, as things happen differently in the real world outside, but it can save you a lot of time on the field by just getting used to the basics of control, orientation, stick movements and so on. Crashing is certainly a heck of a lot cheaper on the simulator, too. More on this subject later.

When the HAL Autopilot was first introduced it caused quite a lot of controversy. HAL stands for horizontal automatic levelling system and is an electronic device for bringing the model back to straight and level flight when the transmitter controls are returned to neutral, that is, the hands are taken off the control sticks. There is no doubt that the system works efficiently. I have tried it and found it fascinating, though it sometimes works against the inputs update of an experienced flyer. It was initially thought by some that, by having this autopilot system on board, the trainee would begin to rely on it to get him out of any flying difficulty and would never relinquish the HAL unit. This has not been found to be the case, particularly where the effect of the autopilot levelling can be gradually reduced by a variable (knob) control on the transmitter. Learning to fly is as much about the confidence game as any other skills and if the fitting of the HAL 2100 gives greater confidence in flying, it must be a positive influence. However, because there is always a risk of a flyaway with automatically stabilized flight when the HAL is fitted (that is, going out of radio range) a fail-safe should always be employed. If the transmitter does not have this facility, it is possible to purchase a simple, engine-cut fail-safe separately.

TRAINING FACILITIES

As noted earlier, if you have a model flying club that is reasonably local, go along and introduce yourself to some of the members and start asking a few questions. Do they have a training scheme (perhaps they have their own training models)? Do they encourage learners to the club? I fear that there may be some clubs who do not accept non-proficient flyers to their numbers – treat them with the disdain they deserve. If they actively encourage you, ask which radio equipment they use. It will probably be a spread of three or four different makes, with a predominance of one manufacturer. More importantly, find out which mode they fly; again there is likely to be a high proportion favouring either Mode 1 or Mode 2. You should bear this in mind when you purchase the radio equipment (*see* Chapter 3). If you ask the members which model they recommend for training you will probably get a dozen different answers, based on the model with which they learned to fly, or have used to train other modellers. You will probably have to make your own mind up in the end.

But what if there isn't a model club near to you? There are flight training schools that will teach newcomers to fly on a one-to-one basis, and some of them also take groups. Naturally, this is a more expensive method, but it would certainly be worth visiting a school, before taking any other action, to give you an idea of what the sport is all about and whether you are likely to enjoy it (*see* Chapter 14 for further information). An alternative is to go on one of the MAA (Model Aviator Association) week-long training holidays, held in the spring and autumn in Yorkshire and Devon respectively. These are residential courses, with accommodation at a holiday park. All flying facilities are provided, down to the fuel, or you can bring your own model.

SITE CONSIDERATIONS

If you will have to fly from a relatively rough grass site you will need a fairly large model with good-sized wheels. It may be that a tail-wheel model, hand-launched, would be the best answer for rough pastures. Conversely, if you are going to be flying from short grass or tarmac, then a tricycle undercarriage trainer will be the easiest to operate. Where there are noise restrictions you may have to opt for electric power, or some sites are restricted to electric and four-stroke IC engines. The last option is slightly spurious as a two-stroke engine can be silenced to give lower noise levels than a four-stroke, some of which can be quite raucous. More normally, the club noise rule will be based on maximum decibel readings of 82db at 7m (23ft) (the DoE recommendation) and most of the engines up to '40' size (0.40cu in) will meet these levels with standard silencers.

Perhaps you are lucky enough to have some hills around you that are suitable for slope soaring (gliding). If they are good for prevailing wind conditions, are accessible and gliding is permitted on the slopes, the chances are that you will have seen modellers slope soaring there. Gliders can certainly be used for training purposes, and are an economical way of learning to fly as they are mostly two channel (rudder and elevator) types. The new EPP (expanded polypropylene) models are almost unbreakable, and while those that are covered with coloured parcel tape may not look particularly elegant, they certainly are functional. Providing that the hill soaring site is within a reasonable distance of home and you can wait for the right wind conditions, consider it as a training option. You can convert to power flying at a later date. Flat field gliding, for example when the model is towed into the air, is less likely to give good conditions for learning to fly; the flight times will either be too short or, if looking to take advantage of thermals for extending flights, the model may be too fragile for the hard knocks of training. Gliders and sailplanes are considered in more detail in Chapter 6.

COSTS

As most of us won't have won the lottery, the costs of our hobby/sport will need to have limitations. However, it is a sound principle with most purchases to pay as much as you can afford and buy the best. For RC aeromodelling this actually means trying to decide how serious and involved you wish to become and purchasing accordingly. Buying something that needs upgrading in a few months is not good economy, but, on the other hand, you do not need to buy top of the range engines if you will only be flying trainer and sports models. (The term 'sports models' refers to designs that are non-specialist and not intended for competition work.) Reading Chapter 3 on RC equipment and Chapter 4 on engines should help you with these decisions.

TRANSPORTATION AND STORAGE

Before buying a 2,400mm (96in) wingspan beauty, give a thought to where you are going to store the model and how you are going to transport it to the flying field. If you have a good-sized workshop – most modellers seem to commandeer their garage and have an estate car (left outside the garage) – all well and good, but if you are trying to operate from a 1,800mm (72in) garden shed and drive a Mini, you must think again. Remember, too, that you will probably soon get to the stage where you will have two or three models to store and carry around. Be practical.

SIZE DOES COUNT

One thing to avoid is to buy a training model that is too small – you should not consider anything below 1,150mm (45in) wingspan. The reason for this is two-fold. One, a smaller model is more difficult to see and therefore orientation may be a problem, and two, because the radio equipment will weigh about the same, regardless of the model size (and the engine not less in proportion) the smaller model will have a heavier wing loading, and so will have to fly faster and may be over-responsive on the controls. Larger models are undoubtedly easier to see and to fly, but there are the practical limits mentioned above and costs to take into consideration. As usual, we have to end up with a compromise.

Although rather larger than the average trainer model, at 1,830mm (72in) wingspan, the author's Filey Flyer has the typical layout for an ab-initio *trainer.*

DO MIND THE QUALITY AND THE WIDTH

Time for specifics. Assuming that you are Mr Average and looking for positive advice on which kit to buy as a trainer, what would I advise? Despite the many hours of pleasure to be had from designing and building models, for the complete beginner I would have to suggest buying an ARTF model, simply because there is a better chance of assembling it to a good standard for flying. The wingspan should be around 60in or over, which should be suitable for about a 40cu in two-stroke engine. Don't go for the cheapest model on the market, and make sure that balsawood is used in most of the construction and not 'box' wood, which will too easily split in a hard landing. There are two types of covering used: one is a sticky-backed material that is difficult to tighten if it goes slack (and is difficult to repair); the other is a more conventional heat-shrink film that can be repaired and tautened with an iron. Keep to a conventional high-wing design at this stage. While you will probably want a plane with a cabin, it is best to be satisfied with a 'painted' cockpit for now. Practicality is the most important factor – the model has to be rugged and fly well.

Relatively new to the aeromodelling market are models that are predominantly injection-moulded from plastic material and these have the great advantage of identical airframe component parts, ensuring that assembly is the same every time. The ARC Ready 2 trainer is an example of the all-moulded aeroplane. However, the weights of these models tend to be somewhat higher than that of the built-up ARTFs, giving a

TOP: *Whether you build your trainer model yourself, or opt for one of the many ARTF designs, will probably depend on the spare time you have available and your handicraft skills.*

ABOVE: *The author has designed dozens of trainer models over the years, mostly with the same basic layout; this one, at 915mm (36in) wingspan, is a little small for serious training.*

Commercial Almost Ready To Fly models have attractive, decorative colour schemes, but it is more important to check out the quality of manufacturing of the kit.

High-quantity manufacturing of the radio equipment, electric motors and batteries, and foam/carbon airframes means that a complete introductory system can sell at less then £100.

ABOVE: Some of the commercially available ARTF trainers are now manufactured by injection-moulded plastic techniques, with the advantage of complete repeatability.

the radio. It is probably a day's work and then you are ready for flying.

COMBOS

Not as popular yet in the UK as in some other countries is the purchasing of RC model Combos, where the model, radio and engine are supplied as a complete package. With these deals the engine and radio are often factory fitted, which reduces the amount of preparation work even further. Look out for some of these special Combo deals, as they can also save you money.

ELECTRIFYING FLYING

How suitable are electric-powered models for the purpose of training? For the answers to that question and further information on electric power, *see* Chapter 5. And finally, do remember that you should be insured before you go out to fly – your household insurance is not sufficient. Your local club will almost certainly include insurance in its membership deal, but Chapter 14 contains addresses of the various associations and indicates if these can supply insurance. The aeromodellers' governing body, the British Model Flying Association (BMFA), provides insurance as part of its membership.

slightly higher flying speed, although the thick wing section helps to minimize this increase. Going by present trends, the most popular trainer purchase is likely to be the built-up ARTF type where your assembly efforts will consist of joining the wings, gluing the tail surfaces in position, fitting the undercarriage and wheels, screwing the engine mount and engines in position and installing

CHAPTER 3

The Heart of the Matter

Writing about the radio-control equipment needed for flying model aircraft and how it works is one of the more contentious subjects in a book dealing with the hobby in general. How much space should be taken in describing the theory of operation, when most modellers simply want to buy the equipment, fit it in the model and go fly? Others, however, may be interested

A three-channel RC system is the minimum outfit you should consider and this should be on 35mHz, with rechargeable batteries. This is suitable for non-aileron trainers and sports models.

in the whys and wherefores of the control system. I don't think that this is a case of a little knowledge being a dangerous thing, more that understanding the basics of the operation of the control system may save you from making some terrible mistakes.

As with other forms of technology there are terms and abbreviations that we must learn to be able to understand the subject. There is a glossary of terms at the end of the book, but we also need some more general explanations of what allows us to control, by remote means, an aircraft through the take-off, through manoeuvres and back on to the ground again. Incidentally, I still find it quite magical that the model flying past is being controlled by me with a little black box.

UP THERE AND DOWN HERE

In simple, basic terms, radio control gives us the ability to control a model remotely, in this case an aircraft, by operating a series of control functions. The control equipment can be divided into two parts.

The hand-held ground equipment, that is, the transmitter.

The airborne system consisting of the receiver, incorporating a decoder, and the servos for actuating the control surfaces. In addition there are batteries and switches.

In the past, there were enthusiasts who built their own radio-control equipment, but now I do not know of one single person who currently builds his own radio-control systems. It is all commercial equipment, purchased over the counter and, in common with many other goods containing electronic circuitry, if it goes wrong there is little chance of carrying out repairs and servicing yourself. It is useful, however, to understand a little of the workings of the equipment, in order to help you to decide what equipment to purchase and to be able to operate your model safely.

The equipment used to fly model aircraft works on a digital proportional system that can be likened to transmitting a series of frames as with a movie film, but instead of light being transmitted the frames are of radio energy with pulses equating to the movement of the control stick on the transmitter. Because these frames of information are sent at rapid intervals the final effect, as with the movie film, is for smooth operation. To complete the frames, after all the pulses have been transmitted, a pause is added to allow the decoder in the receiver to reset before accepting the next frame. There is also a constant checking of the frames to ensure that no outside interference is disturbing the controls.

At the receiver end, the signal is accepted as a series of on and off pulses and acts as a switch. This chain of 'ons' and 'offs' is still contained in the frames of information as dictated by the operation of the transmitter. The information is passed by the receiver to the decoder, which, by a 'logic' system, separates the individual control pulses and allocates them to the various channels or functions. These separated control pulses are amplified and passed on to the servos, which compare the pulses with those internally generated and result in a movement of the control arm of the servo, or stay at the neutral point. Because, in practice, the information is being sent at many frames per second, the resultant action of the servo is continuous and extremely sensitive.

SIGNAL TRANSMISSION

There are three methods of transmitting the signal: AM (amplitude modulation); FM (frequency modulation), also known as PPM (pulse proportional modulation); and PCM (pulse code modulation). AM is not widely used and is generally confined to the two- and three-function inexpensive models at the toy end of the market. FM (PPM) might be considered as the 'sports' system for the average modeller, while PCM is used on top-of-the-range equipment, as it has certain advantages in being less susceptible to interference, and, if this does occur, has the ability to switch the airborne system into a fail-safe mode. Most of the PCM transmitters are also capable of transmitting on FM (PPM) so that they are compatible with the less expensive receivers.

The introduction of PCM caused a few misunderstandings and concerns. It is firstly important to understand that it is only safe to operate one radio outfit on any given frequency, irrespective of whether it is an AM, FM or PCM system, as these only vary the method of transmission of the signal. Before PCM became commercially available for modelling purposes it was thought that the equipment might be so technically advanced that it would allow all modellers to have their own individual frequencies. Such ideas, and those of having total interference rejection, were soon dispelled – to achieve these ideals would cost many thousands of pounds and result in equipment weighing more than our models could carry. What PCM has allowed is the use of synthesized frequencies, that is, dialling in the required frequency instead of having to change crystals and frequency scanning, whereby the transmitter will search the frequency spectrum and select a vacant spot frequency.

However, laudable as these advances may seem, they can also pose safety problems. One of the essentials for flying-field safety is a frequency peg system, whereby only one modeller is operating on a spot frequency and the indication of that frequency is by having a pennant displaying that frequency number on his transmitter. Having synthesized frequency dialling is convenient, maybe too convenient, and it is easy for the operator to forget to change the peg and frequency pennant. Even easier, and potentially more dangerous, is the scanning system. Sure, the scanner will find a vacant frequency, but unless the operator is very diligent and obtains the appropriate peg and changes pennants, an unsuspecting modeller may switch his outfit on, without knowing that he was on the same frequency as the other operator. If everyone was operating scanning equipment there would be no problem, but it is unlikely that this situation will arise in the foreseeable future. Governing bodies of aeromodelling are rightly concerned about the availability of synthesized frequency and scanning systems and they may be banned in some countries, or limited in their uses. Clubs and individual modellers should also be aware of the potential dangers – shooting down another model through switching on to the same frequency can be both costly and life threatening.

Pulse code modulation was made possible by the introduction of microprocessors, and as these have been developed over the years, so it has been possible to increase the number of functions programmable on the PCM transmitter and to improve the speed and accuracy of the data transmitted to the receiver, and from the receiver to the servos. Although operating digitally, the PCM signal is transmitted by the binary system using a code composed only of the numbers 0 or 1. The receiver only has to detect an 'on' or 'off' situation and is less prone to interference; also, because of the super-speed of the microcomputer, it not only transmits the combinations of 1s and 0s in nanoseconds, but also has ample memory capability to decipher the code and to check for interference. The latter process involves checking whether the 'off' signals are totally clear, comparing them with previous 'frames' of signal, and deciding whether there is sufficient interference to warrant switching off the signal from the receiver to the servos. If the receiver decoder decides that the signals are obviously spurious, then it will go into a 'fail-safe' mode. The transmitter can normally be programmed so that the fail-safe retains the servo positions in accordance with the last true signals, or moves them to a predetermined setting – for example, moving the throttle servo to cut the engine.

Whereas the AM and, to a lesser extent, the FM systems produced 'glitching' (with control alternating between 'on' and 'off'), which is frequently visible as the model moves erratically, the PCM equipment will give full control – or nothing. On receipt of interference the receiver will, once it has determined that a major signal problem has occurred, switch into the fail-safe mode and only return to normal operation when the interference has disappeared and a short delay has occurred. The delays, perhaps half a second, before switching in and out of fail-safe are there to confirm the situation and to prevent an oscillation of 'on' and 'off' that could be caused by intermittent interference.

For the RC aircraft enthusiast, more so than surface vehicle operators, the model going into fail-safe is of great concern, and it can be frustrating to stand with a transmitter that is having no influence on the flight pattern of the model. It is, however, important to realize that with a non-PCM outfit there could have been a number of previous occasions when the model might have crashed through interference. The PCM system, by only cutting out when the interference has reached an intolerable level, may well have maintained operation when other systems would have failed.

Top of the range systems will have more model memories, more channels and a whole range of functions and facilities suitable for fixed wing aeroplanes, sailplanes and helicopters. Prices of these nine- and ten-channel outfits may exceed £1,000.

Such is the speed of the transmitting and decoding information that we can now take advantage of using faster and more accurate servos. The latest are more responsive and have smaller, or zero, 'deadbands' to take advantage of the improved data transmission technology – but more on that later.

As AM outfits have gradually been phased out in favour of FM, so probably will PCM be introduced at the basic levels of RC outfits in favour of FM – until an even superior method of radio signal transmission is devised.

PCM, then, is not interference proof, but, because of its internal checking system, it is less likely to be affected by external interference. If the receiver does lock-out because of interference, it will go into fail-safe mode. The temptation then for the modeller is to set the servos to a neutral setting in the hope that this will result in the model continuing to fly, and that the signal and thus control will eventually be regained. This, though, is a prescription for disaster as the model may fly great distances without control and crash in vulnerable areas. Although it may sadden the operator, the safest fail-safe setting is to cut the engine completely (a rotating propeller can be a nasty implement), and to arrange the control surfaces so that the model will crash in the shortest possible distance and as slowly as possible. This will be achieved by programming for full up elevator, full right aileron and rudder; if you are then flying the model at a safe distance from fellow modellers and the public, there should be no risk of a model in fail-safe reaching them.

It would seem likely that in the future there will be a dual-frequency system, in which the transmitter and receiver will automatically cut from the primary to a reserve frequency in the event of interference, especially with larger models. This is not a new idea; it has been used on an experimental basis for a decade, but has yet to be introduced commercially.

FREQUENCIES

Very precise frequency control is necessary because modellers are only allocated relatively narrow wavebands by the regulatory authorities. Why can't we operate over the full frequency spectrum as used in domestic radios? Because we are transmitting as well as receiving and the result would be chaos. There have been a few problems over the years with our radio-control transmitters interfering with television receivers at close range, but, thankfully, these problems seem to have disappeared. For similar reasons, the outputs of our transmitters are limited to give a range of about 1.6km (1 mile); if it were greater then there would be the risk of having interference from one set of radio-control fliers to the next. Even so, if clubs, or groups of modellers, fly in relatively close proximity, say 2 miles or less apart, there should be co-operation between the modellers as to flying times so that there is no risk of interference on common frequencies. Having a limit of range of a mile or so is not a problem with flying – even the largest of model aircraft begins to look small at less than half this distance.

The history of international allocation of frequency bands for modelling activities is both interesting and confused. There has been no absolute international agreement and allocations vary from country to country. The 27mHz band was one of the early allocations for modelling purposes, but this had to include both aircraft and surface vehicles (cars and boats). This was bad enough, but then misguided government legislation also allowed CB (Citizen Band) to be operated on 27mHz, with the dangers being increased as a result of many CB operators using illegal boosters on their transmitters. The craze for CB has now died away and 27mHz operation is safer than it was, but you should still ensure that you fly on these frequencies well away from model surface-vehicle operators and highways where truckers may still be using CB equipment. Commercially, it is only the lower-cost, ready to fly, small electric models that now operate on 27mHz.

Internationally, the most popular frequency band for aircraft is the 35mHz band and this is subdivided into 10kHz spot frequencies. The allocation for the UK band is included in the Appendices, but it will vary from country to country and is often augmented by additional wavebands. Fortunately, the 35mHz allocation came in at the time when aeromodellers were having problems with CB operators on the 27mHz frequencies, and at the same time a separate allocation (40.665 to 40.995mHz) was designated specifically for surface vehicles. It is important to realize that these allocations are specific to the particular disciplines and should not be used for other purposes. If, for instance, you purchased a radio outfit on a 35mHz frequency to fly in a model aeroplane, this system should not be used for a car or a boat, as it could cause interference to aeroplanes flying in a similar area. Nor is it possible to change crystals in the transmitters and receivers from 35mHz to 40mHz, and vice versa; the electronic tolerances in the systems will not allow this.

Frequency pennants, as mentioned earlier, follow specific colours and numbers. For instance, surface vehicle frequency pennants have a green background, whereas the 35mHz aircraft band is signified by an orange background with the spot frequency number printed on in white. Frequency 35.020 will have the pennant number of 62.

In addition to the VHF (very high frequency) band allocations, aeromodellers also have the use of a UHF (ultra high frequency) band from 458.8 to 459.5mHz. The advantage of equipment on this band is that it is used by very few modellers and there is, therefore, a minimal risk of accidental interference from a modeller on the same frequency; a risk that is ever present on the 35mHz band in spite of the precautions taken. Against this advantage must be set the additional costs of producing the UHF equipment, and the fact that it is not readily available or easily serviced. Major radio-control equipment manufacturers have been reluctant to produce this equipment because of the extra costs and because it is not a legal frequency in all countries.

THE OUTFIT

For the first-time buyer the radio-control system is likely to be bought as an outfit consisting of:

- transmitter, complete with frequency crystal and frequency pennant
- receiver, with matching crystal
- servos, usually four in number, with accessories
- airborne battery pack and switch
- battery charger
- instruction manual.

At a later stage the modeller will purchase additional items separately and these are readily available from retailers and mail-order outlets. When the time comes to fly a second model it may be inconvenient to have to transfer the receiver, servos, battery and switch from one model to another, and so these items will be bought separately, but the transmitter will be common to both models.

Transmitter

Perhaps, one day, we will have a mock-up of a full-size aircraft cockpit, where we sit and operate the controls of our radio-controlled model through a joystick, rudder pedals and throttle quadrant. Until that time we will have to be satisfied with operating a hand-held transmitter, which, although it may have a few curves and fancy corners, will be a basic box with two axis control sticks and a number of knobs, levers and slides to operate the auxiliary functions. The advertising blurb may talk about ergonomic design and advanced styling, but what is important is whether it is comfortable in the hand, that the controls are easily reached, that it is well balanced and is not too heavy and unwieldy. In essence, all transmitters perform the same functions, although some may have more control operations than others.

With human hands being similar in size and execution there are only a limited number of design arrangements for the transmitter if all the controls are to be comfortably operated. By all means check out the transmitter before you buy it – assuming that you are purchasing it from a local retailer, extend the aerial and get the feel of it. Does it feel comfortable? Just to confuse the issue further, some modellers prefer simply to hold the transmitter in both hands and operate the control sticks with the thumbs on top of the sticks, while others feel more comfortable having the transmitter supported by a neck strap and holding the sticks between finger and thumb. Many helicopter pilots, and some fixed-wing-model flyers, are happier with the transmitter fitted in a tray, again supported by a neck strap, somewhat similar to the ice-cream sales people at the theatre. The transmitter may come with the outfit, and some also include neck straps, but these and the transmitter trays are also available as optional extras.

Receiver

The receiver is supplied to match the transmitter, that is, AM, FM (PPM) or PCM, and with a matching crystal. It may have a matching number of functions, although this is not always the case. You might purchase an outfit with a transmitter capability of eight channels, whereas the receiver is only suitable for six channels. It is unlikely that, in the first instance, you will require more than four or five functions to operate your model, but it may be worthwhile thinking about the future and have a transmitter capable of operating six or eight functions. This will give you the basic controls of elevator, ailerons, rudder and throttle, plus flaps and retracting undercarriage and additional operations such as bomb dropping, glider release, camera control and so on.

Receivers are commendably small; the limiting factor in size for standard receivers is the sizes of the servo and battery plug sockets and the holder and crystal. Servos are connected to the receiver at a terminal block and the battery switch harness is also plugged into the terminal block. You may find that the last servo connection is on a common connection with the battery socket, through a 'Y' lead.

Receivers have tough plastic cases, but these must be well protected with foam when they are installed in the fuselage. Care should also be taken to make sure that the servo leads and plugs are not strained, and the same applies to the aerial lead, which can be easily wrenched out of the circuit board unless it is restrained. A reminder, too, to unwind the aerial lead when the receiver is installed in the model and routed to a convenient point. I would guess that nearly all experienced pilots have, at some time, attempted to fly the model with the aerial neatly coiled by the receiver. If you are lucky you might be able to land the model before it gets out of radio range; the chances are, though, that the penny will drop at the same time as the model strikes the ground.

Servos

Servos come in a wide range of sizes and performances – and prices. At one time it was possible to purchase servos with linear outputs, but it now seems that all of them have a standard rotary output, although it may be possible to purchase a conversion unit that will change the servo to a rack-and-pinion style output with two arms travelling in opposite directions. The advantage of having a true linear output was probably outweighed by it being more vulnerable to damage and being more costly to manufacture and assemble. All servos operate in the same direction and rely on a transmitter servo-reversing facility for correcting the direction of movement; this resource is included on all the transmitters,

even the inexpensive two-channel versions. By having this facility it enables you to fit the servos in the model and then switch the direction of control to suit the model. It should be remembered, however, that using the same transmitter for more than one model will require checking to see if the servo directions need changing. It sounds like an obvious check to make, but it is surprising how many experienced fliers have overlooked the obvious and finished up with egg on their faces – and models in the ground.

Programmable computer transmitters overcome the problems of having to change the servo switches and adjust the trims, by having separate memories for individual models. All you need to do is to call up the model to be flown and the controls will automatically be set to the positions of the last flight.

Airborne Battery Pack and Switch

A few outfits can still be bought with dry, alkaline batteries of the AA type used in toys and torches, but that is the proper place for them and not in radio-control equipment. The only reason for supplying an outfit

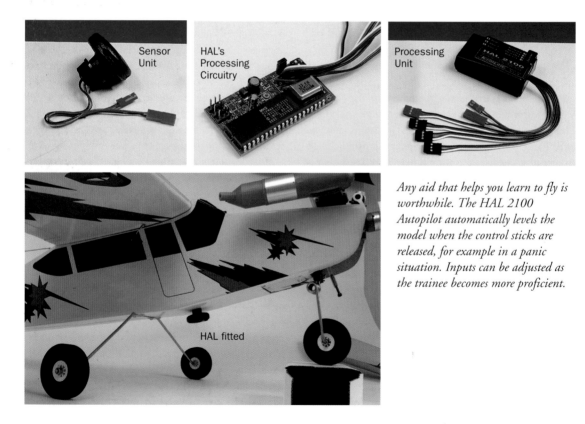

Sensor Unit

HAL's Processing Circuitry

Processing Unit

HAL fitted

Any aid that helps you learn to fly is worthwhile. The HAL 2100 Autopilot automatically levels the model when the control sticks are released, for example in a panic situation. Inputs can be adjusted as the trainee becomes more proficient.

Servos come in a bewildering variety of plain bearing, ball-raced, metal-geared, coverless motors, digital-powered and in all sizes and torque outputs. Standard servos will suffice in the early flying stages; later you will have a better idea of your new servo needs.

Standard fourteen-hour chargers are supplied with outfits for receiver and transmitter batteries but, as you become more involved in the hobby it is worthwhile investing in a charger/cycler to keep your batteries in tip-top condition and/or a multiple charger.

with dry batteries is on the grounds of expense, as the batteries are not supplied with the outfits and the manufacturers do not have to include a charger with the sets. Fortunately, it is usually possible to replace the dry cells with rechargeable types, but any receiver battery box should be replaced with a pre-wired battery pack. Nickel cadmium (NiCads) rechargeable batteries have now been in use for many years; they can be charged and discharged hundreds of times and are extremely reliable. If there is going to be a failure – and this applies to all parts of the radio-control system – it is likely to happen during the first few hours so, for this reason and to increase the maximum output of the NiCads, cycle the batteries through three or four operations of charging, followed by operating the system until the batteries are exhausted, before you fly the model.

Transmitters are usually designed to operate on 9.6V (eight 1.2V battery cells) and 600mAh capacities, although some may use larger capacity batteries. Ideally, the battery pack will be a separate unit with a plug that is attached to a socket in the transmitter. Where the transmitter was originally intended for dry battery operation the batteries will be of the push-in, sprung battery box arrangement. Rechargeable cells, of the same dimensions as the dry batteries, can be used as direct replacements (a charging socket is usually fitted in the transmitter), but regular checks should be made to see that the connections are sound and that the contacts are clean.

For the receiver, the battery voltage is normally 4.8V and the pack supplied rated at 600 to 800mAh. The size, output and cell combination for receiver/servo packs can vary enormously. For lightweight indoor flying a 50mAh 4.8V pack may be used, but for a helicopter, where five servos are in near constant operation, it would be prudent to use a 1,200mAh battery pack. It is also possible to use 6V, five-cell battery packs for the receivers and servos, although checks should be made to be sure that the receiver and servos are suitable for operating at these higher voltages. Also, remember that the initial voltage after a full charge may be in excess of 7V, so operate the system for a minute or two before committing to flying.

The general efficiency of NiCads has improved considerably and they have now been joined by the even more efficient nickel metal hydride cells, which, incidentally, are more environmentally friendly through having no mercury content. Virtually all of the cells are capable of being fast-charged, although the preferred method is to use the standard (14-hour) overnight charger for the transmitter and receiver batteries. Using this slow charge method is likely to improve the life of the battery and it is only when the receiver battery is also used for powering an electric motor that the need for fast charging is likely – unless you anticipate doing more than a couple of hours flying in the day.

There is one danger associated with the use of rechargeable batteries, more so with the airborne pack, and that is a phenomenon known as 'black wire corrosion'. No one seems to know for sure how and why it occurs, but it is certainly a fact. It only happens on the negative (black) wire and usually only between the battery and the switch, although if left unattended it may creep further into the system. Black wire corrosion is unlikely to be present in new equipment and seems to take a couple of years to manifest itself; leaving the battery in a discharged state seems to accelerate the process. Many theories have been propounded as to the cause of this worrying occurrence, ranging from the unlikely effect of the black plastic coating, to damp and chemical discharges from the battery, but none have been proven. If the model or transmitter is not to be used for a lengthy period, say three months or more, a wise precaution would be to disconnect the receiver battery from the switch harness and the transmitter battery plug from its socket and store them in a warm, dry environment. What is annoying is that the military do not seem to suffer these same corrosion problems as we do. Perhaps it is because of the special nickel wire that is used in their equipment; if so, it seems a pity that the manufacturers of our radio-control equipment cannot use wire of a similar specification.

Switch harnesses comprise of a switch, a socket to receive the battery plug, a plug to go into the receiver terminal and another plug for the charging socket.

The switch must always be kept clean and free from oil and fuel, and take care not to stress the wires when installing the switch. Special switches can be obtained that incorporate the charging plug and these are useful for one-piece models, or small models.

Battery Charger

The charger supplied with the outfit will have a dual output, for the transmitter and receiver batteries, and will operate at a standard rate of $\frac{1}{10}$ of the battery capacity, that is, it will charge at 60mAh for 600mAh batteries. It is normal to charge the batteries for a 12-hour period and it is virtually impossible to over-charge the batteries with these types of chargers. Therefore, we do not need to worry about how long we have operated the equipment before charging and it would not matter if the batteries were on charge for a 24-hour period. The one danger is that of totally discharging the batteries and leaving them in that state. This is where the cyclers come into their own, because they will not only take the battery through a full discharge and charge cycle, but most of them will indicate the state of the battery. For instance, if a 600mAh battery is cycled and it only indicates a fully charged 450mAh, it is time to discard the battery – although only after putting it through a further two cycles to double check. The other great advantage with cycle charger units is that they will cope with batteries of different outputs and numbers of cells. Although they are an extra to the basic outfit, they are worth the purchase for the peace of mind they give.

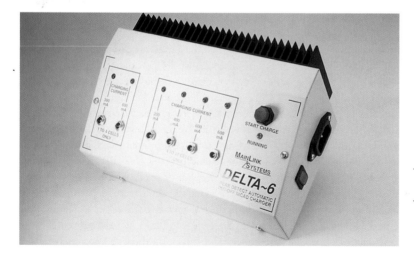

12V Delta Peak field chargers are essential for serious electric flying where the motor batteries have to be fast-charged between flights. A facility for also charging transmitter, receiver and glo-start batteries is a useful addition.

With the growth of indoor RC flying receivers, servos and speed controllers are getting ever smaller, but miniature receivers for outside flying should have a full-range specification and have the same type of frequency crystal as the standard receiver.

Instruction Manual

It used to be a case of a simple instruction leaflet, but now, with advanced computer outfits, it can be a manual of a hundred pages or more. The vital factor, whether it is a simple two-channel outfit, or a top of the range ten-channel computer system, is that the instructions should be easily understood. That is easier said than done when it comes to the 'all-singing, all-dancing' computer transmitters with a vast range of facilities for fixed-wing, glider and helicopter models. In this computer age the programming will probably seem simple to those dealing with the computers from their junior school days, but for the more mature person it may take a little more reading, and re-reading, and looking at the diagrams, before the right buttons are pressed and the right results achieved. In fairness, the computer systems are becoming more user-friendly and they are getting easier to program, certainly at the basic stages.

Sometimes the manufacturers get so carried away with the technicalities and complexities of the system that they overlook the basics. It is still vital to know how to install the equipment, how to protect it, where and how often to get it serviced, insurance requirements and general action needed before you go to fly the model. If such actions are not addressed in the instruction manual, it is hoped that this book will go some way to providing the essential information.

Before moving on to advice on selection of the radio equipment, a word of warning. Radio-control outfits are very attractively packaged and it is often a case of 'Yes, I want one of those!' Remember that the radio-control outfit is a utilitarian piece of equipment – it is there for a purpose, not as a decorative item. Try to keep in mind, when you are purchasing the equipment, what your actual needs are and buy according to those requirements. Do not be seduced by glamorous appearance or promises of instant pleasure!

CONFUSION – HE SAY!

In days of yore, before proportional equipment was invented, outfits were described as having so many channels. With single channel you had literally that, one operation of a rudder control, and with a sequential actuator the first press of the button would give left rudder, the next right rudder, and so on. Compound escapement would select left rudder with one press and right rudder if you pressed the transmitter button twice. Reed equipment was described as having, say, ten channels and these were paired for elevator, aileron, rudder and engine throttle, for movements in each direction, plus an auxiliary control. When proportional equipment came along it was talked about as having a number of functions, so a four-function outfit would have the four basic controls. For some reason the fashion of referring to each control as a function lost popularity and began to be determined as channels again. This remains the present situation and if you hear someone talking about a two-channel outfit, he will be referring to a system with proportional control on rudder and elevator. Function is more used to describe the application of a channel, for example throttle, flaps, undercarriage, elevator and so on.

But how do we know how many channels we will need when we buy our first set of radio-control equipment? The simple answer is that we don't. No one can tell you, in advance, how involved you are likely to become in the hobby and it is unlikely that you will know yourself. If you feel certain that you will want to go on and fly sophisticated scale models that will demand a number of auxiliary functions, then you should go for the top of the range equipment. Perhaps, though, you simply want to try radio-control model flying, but then find out that it is not for you. To make an outlay of some hundreds of pounds and then have it as so much wasted equipment is not a good situation. There are ways of helping you to come to a sensible decision, and visiting your nearest model club is one of the best. Find out where they fly, go along and talk to some of the active modellers, most of whom will be only too pleased to welcome you. With luck, the club may have a communal training model, complete with a buddy-box training system, whereby the instructor's and pupil's transmitters are connected by an 'umbilical' cord, and let you try your hand at flying. Even if there is no training model available just watching and talking will give you a better idea of what the hobby is about, and what is in store for you if you take it up.

Mode 1 or Mode 2?

One other term you will certainly come across when you go to purchase your radio outfit is 'mode': 'What model do you want your transmitter on, Mode 1 or Mode 2?' Without forewarning you will probably look blankly at the salesman and be unable to give a qualified answer. What mode entails is which functions the control sticks on the transmitter command. On Mode 1 the right-hand stick controls the ailerons, left and right, and the throttle, up and down. The left-hand stick is for elevator, up and down, and the rudder control, left and right. Mode 2 differs in that the elevator is controlled on the right-hand stick, with the ailerons and the throttle is on the left-hand side. Which is best? There isn't a best, it is mainly a matter of which mode you learned to fly in the first instance, although some modellers do find one or other of the modes easier. As

far as control of the model is concerned there is little to choose between the two methods, world champions in various types of radio-control competitions are equally divided between the use of the two modes, and it is only when you get to helicopters where there seems to be a preponderance of Mode 2 fliers.

So how do we decide on which mode to fly? Go along to the club where you will fly and see the mode that is most popular there. Remember, you will be looking to them for assistance when learning to fly and it is only sensible to choose to fly on the same mode. While you are investigating this aspect of transmitter arrangement, take a note of the radio equipment they are using, which manufacturers are popular and how many channels they are using. Most radio-control transmitters, but not all, have a facility for a buddy-box trainer lead attachment, but these are not interchangeable between different manufacturers' equipment. Therefore, if you are hoping to receive some tuition from fellow club members, you will have to be using the same make of equipment and probably have to buy the buddy-box lead, too.

ON YOUR OWN?

If it is impossible to obtain the advice and opinions of club members, or other experienced modellers, you will have to make an informed decision from certain facts and considerations. Here is a table showing the general usage of control functions between two and six channels. Anything over six and you are in the realms of specialist functions, normally with scale models, such as bomb drops, hood opening, wing folding system, landing lights, and so on. Helicopters use similar control functions, but the elevator becomes fore/aft cyclic, rudder is tail rotor control, and so on.

No. of channels	Control functions employed
2	Rudder or ailerons and elevator
2	Rudder and engine throttle control
3	Rudder, elevator and engine throttle
3	Aileron, elevator and engine throttle
4	Rudder, elevator, ailerons and throttle
5	Rudder, elevator, ailerons, throttle and undercarriage
6	Rudder, elevator, ailerons, throttle, undercarriage and flaps

For the trainer model and sports models the basic four functions of rudder, elevator, ailerons and engine throttle are all that is normally required, but you may well progress to more advanced sports and scale models where one or two extra channels will be required. Going back to the opposite end of the limited channels, just two functions, rudder/ailerons and elevator, or rudder and engine, can provide a tremendous amount of fun and challenge. At one time it was the norm and I can assure you that we had a ball and didn't feel in the least bit deprived.

It is not only scale models that might require more than the four basic functions. Sports models – a very general term – may be developed to carry a still or video camera, to tow gliders or carry gliders or to drop sweets for children. 'Toffee bombing' at fêtes and fairs is a great way of getting children actively engaged in the sport.

Competition gliding is another, perhaps surprising, area where you might require more than four functions. In addition to the three basics (no throttle) there are spoilers, 'crow' brakes, variable camber wings and complex trim settings.

COMPUTER LITERATE?

The cost of computer outfits at the introductory level has dropped significantly and they now sell for the same price as the equivalent non-computer sets of a few years ago, the latter having fallen in price even further. Do you absolutely need a computer outfit for normal and advanced flying? The answer, obviously, is no, because for many years we did not have the luxury of such things and it is true to say that we can still manage without them for all models, but it does make life a lot easier in many cases. For instance, we can program into the computer such functions as control surface movement directions (without having to move over any switches), control surface movement limits, proportional control movement for dual rates, mixing of two functions, trim settings and so on. We can do this not for just one model, but according to the number of model memories, for a series of models. It is obviously a whole lot easier just to operate one control on a transmitter – Model Select – than a number of reversing switches, trim settings and so on. It used to be the case that modellers were careful to install the radio so that servos all moved in the correct direction and then made trim adjustments mechanically. Now, the modeller expects to be able to carry out all his function corrections from the transmitter. But, beware, it needs even more checking that you have all the controls moving in the right direction and that you are flying with the correct model selection. The number of accidents resulting from a failure to check the last two items – and particularly the correct movement of ailerons – is legion.

If you decide to purchase a second-hand radio outfit from a swap meet ensure that it is on the basis of either being flight demonstrated, or on a money-return basis within one month if the system proves to be faulty.

STARTING POINT

How easy you find it to learn to fly will depend more on your aptitude and the standards of training – plus the choice of model – than it will on the make of radio equipment and how many 'bells and whistles' it has. Try to analyse your requirements, admittedly not easy at the beginning stage, and purchase with a view to the next couple of years' flying. This does not mean that the initial purchase will become redundant, merely replaced for certain types of models.

For the newcomer wishing to become quite involved in the hobby and with a reasonable budget the following are desirable items for an initial outfit:

- a minimum of four control channels, but as five- and six-channel outfits are not excessively dearer, it's preferable to go for the six-channel (function) outfit, even though the receiver may only be four or five channels;
- computer systems do have sufficient advantages, when you get to the stage of having a number of models, to warrant the extra cost involved; the more model memories in the computer transmitter the better – three is the minimum, six or eight is preferable.

Any introductory level outfit should have the following facilities:

- trims on all four basic functions
- servo reversing on all channels
- dual rates for elevator and ailerons
- basic mixing of rudder and ailerons
- end-point adjustment, also known as adjustable travel volume
- trainer switch and socket for provision of a trainer lead (buddy-box system)
- NiCad battery for transmitter and airborne system is essential and a mains charger
- electronic indication of battery or signal output state on transmitter
- narrow band (single or dual conversion) receiver
- switch harness with charging socket
- three or four standard servos
- aileron extension lead
- frequency pennant
- instruction manual.

Anything in addition to this list – and there will be plenty more functions to program on the computer transmitter – is a bonus. Most of the computer transmitters, even at the introductory level prices, are switchable from PPM to PCM and this may be a useful attribute for the future. Bear in mind, though, that PCM receivers tend to be considerably more expensive than the PPM (FM) types.

Having made your initial outfit purchase (they are all tested for European standards), do take the trouble to read the instructions thoroughly, to fill in and send away the guarantee and to become accustomed to the operation of the transmitter and model controls before going out to fly. If, and it is very unlikely, there is a fault in the system, it is likely to show up in the first hour or two of operation, so testing it out on the ground also makes good safety sense.

Look after your equipment, send it away for servicing after any damage and get it checked every year or two as a matter of routine.

Advances in the design of radio-control equipment come at such a rate that, by the time that this book is published, there will already be additional functions and higher specifications of the radio-control outfits. The one area where specifications may vary is with the supply of servos in the outfit. There is a wide variation in the types of servos used on models: some are high torque, some high speed, some coreless, some digital, with high-centring resolution, some waterproof, some plain bearing, some single ball-race, some dual ball-race, some vibration resistant, some for undercarriage retracts, some miniature, some subminiature, and so it goes on. Outfits for beginners and sports model enthusiasts will be supplied with standard servos, possibly with plain output bearings, or a single ball-race, with moderate speed and torque capabilities. These are perfectly adequate for most normal-type fixed-wing models, but may not be suitable for specialist subjects. Because the manufacturers of the advanced radio-control systems do not know the type of models to be flown by the purchaser, the outfit is often sold as a 'combo', that is, just the transmitter and receiver, and in this way the modeller can add the servos, receiver battery and switch harness to meet his own demands.

Do take your time and consider carefully the options before you purchase your first radio outfit, as it represents one of the biggest expenditures.

CHAPTER 4

The Power and the Glory

Until efficient electric motors and rechargeable batteries came on to the scene the only way of powering a radio-controlled model aircraft was with an IC (internal combustion) engine. Prices, initially, were high, certainly in comparison with a weekly wage, but in real terms prices have dropped, quality and reliability standards have improved and there has never been a greater choice of sizes and types of motors. How have these improvements been achieved?

Mass production and global sales have certainly accounted for most of the advances, not least with the introduction of CNC (computer numerically controlled) machinery. At one time, the major IC engine manufacturers for model aircraft were to be found in the USA, Germany, Japan and the UK, but now the engines are more likely to come from China or Russia. Because of the improvements in manufacture, and, being cynical, the fact that some of the newer producers may have 'borrowed' a few of the design features from the more established companies, it does not follow that these less expensive motors are substandard. Perhaps it is because of my memories of trying, sometimes in vain, to start recalcitrant engines of years gone by, that I am amazed at how many of the modern engines start, virtually first flick, straight out of the box. Nor do they need the lengthy running-in period of earlier engines; they are machined to much closer tolerances and high specifications, so minimal running-in is required.

A superb scale model of a World War II Handley Page Hampden deserves engines of the highest quality and reliability. Fitted with two Laser 150 four-stroke engines, the model has made hundreds of successful flights.

Large spark-ignition engines require a good healthy swing of the propeller, not unlike full-sized Tiger Moths. Because of their reliability and cleanliness they are regularly used in large-scale models.

Having said that, the next question is usually, 'Well, if I can buy an engine for £50, why should I fork out £100 for another make of motor that appears to have the same specification?' To some extent you may be paying a premium for the name; after all, someone has to do the research work and it may be that the more expensive engines are being produced in a country where labour and factory costs are higher. However, there is probably a little more to the cost difference than that. Perhaps the quality of the ball-races is higher in the expensive engine and the carburettor may be just that little more efficient and smooth in operation. If you are operating a £500 helicopter it makes good sense to have the most reliable engine, with good throttle control through the full range. Certain aeromodelling environments, such as helicopters and ducted fan jets, are hard on engines and only the top quality will give you reliability. If you are only flying a trainer or sports model once or twice a month, then the longevity of the engine is less of a worry; it is very unlikely that you will go beyond the useful working life of the motor.

Engine reliability is important and if you take the trouble to take care of the engine during the first hour of its running and set up the needle settings correctly it is unlikely you will have problems. With a sports model the smooth operation of the carburettor through its complete range is not so important, providing it keeps running at the lower speeds and opens up to full throttle without cutting. I know of very few mechanical failures in the economy priced engines, except where they have been operated in helicopters

and ducted fan models. Going through current model-magazine advertisements, there are very few engines listed that I would not recommend, but have a word with your friendly model club to see what they use. Some engines might have been a little 'iffy' a few years ago, but have now benefited from modern production methods. I do believe that quite a few of the makes are made in the same vast factory and are 'badge' engineered. Overlooking, for the moment, the more specialist CO_2, electric and jet-type motors and engines there are three basic types of model aeroplane engines:

- glow motors
- diesel
- spark-ignition engines.

They all have their own devotees and each has a particular use for certain models. By far the most popular type of miniature IC engine for aeromodelling purposes is the glow motor. Before World War II the only commercial engines were of the spark-ignition type, but in the 1940s two revolutionary model engines were introduced, first the diesel and then the glow motor. Both had the advantage of dispensing with the batteries and coils needed for the 'sparkies' and resulted in much lighter and less-complicated engines, which were simple to operate and considerably more powerful. Diesels operate by compressing the fuel/air mixture between the piston and a variable position contra-piston. To achieve this 'firing' the fuel contains ether, which when mixed with kerosene and lubricating oil ignites without any form of ignition plug.

They don't come much larger than this; in fact this 'model' is only a few millimetres less in wingspan than the full size prototype – which is quite small for an ultralight twin.

In the glow motor the spark-ignition-style plug is replaced by a plug that has a coil of platinum wire, the element, in the plug body. To start the engine the plug is energized from an outside battery source (1.5 to 2V), which causes the element to glow brightly. On rotating the propeller the fuel/air mixture (methanol/oil) is discharged into the combustion chamber and ignited. Once the engine is running, the battery can be

Four-stroke model engines are very popular as they tend to have a more acceptable exhaust note than the two-stroke types, and they are also more fuel-efficient.

disconnected and the compression of the firing stroke is sufficient to keep the plug glowing and the fuel mixture igniting.

Although spark-ignition engines fell from favour for many years, the petrol engine made a comeback when larger capacity, more powerful engines were required for 'mammoth' models. Engines used in chainsaws, strimmers and other commercial motorized gardening products were converted so that they would direct-drive a propeller and could be used in model aeroplanes. Although there are now purpose-designed spark-ignition model engines, many of them still rely on the commercial-use engine as a basis for the new petrol engines. Electronic-ignition systems are also available for converting large glow motors to spark-ignition operation; the advantages given include cheaper fuel and cleaner running.

WHICH TYPE OF ENGINE?

Spark-ignition motors are only for the large models and by the time you reach the point of building and flying these types you will have more knowledge of the engine types.

Diesels

Diesels are like good wine, an acquired taste. They are somewhat dirty and smelly to operate (not the flavour of the month with wives), and have two principal

The two-stroke single-cylinder glow-plug engine, with front induction and side exhaust, remains the most frequently used engine for model aircraft. Although the basic design has remained unchanged for many years the performance and throttle response have improved dramatically.

Large capacity competition two-stroke glow engines now feature fuel injection, which is computer controlled for the most efficient carburettor control. In 1940 a four-cylinder 40cc model engine would have a rating of 1.6hp; this 23cc OS engine produces 3.5hp.

Diesel engines (compression ignition) started to fall out of favour when the glow motors were introduced, but there are still devotees of this type of engine, particularly free flight and control-line enthusiasts. The engines are available in standard and RC throttle versions.

controls to adjust (needle valve and the compression screw); they also require a special 'diesel flick' of the propeller to start them. If they are more user-unfriendly to operate, why bother with them? They have definite advantages when operated in small models, especially free-flight types where the variable compression allows the engine to be adjusted reliably to give slow or high propeller speeds. Also, you do not need to lug around a battery for starting the engine. To extol the praises of the diesel engine in any other positive terms is difficult; you tend either to be a diesel freak or not – I'm one.

Glow Engines

Nine out of ten motors you see on the flying field will be glow engines and these come in two basic types, the two-stroke and four-stroke engines (it is technically more correct to term them as four-cycle engines). Four-stroke model engines are by no means new, as there were examples powering model aeroplanes pre-1914, but it is in the last ten years or so that they have regained popularity. The distinction between two-stroke and four-stroke engines is that, to perform a full cycle of operations, that is, recharging the contents of the cylinder and effecting combustion, the four-stroke requires four movements of the piston in the cylinder (up, down, up, down), whereas the two-stroke requires two. Because of the valve mechanisms and machining content, the four-stroke is more expensive than its two-stroke counterpart. It also tends to be a little less powerful and slightly heavier. On the plus side the four-stroke has a much more pleasant and environmentally friendly exhaust note. This is not the same as saying that it is quieter, as the two-stroke can be silenced (with add-on silencer devices) to a lower decibel level than the standard four-stroke, but the high revs of the two-stroke will always make it sound more frenetic.

Fuel consumption is more efficient with the four-strokes, although they may require a fuel with a nitro content, which increases the cost of the fuel. Few of the modern IC model engines give trouble in starting or running. Some may be a little more critical with respect to the positioning of the fuel tank and others may have a more sensitive needle-valve setting, but it is rare for them to fail to function. For the beginner an inexpensive two-stroke engine (it doesn't even have to be a version where the crankshaft has ball-race support) is probably the motor to go for. From that, you can learn the basics of starting, operation and care and maintenance. After this, your selection of engines will depend on the models to be flown and your individual preference; a scale model, for instance, will nearly always benefit from the sound of a four-stroke engine.

ENGINE MOUNTING FOR TESTING

When you have purchased your engine, got it home, admired it and watched the piston go up and down, it is time to read the instructions diligently. This is important, if for no other reason than that in by not abiding by them you might invalidate the guarantee. More than

ABOVE: A classic British success story, the Laser four-stroke engines, both single and vee twins, are used by a high proportion of the World RC Scale entrants. These overhead-valve glow engines run on straight methanol/oil fuel, which reduces the risk of internal corrosion.

Most commercial engines incorporate castings for the crankcase, cylinder and cylinder head, but the Laser is fully machined from the solid. CNC machinery is used throughout the model engine manufacturing business and this has revolutionized the running qualities of modern engines.

that, though, there is usually some sound advice on the installation, running and maintenance of the engine.

If you have just bought your first engine you will have two options for test running – in the model, or on a separate test bench. The latter is undoubtedly preferable for the novice, as it allows him to get to know the engine in a safe environment without having the model to worry about. For bench running you will need a special test bench, or the engine can be mounted on a heavy plywood board, which, in turn, must be secured to a very solid table, post or some other immovable object. If you are unsure whether the engine is firmly enough secured give it an almighty pull – if it moves, do not start it. Remember also that vibration can also cause nuts and bolts to work loose, so keep an eye on the fixing bolts. If you are testing the engine when it is fitted to the model, get a helper to restrain the model when it is being started and never run the engine with

Radial engine mounts are available for all engines except the largest capacities, and are manufactured from glass-reinforced nylon, or cast aluminium alloy. Smaller engines can be retained by the use of self-tapping screws, while larger capacity, more powerful motors should be bolted in position, with lock-nuts on the underside.

Although modern engines only require short periods of running-in to bed down the moving parts, this action is vital for the longevity of the engine. As an alternative to bench running, or risking an important model, it is sensible to use a simple model for the running-in period.

the model standing on dusty, dirty ground, as this will find its way into the engine intake. Wear safety glasses and heavy duty gloves when running the engine, even though you will have to remove a glove to adjust the needle valve. Always bear in mind where the propeller arc extends, and keep clear of it at all times. You only need to inspect the edges of moulded propellers to realize that they are potential 'bacon slicers', so treat a running engine with great respect. Ear defenders are a sensible precaution when running an engine in a confined space, but don't let them lull you into a false sense of security. Perhaps it would be wise to let your neighbours have the use of the earmuffs.

STARTING AND RUNNING-IN

With full operating instructions supplied with all engines there is little point in repeating the words or diagrams.

SILENCING

Noise levels from engines will vary considerably in relation to the speed of the engine and one of the easiest ways of making an engine less noisy is to fit a larger propeller. Some engines, particularly some of the higher performance motors, are not happy running at lower speeds and these may still give noise readings in excess of the recommended 82 decibels at 7m (23ft) (in the UK). When this happens, and in the interests of retaining our flying sites, an add-on silencer should be fitted. Another method of reducing noise levels is by using an isolating engine mount, which features rubber bush resilient inserts to reduce vibration.

SAFETY

Treat any engine, even the small capacity ones (they can 'bite' too), with the greatest respect. Once the engine has started make any adjustments from behind the engine (some of the latest engines are being supplied with the main needle mounted to the rear of the engine as an added safety feature); if the propeller does fail, the blades will be thrown sideways and forwards. Before any flight, lift the nose of the model high to ensure that the engine will not lean out – that is, speed up and labour or stop – in this attitude. Lean runs, where the needle valve is closed too much and so insufficient fuel gets to the

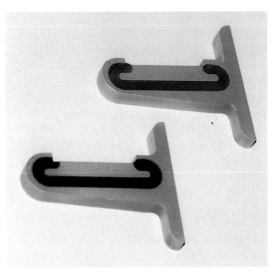

Larger single-cylinder engines will benefit from being installed on anti-vibration mounts, which will reduce the noise levels as well as preventing the transmission of vibrations to the airframe.

engine, leading to high temperatures and oil breakdown, are your biggest enemy. If you do have an engine cut out and the model lands in dirt, never turn the engine over until you have had a chance to get it home and clean the dirt away. Get to know your engine. If you watch other modellers, you will soon be able tell those who are in sympathy with the motor, which will as a result always start quickly and run consistently. They will also be the ones who empty the fuel tank at the end of the day, clean the engine down and add a few drops of oil to the intake before putting the model away.

MAINTENANCE

Apart from the actions mentioned above, the engine will not require much maintenance and servicing, just a general external cleaning and, possibly, a stripping of the carburettor to remove small pieces of debris that manage, despite filtering of the fuel, to get in and cause erratic running. If there is any major fault, such as a broken conrod or a failed bearing, send the engine back to the servicing agent to have it properly repaired. You can, if you are mechanically minded and have the correct tools, strip the engine to clean it after prolonged running – a cookware cleaner (*no* caustic soda) and boiling water will do the cleaning. The biggest enemy for a model engine is corrosion, which is more prevalent in four-stroke engines where nitro-based additives are used in the fuel mix. Avoid nitro composition in the fuel if this is feasible, but if it must be used ensure that you use an 'after run' product in the engine at the end of a flying session. When the engine is to be put away for a few months it should be well swilled out internally with petrol and then treated liberally with oil.

MORE POINTS ON SAFETY

The author, after fifty years of operating model engines from 0.2cc to 200cc, finally managed to put his hand in the propeller while the engine was running. I was about to pick up a free-flight model to launch, when another model flew in my direction, I ducked and my left hand attempted and failed to stop the PAW 1.49 diesel from running. Eleven stitches and a considerable scar was the result. Be warned and be very vigilant.

Probably the highest number of bad accidents in operating engines fitted in models is by the operator putting his hand through the rotating propeller disc when attempting to adjust the needle valve. Because the propeller is near invisible when it is running at speed it is all too easy to forget it and move your hand through it and towards the needle valve. Hence, another reason for making all adjustments from the rear of the engine; although you will probably witness many modellers taking the alternative, potentially dangerous, option at the flying field.

FUELS

Engine manufacturers, in their instructions, will normally specify the types of fuel suitable for their engines. For diesel engines they may well suggest a home brew, consisting of ether, kerosene (paraffin) and a lubricating oil, in roughly equal measures. There may also be the addition of 1 or 2 per cent of isopropylnitrate to give greater flexibility and easier starting. Except for the very smallest capacity engine (less than 0.5cc capacity), where the fuel needs to be as fresh as possible and preferably mixed immediately before flying, the commercial mixes are far more convenient. Go into a chemist shop these days and ask for some ether and

they will look at you sideways! Commercial blends are available for small, larger and racing diesels.

For glow engines there is no consensus with regard to the types of lubricating oils to use, or the percentages of nitromethane to include – or the lack of it. Castor-based oils were the staple diet of glow fuels for many years because they mixed readily with the methanol and only broke down at extremely high temperatures. Then along came the synthetic oils, which promised better overall combustion efficiencies from the fuel and cleaner operation. Regrettably, some of the synthetic oils were not up to the job, broke down at relatively low temperatures and caused engines, particularly new and 'tight' engines, to seize. This gave synthetic oils a bad name, one that is still to be overcome in many cases. The truth is that some of the synthetic oils are now superior to castor oils, particularly when fuel manufacturers use an inferior castor to the 'first pressings' oil. We now have the anomaly of some engine manufacturers insisting that only castor-oil-based fuels be used, some dictating that only synthetic oils are permitted, and yet others who recommend a synthetic oil with a small percentage of castor as a safety measure. You should check whether the engine's guarantee or warranty stipulates using a particular fuel type otherwise the guarantee will be null and void. If this is the case, be warned.

Nitromethane is added to glow fuel to increase the performance of the engine, which it does roughly in relation to the percentage added, providing that the design of the engine is suited to higher power. It is pointless adding high percentages (10 per cent and more) to a sports engine; if you want more power for a model in this case you should be using a larger capacity engine. Nitro, as it is normally known, not only increases performance, but also has other advantages. It tends to make engines easier to start, especially in cold weather, and gives a more reliable idle speed. Small capacity glow motors (.020 to .049cu in) will only run consistently with nitro contents of 15 to 20 per cent and engines a little larger (up to .06cu in or 1cc) will certainly benefit from a 10 per cent nitro content.

Still confused? For the average-sized glow engine of between 0.25cu in and 0.40cu in capacity, a fuel with 18 per cent castor oil, or 15 per cent synthetic, and 5 per cent nitro should be suitable for year-round flying. Always buy your fuel from reputable dealers, ones that have been around for a few years, and who use good-quality materials. Although it is possible to buy glow fuel in small quantities, for example by the pint (0.6ltr), it is always more economic to purchase it in gallon (5ltr) containers. However, bulk quantities of glow fuel should be stored in a safe place, not in the house, due to the fire risk. Diesel fuels are rarely supplied in larger quantities than 0.25ltr (0.6gal), as the engines tend to be of smaller capacities than glow motors and the ether evaporates when left over long periods.

GLOW PLUGS

Most engines are supplied without glow plugs, which is an odd situation because there is no way that the engine can be run without a plug fitted. However, the type of plug to use will be stipulated in the instructions, usually the type made by the engine manufacturer. Plugs come in a graded rating of temperatures, for example from Hot to Cold for two-stroke engines, and the normal advice is the hotter the engine, as for racing engines, the cooler the plug rating. For four-stroke engines there is usually a 'four-stroke plug' and most manufacturers' plugs can be used in any four-stroke engine, as they rarely have separate temperature ratings.

If you experience starting, or running, problems with your engine you should examine the easy options first, and changing the plug is the easiest option of all. It may

be that the plug element has been damaged, or is burnt out and a simple replacement is all that is required. It may also be that a change of fuel or extreme ambient temperature changes require a slightly different plug specification for reliable running. It is always worthwhile experimenting with glow plugs and fuel and propeller combinations to get the best out of an engine.

PROPELLERS

Again, the engine manufacturer will suggest a range of propellers suited to the engine and may suggest their uses in terms of the models suited to the propeller sizes. Glass-filled nylon is the common material used for propellers of sports models, with the advantages of moulding to precise limits and repetitive accuracy. The balance of these propellers is normally quite good, but it is worth checking, on a propeller balancer, to be sure that one blade is not heavier than the other. With this condition, undue vibration can be set up, leading to possible damage to the airframe and radio equipment. To balance a propeller that is out of true, the rear of the heavier blade should be skimmed with an abrasive material (wet and dry paper, for instance), until a correct balance is achieved.

How do we decide on the diameter and pitch combination for the propeller? The deciding factor here is

To start a glow engine the glow plug has first to be energized and this can be done from the field box panel, or from a separate plug energizer, with an integral rechargeable battery. This is handy if the model has to be hand restarted at the flight line.

Standard sports propellers are moulded from reinforced nylon; they tend to be quite well balanced, but benefit from final weight distribution by using a commercial propeller balancer.

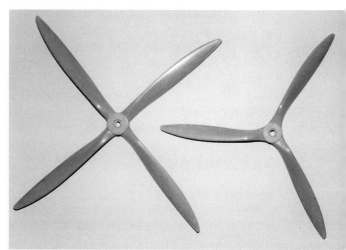

To reduce noise levels on high-performance full-sized aerobatic aircraft three- and four-bladed propellers are used. For the same reasons, three- and four-bladed propellers have been developed for powerful model engines.

the type of model to be flown. A large, heavy and slow-flying model will need a propeller with a large diameter and low pitch, whereas an aerobatic design will fly better with a smaller diameter, larger pitch propeller. The latter type would also suit fast-flying models and semi-scale jets. Take a typical '40' size engine ('40' referring to a 0.40cu in capacity engine): for a trainer we might opt for a 254mm × 153mm (10in × 6in) (diameter × pitch) propeller; for a vintage-style model a 280mm × 127mm (11in × 5in) propeller; and for a fast aerobatic type, a 230mm × 170mm (9in × 7in) propeller. We go for the lower pitch for a slow flier because we are interested in acceleration and a low maximum speed, the acceleration being needed to haul a fairly bulky model, with plenty of drag, into the air. Opposite requirements are needed for a small, highly aerobatic model; because it is small and reasonably light it will not have any problems in getting airborne, and once up we need good speed and pulling ability through manoeuvres.

An easy way to reduce noise levels on a model is to fit a different propeller. Quite a high degree of noise is generated by the propeller, so, if we slow it down by increasing propeller pitch, we also reduce the level of noise created. Yes, we will lose a little power, but not normally enough to be critical. Also good for noise

attenuation is the fitting of a three-bladed propeller, which is a common cure in full-sized aircraft and works just as well on models.

STARTERS

Electric starters are a standard part of most modellers' field equipment and they are an absolute requirement for helicopter fliers (no propellers to flick). Most modern engines will start by hand and there is still something satisfying in flicking the propeller and the engine roaring into life. Indeed, it is the sign of a modeller with a reliable and well set-up engine if it is regularly started by hand. There is, though, no absolute virtue in flick-starting the engine, as the electric starter will do the job very well and will certainly be superior for engines that require a bit of coaxing into life.

There are a few dos and don'ts when using an electric starter. Never use a starter on a diesel engine of less than 0.19cu in (3.2cc) capacity as there is a real chance of the engine becoming over-compressed, with consequent damage to the conrod. Even with moderate-sized glow engines one should take care before applying the starter. Before the glow clip is attached, flick the engine over by hand to ensure that it is free and then give a short burst with the starter. If this is satisfactory and there is no excess of fuel being discharged from the silencer outlet, or spitting out of the carburettor, then the glow clip is connected to energize the plug and the starter applied; the engine should burst into life.

Hand starting is, or should be, possible with all engines. It is simply a matter of getting to know your engine and taking the sensible precaution of wearing a protective glove, or finger stall. In many ways, you can get a better feel of the condition of the engine, whether it is dry or flooded by hand starting. You will

see, quite regularly, a modeller trying to start a flooded engine with an electric starter, but all he is doing is drawing more and more fuel into the engine and decreasing the chance of it starting. By hand, you can feel that the engine is flooded and have a better chance of it starting, as a single flick of the propeller will not induce more fuel into the engine.

One of the near foolproof ways of starting an engine by hand, when it is fitted in a model, is to place your finger over the air intake, turn the propeller over a few turns to ensure that the fuel has reached the carburettor and then rotate the model slowly clockwise (viewed from the front) until it is inverted. This will ensure that the fuel will have travelled down the transfer ports in the cylinder and reached the combustion chamber. Now, return the model upright, connect the glow lead and, with a gloved hand, hold the propeller blade tightly and pull it over top dead centre. As the piston moves through the top you should feel a 'kick' as the fuel mixture ignites. Now, with the throttle opened about a quarter from closed, flick the propellers smartly – the engine should be running within a few flicks. Quite simply, if there is fuel at the combustion chamber and a healthy glow, then the engine should fire. If there is the correct amount of fuel reaching the head, then the engine should keep running. If it does not, then look (after a check on the plug) at the fuel system. Are there any leaks in the tubing, or is the clunk weight correctly at the rear

ABOVE: A typical two-stroke engine installation in a trainer model, the side-mounted silencer has a rotatable rear section to direct the exhaust away from the model. Note the accessibility of the needle valve and, under a hatch behind the engine, the fuel tank.

An unusual combination. A Laser engine, normally a glow motor, adapted for diesel operation. Not generally available, it nevertheless proved to be very practical and fuel-economic.

of the tank? The purpose of the clunk, fitted to the rear of the fuel feed tubing, is to allow fuel to be delivered to the engine irrespective to the attitude of the model. Are the back-plate bolts tight? If not, there could be air getting in and this will cause erratic running. Check the carburettor for blockages. Assuming that there are no actual mechanical faults, there has to be a logical reason for the engine not to run.

TACHOMETERS

Tachometers, or rev counters, have their uses, but those uses are limited. To see someone holding an electronic tachometer to check the rpm of the propeller of a sports model engine seems to me pointless. Perhaps, for pylon racing engines, where the last 100rpm might mean the difference between winning and losing, yes, but with your average model it is a waste of time. By all means do check on an annual basis, with an identical propeller, to see whether there is any deterioration in the performance, as a loss of a few hundred rpm might well indicate that the engine needs dismantling and cleaning. What is far more important is that the engine should be running reliably, idling safely, picking up through the rpm range smoothly and running through a tank-full of fuel without hesitation. It is far more important to take time in achieving these aims than 'tweaking' the needle valve to get a few extra rpm.

You will frequently see fliers using a tachometer on a multi-engined model. What they are attempting here is to have the engines running at the same speed and often peaking out the slower engine to match the fast one. This is potentially fatal as it will probably lead to the 'slow' engine being leaned out to the stage where it will cut in the air – with nasty consequences. An engine tends to unwind (increase in rpm) in the air and it therefore needs a slightly richer fuel setting on the ground. For multi-engined models the only safe way of setting the engines is to run each engine independently, lifting the nose of the model to check that it will not result in a lean run during a climb. If one engine is doing a few hundred rpm more than the one on the opposite side it will not matter, as you almost certainly will not notice the difference in the flying of the model. You will certainly notice the difference, however, if one motor quits, so reliability of operation of the engines is everything. If the different speeds of the engines offends you aurally (although the engines will

only sound 'on-beat' at certain attitudes), the best way of obtaining equal speeds is by trimming the propeller tips of the 'slow' engine, but remember to rebalance the propeller after trimming. Then you can use the tachometer to check propeller speeds.

Occasionally a manufacturer will go out on a limb and produce an exotic design, such as this four-cylinder in-line four-stroke engine, based on the de Havilland Cirrus engine. This engine was fitted in a DH Cirrus Moth scale model.

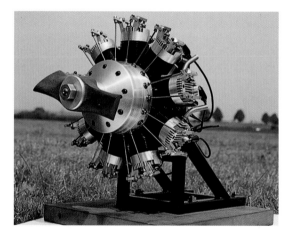

Multi-cylinder radial engines and rotary engines are normally the province of the model engineer and although these superb examples are regularly bench-run and demonstrated, they rarely find their way into flying models; perhaps not surprisingly considering the number of hours spent constructing them.

CHAPTER 5

Electrification

No noise – nearly – no smell, no dirty exhaust residues, no spilt fuel on your clothes, instant starts and instant stops, these are some of the electric flight characteristics that appeal to, or appal, aeromodellers. If you are the sort who enjoys going out to fly on a Sunday, taking the wife with you (no risk of dirtying the car, or having the interior smell like a mixture of an uncleaned corner of a garage and an operating theatre), arriving back home and still not having to wash, then electric-powered model aeroplanes are for you. If, on the other hand, you like to hear the growl of an engine, find a challenge in getting the diesel or glow engine started and don't think that you've had a good day unless you get back home all smelly and dirty, then you'd better stay away from the electric path.

First though, let's dispel a few misconceptions.

1. *Electric power might be all right for 'powered gliders' and sports models, but it is always second best when it comes to 'real' power.*
   WRONG. With the advent of high-performance motors developed, initially, for cars, ever increasing battery efficiencies, the use of gearboxes to enable larger, more efficient, propellers to be used and field chargers that take all the guesswork out of giving the battery packs a full and complete charge, the power is certainly there. We may have to look at the use of that power in a different way, accept a shorter flight time and redesign the airframe, but electric flight should no longer be looked upon as a poor cousin to IC power.
2. *Electric flight makes for 'lightweight' flying – no starter, no starter battery, and no fuel.*
   WRONG. Try lugging the charging batteries, especially for the larger battery packs, across a couple of fields

The quiet operation of electric-powered models allows them to be flown in noise-sensitive areas where an IC-powered model would be objectionable.

45

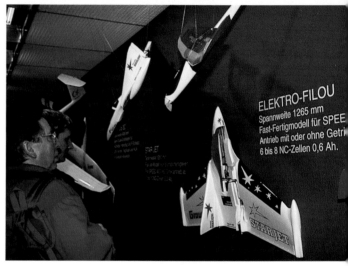

ABOVE: Many model designs now have the option of being powered by an electric motor or a glow engine. Although the battery weight is a slight drawback to comparative performance, the ever improving efficiency of electric motors and batteries is rapidly reducing this differential.

ABOVE RIGHT: You can have the best of both worlds with electric-powered gliders. The motor is used to climb to height and then switched off, the model then reverts to a glider and the propeller folds back to the fuselage sides.

ELEKTRO-FILOU
Spannweite 1265 mm
Fast-Fertigmodell für SPEE
Antrieb mit oder ohne Getri
6 bis 8 NC-Zellen 0,6 Ah.

ABOVE: Futuristic shapes are practical with electric power; flying wing-style models are appropriate as they have good aerodynamic efficiency and a pusher motor power can be incorporated.

Electric ducted fan units allow for a wide range of scale prototype jet aircraft to be modelled. There is very little risk of one motor failing and giving asymmetric thrust problems.

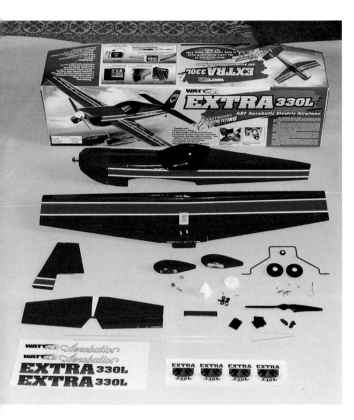

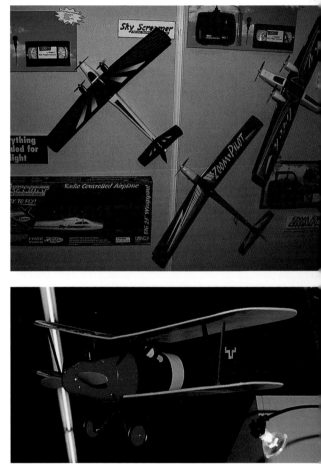

ABOVE: ARTF electric kits may, or may not, include the motor, but should include all the hardware, decals and control linkages to complete the model. It is possible to convert some electric kits to IC power and vice versa.

TOP RIGHT: More moulded-foam electric-powered ARTF models – the range and variety are enormous and growing all the time. Everything from a Fokker triplane to a Eurofighter jet is on the market.

ABOVE RIGHT: This diminutive World War I Albatros fighter can be flown indoors or outdoors and has a flight time of around eight minutes. It is always worthwhile experimenting with different battery packs and propellers.

and you will understand. If you can get your car close to where you are flying the model and can use the car battery for charging, then you have got a 'lightweight' flying-field support pack (providing you don't have to push the car because of a flat starter battery!). In this case, however, the same conditions could apply to IC power and the chances are that you are breaking the BMFA recommended safety code by flying the model so close to your car.

3. *Electric flight is a cheap form of power.*
   WRONG – or at least partly wrong. Yes, you can buy

an electric power set, consisting of a 600 motor, propeller and propeller adapter, for less than £14, a battery will cost around £20, a speed controller another £25 (depending on motor size, less if you only use an on/off switch) and have an outfit that will adequately power sports and semi-scale models. But, if you want serious power levels, for competition duration purposes or large multi-engined scale aircraft, then you will have to dig deep into your pocket. It should be expected that an efficient electric package is likely to cost the equivalent of a

You would be very hard put to construct and finish a model by traditional methods to rival the standard of this electric ducted fan F-16. Assembly of the kit only takes a day or so.

BELOW LEFT: This four-engined B-29 bomber is an example of the type of model that has been made possible by the introduction of miniature electric motors and radio equipment.

BELOW: Yes, you can have your Spitfire, though it is still not recommended for a first, or even second, RC model, but once you have mastered the control of a high-wing and low-wing trainer, go for it.

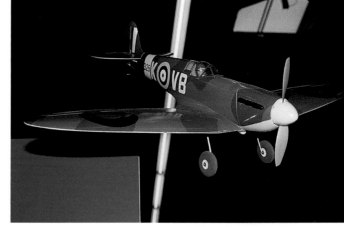

four-stroke engine, but with the benefit of fuel costs being eliminated in exchange for some addition to the home electricity bill.

4. *Electric flight is safe.*

WRONG. It is no more and no less safe than flying IC powered models. In some ways, it might be considered as slightly less safe – because it is quieter, the innocent spectator might not hear the model coming towards him or her and therefore there is an increased risk of being hit. And don't be fooled by the quietness of the motor/propeller. If you are in contact with the propeller, except on the smallest motors with push-on, soft plastic propellers, the results can be very nasty. Not only will

the glass-reinforced plastic carbon-fibre propellers cut you, they will continue to cut you, as there is no engine stoppage as you might experience with an IC motor.

Whether you fly IC or electric – or gliders – you must always exhibit extreme care when flying. There is the temptation to fly electric models in public areas, simply because they are quiet and do not annoy the public. First check that the flying of models is permitted (or not banned) by the local by-laws and if you do fly, have someone standing by you to keep you aware of any other persons in the flying area. Making sure you have the necessary insurance cover is an essential action.

5. *Electrics are only for slow models.*

WRONG. One of the best competition classes for electric power is pylon racing. Here you have a limited race time, less than two minutes, so you can get all the 'juice' from the battery in a short period and obtain maximum power from the motor. The end result is high speeds that are comparable with IC-powered models, although it is one time where the lack of noise reduces the effect and enjoyment of the action. The adrenaline-making time of pylon racing is when the engines are screaming away on the start line, waiting for the flag to drop – with electrics there is an unhealthy silence. Imagine a Formula One Grand Prix with all the cars on the starting grid, red lights showing and no noise – it would be enough to silence even Murray Walker!

6. *Electrics have virtually reached the limits of their development potential.*

WRONG. On the aircraft side we haven't done a fraction of the experimentation and development of the car racing fraternity, who have invested tens of thousands of pounds to produce higher performance motors and more reliable speed controllers. The battery manufacturers have been concentrating on increasing the outputs of the cells while reducing their size and weight. We, as aeromodellers, are now benefiting from all this development work; manufacturers of electric motors are beginning to release them, modified for aero work.

We can expect more improvements to motor and battery efficiencies, and one day we might reach the stage when an electric motor and battery will produce the same power as a glow engine and will weigh the same as the engine and fuel complement combined. Then, it may well be goodbye to the IC model aero engine.

BE GUIDED BY THE KIT MANUFACTURER OR DESIGNER

Looking at the number and variety of electric motors listed in a catalogue makes you realize what an impossible task the beginner could have in selecting a suitable motor for a particular model, how many and what capacity battery cells to buy, whether to use a gearbox and what propeller sizes to use. In comparison, the selection of an IC engine and propeller is simple.

Fortunately, designers and manufacturers have recognized the problems facing the aeromodelling newcomer and either include the required motor in the kit (fixed-wing and helicopters) or specify the equipment required. One of the biggest revolutions in electric models has been with the 'Park Flyers' and indoor models. These lightweight, sometimes ultra lightweight, models of less than 100g (3.5oz) total weight, are slow flyers, although they can also be highly manoeuvrable, making them suitable for relatively small indoor venues. There is no doubt that one of the biggest growth areas in aeromodelling will be in the ARTF indoor RC electric models.

Absolutely staggering are the number of moulded foam ARTFs, which allow you to fly all types of aircraft at affordable prices. If you had any doubts about the popularity of electric-power models take a look through the kits available; you will find a greater variety than in any other department and growing at a rapid rate – Spitfires, Hurricanes, WWI fighters are all with us.

WHAT'S WATT

If you are new to RC aeromodelling you will want to know what is required for electric-powered models and whether this form of power is suitable for a first trainer model. Answering the last point first, yes, electric-powered models are suitable for basic training, but within certain limitations. Most of the models intended for training purposes are ARTFs (almost ready to fly) either from moulded foam, or built-up construction and ready covered. With a few exceptions, they are of the powered glider type, for two- or three-channel radio and frequently supplied with the motor, sometimes the propeller as well. The advantage of the two-channel models, which do not have any speed control for the motor, is that they can be operated from the inexpensive two-channel radio outfits. Going down this route allows you to get started in RC flying for a little over £100, but you must accept that it will not be possible to fly the models in all types of weather. One step further, to operating three functions, for example rudder for turning, elevator for climbing and diving, and motor control for ascending and descending, and you have a more versatile electric sailplane, or a potentially greater selection of model types, including the chance to go for the conventional high-wing, semi-scale model.

IS IT A BIRD – IS IT A TOY?

Differentiating between a toy aeroplane and a model aeroplane is now almost impossible. You can go into a toy shop and buy a completely ready to fly, two-channel electric-powered model, complete with motor, rechargeable batteries, transmitter, the lot, for around £50. Yes, it may not have proportional rudder control and ascending and descending may be via motor control and not elevator – which, in any case, is the correct way – but the models are capable of reasonable flight. So, if it flies, does it matter whether we call it a model or a toy? The sad aspect of these inexpensive toys is that they are often broken on their first outing. They are only truly suitable for flying in calm weather conditions and how often do we get those? The temptation will be to charge the model, go out to the local park or recreation ground and for a totally untrained person to throw the model into the air, probably out of the wind and far too steeply. Even if the launch is good, the equally untutored operator of the transmitter has to become a qualified pilot from the moment that the aeroplane gets into the air – and with the aeroplane almost certainly being on 27mHz, did he check first to see whether any other toy cars or boats are being operated in the vicinity on the same frequency? If there happened to be one on the same frequency, there could be a disaster. For the experienced model flyer the control of these small electric models is not necessarily easy, so how much more difficult it is for a complete novice to complete a successful flight?

I am not decrying these 'toy' models – they are incredibly ingenious and some of the more way-out and unusual designs fly the best. But are they a good introduction to radio-controlled model flying? Anything that makes young people more air-minded has to be good, and if they achieve a modicum of success it may well lead them on to greater things, but in all honestly their success is likely to be limited. If only the salesperson would point them in the right direction – to a model club – and the members of the club would be open-minded about these 'toy' aeroplanes, we would end up with many more satisfied aeromodellers.

There are more advanced electric models on the market. These are also in the virtually ready to fly category and may be sold as a complete package, or alternatively without the radio gear. These can be highly attractive and seductive, with models of Reno racers, modern jet fighters, multi-engined types and scale models from all eras. If you are a beginner, please put them on your next year's Christmas presents list and not this one, or it could all end in tears!

BACK TO THE BASICS

For any power output (propeller size and rpm) the electric motor/switch/battery package will be heavier than a modern IC engine and fuel tank. For this

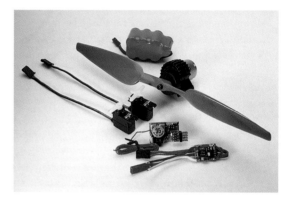

Electric flight packs, containing the motor, battery, receiver, speed controller and servos, are available, or the items are available separately.

The selection of an electric motor for a specific model can be bewildering. If no positive recommendations are made with the plan or kit, you will have to obtain advice, or experiment, which can be an expensive option.

Micro-receivers can now be purchased with weights of just a few grams, but ensure that it has specifications to suit your needs, for example operating range and number of channels.

Motor speed controllers have to be matched to the motor being used and the current drawn; it may also be necessary to match the controller with the specific motor/s.

reason it is important to minimize the weight of the air-frame and of the radio/motor complement, in order to keep the wing loading of the model reasonable and the flying characteristics good. It was normal practice, with the smaller and less expensive electric models, to have an on/off switch for the motor, whether servo-operated or electronic. The cost of electronic speed controllers and the weight of them have now reduced to the extent that the fitting of a speed controller is standard for three- and four-channel electric models. Nickel cadmium and lithium polymer nickel metal hydride batteries have also been improving in capacity/weight terms and this gives the modeller the option of having separate batteries for the motor and the radio.

An alternative would be to use a BEC (battery eliminator circuit), which allows a common battery to be used for both the motor and radio receiver and servos. The disadvantage of the BEC, which cuts off the battery supply to the motor when the voltage of the battery drops to a predetermined level, is that it gives a limited period of control for the radio side and it is not easy to define the safe operating time. For high-efficiency powered gliders, where 'hooking' a thermal is quite likely, it would be safer to have a separate small-capacity receiver battery. Whether you use a mechanically operated switch, electronic switch with BEC, speed controller or separate batteries it is a wise precaution to have a fuse in the line from the battery to the motor to prevent the motor being burned out if the propeller is stalled accidentally. One other precaution to take is to suppress the motor to prevent

radio interference. This will already be done on many of the supplied-in-kit motors, and instructions will be included with motors supplied separately.

Once bitten by the electric bug you will have plenty of motors, gearboxes, propeller types, speed controllers, battery types and numbers of cells and chargers from which to choose and experiment.

THE FUTURE

With such rapid developments in the field of electrics and electronics it is difficult to keep abreast of all the new products coming on to the market. You should read the model aeroplane magazines to keep in touch with new developments; motors, batteries and control systems are constantly improving, becoming more efficient and getting smaller. To give one example, at the time of writing this book I visited an indoor flying meeting where many experimental radio-control electrics were being flown. One example was a small model constructed from expanded polystyrene foam sheet of the type used as wallpaper insulation. Powered by a miniature electric motor from an electronic pager, using a lithium polymer rechargeable cell, the control was via an infra-red transmitter and receptor, the controls being proportional rudder and motor speed. The total flying weight of this micro model was just 7.5g (0.3oz), little more than a pound coin, and it was capable of a flight of more than fifteen minutes. Such achievements would have been unthinkable a few years earlier and what the future will bring is equally unimaginable.

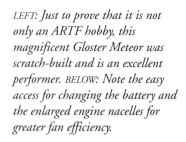

LEFT: *Just to prove that it is not only an ARTF hobby, this magnificent Gloster Meteor was scratch-built and is an excellent performer.* BELOW: *Note the easy access for changing the battery and the enlarged engine nacelles for greater fan efficiency.*

BELOW: *Electric-powered models do not have to be small. There is no theoretical limit to their size or scale, it is simply a matter of increasing the battery complement and motor ratings.* INSET: *The SE5 biplane is quarter-scale and has a geared motor.*

CHAPTER 6

Silent Flight

Glider pilots are sometimes a breed on their own. For them, the real challenge is to pit their skills against the elements and they do not want the additional encumbrances of engines, fuels and batteries. It is the beauty of the model being kept aloft by the action of a thermal or the upcurrents of wind from a hilly terrain. Gliders can almost be taken as a subject in their own right, as the variety of models virtually rivals those of powered aircraft, with the exception of helicopters. There are trainers, sports, racing, scale and aerobatic gliders, just as there are the powered versions, but one of the principal differences is that the flying is usually undertaken in areas of great beauty. A wide open, windswept airfield is rarely a place of loveliness, but a windswept hill, with views of valleys and, maybe, the sea, now that's a different proposition.

Gliders, or sailplanes (they are the same thing, a sailplane just sounds a little more exotic and upmarket), provide some of the purest forms of flying. With these unpowered models we are relying entirely on the elements and our own skills to be able to keep them aloft. When I have given talks to young people I usually ask them what keeps an aeroplane flying in the sky. The answer used to be that it was being pulled along by the propeller, now it is more likely that the jet engines are pushing it through the air. How does a glider stay in the air? That would normally stump them, as it was considered to be some sort of unnatural magic that achieved this flight. In some ways these youngsters were right, it is magic to watch a glider making its silent way through the air without any apparent form of support – but all based on good aerodynamic principles.

Scale sailplanes are undeniably beautiful and there are a number of different methods of getting them into the air. They can be towed by a powered tug, hand-towed, bungee launched or slope-soared from hills.

There are two principal types of glider flying, flat field and slope soaring. The former relies on rising air currents (thermals) to keep the model airborne – and avoiding the corresponding areas of 'sink' – while slope soaring involves upward air currents produced by the wind blowing on to a hill slope or cliff.

SLOPE SOARING

If you are lucky enough to live near to good slope-soaring sites, and they can vary from quite small hills or dunes to huge cliff faces, it would be almost criminal, as an aeromodeller, not to use them. The quality of lift produced from a hill site will vary according to the angle of slope, the horizontal contours, the terrain in front of the site and how 'square-on' it is to the prevailing wind. There are many recognized gliding sites around the country and details of these are available from the governing body of aeromodelling, the BMFA, or there may be a local club or group that operates on a regular basis from a slope-soaring site. Not all the suitable sites are listed or used; you may be able to locate one that gives good lift, with certain wind directions, but, before flying, do check and get the requisite permission to use the site and never fly without having third-party insurance.

Hills, cliffs and mountains are generally in relatively uninhabited areas and any budding RC flyer living in such a domain is not likely to have a model club close to hand. Learning to fly on your own is fraught with dangers and the chances of taking a powered model for its and your first flight and getting it down in one piece are not too good. One recent advantage in going it alone with a slope-soaring model is the introduction of EPP (expanded polypropylene). This black foam material is very tough and has the properties of normal expanded polystyrene, white foam material, but does not need to be veneered with balsawood or obechi veneer. Instead, the wing panels are joined, sometimes with carbon-fibre tube reinforcement inserted into the wings and the joint strengthened with reinforced parcel tape, the sticky-backed type used for strong packages. This tape is then applied over the whole wing surface, even being used as a hinge material for the ailerons, where fitted and overlapped at the edges. More for attractive effect, although also for reducing the destructive ultra-violet rays from the sun, the white reinforced tape is then covered with coloured vinyl tape, a thinner tape

An example of the scale sailplane modeller's art, where the model is built from scratch and features full-sized construction techniques, rib for rib and former for former replication. These large gliders are sheer elegance in flight.

EPP is popular with slope-soaring enthusiasts because of its rugged, near unbreakable qualities. It requires a different finishing technique, using parcel and reinforced tapes.

similar to brown parcel tape. Perhaps the overall effect is not that expected by a traditional aeromodeller; it results, though, in a near indestructible model, which will take a tremendous amount of punishment.

I have witnessed, at public displays, EPP models being purposely dived vertically into the ground from a height of 10 feet or so, with no more apparent damage than a squashed nose, which recovers. This is an irresponsible piece of 'showing off'. While the model might withstand the crash, the radio equipment is vulnerable. Not all of the RC components are solid state, the servos have moving parts and gears and the receiver has a fragile frequency crystal. At all times, whether on powered models or gliders, we should try to protect the radio equipment and check it thoroughly after any crash. To purposely abuse it can only lead to problems.

Having given the warnings, it remains true that the EPP glider way of learning to fly has much to be recommended. The fact that the models will take severe knocks ensures that flying can usually continue and there is less repair work to carry out. Flying-wing models, without any conventional tail surfaces, are popular subjects for EPP structures; they are very efficient, responsive and great fun to fly. For the beginner I would still recommend a conventional layout, that is, with a fuselage, wings and tail surfaces, as these make keeping orientation easier (which way the model is flying) and can be made less responsive more easily in respect of control surface movements and effects.

UP LIKE A LIFT

Having found a suitable slope-soaring site, and if it is being used by other flyers, having made yourself known, elicited their help and ensured that your frequency is not being used by anyone else, you are ready for a truly exciting experience. But if you are on your own, and assuming that you have carried out all the necessary model checks – checked the balance point and that there are no warps, that everything is fixed together properly and the radio range is okay – it is time to take those first hesitant steps. Try to weigh up the possible lift that is available, not easy because it is always invisible, but if you have a good long ridge, no trees or hills immediately in front, a moderate breeze that is blowing at 90 degrees to the ridge, then you shouldn't have too many problems. The lighter the model or, more correctly, the lighter the wing loading,

Flying-wing gliders, using EPP materials, find favour with sports slope-soaring flyers, who often participate in aerial combat contests – providing that it is in a safe area, with no general public around.

the calmer the conditions can be to maintain flight. Take a good look at what is in front and at the bottom of the hill, just in case you finish down there. If the wind is rather stronger than you would wish you can always launch the model from part of the way down the hill, where the wind effect will be less. Cliff sites offer some of the best and smoothest lift conditions (there are no obstructions in front to cause disturbances), but wait until you have some experience or a tutor to use these; it can be very disturbing to see your model halfway between the cliff top and the sea and not know in which direction it will go.

Firmly launch the model or, preferably, get someone else to launch it, directly into wind, nose slightly down and with the controls at neutral. Don't be tempted to hold up elevator on to make the model climb, as it is more likely to go straight over your shoulder on to the ground behind you. (Have you checked that the approaches behind are clear of trees and the ground free of boulders?) The initial aim is to get the model tracking, with wings level, away from the hill; once out there the natural air currents will lift the model higher. Once at a safe height and away from the hill, we can start to check out the turning of the model. With ailerons the model will bank over

A simple two-function (elevator and aileron) glider can get you flying from a suitable slope for a very modest outlay. However, if you live miles away from a slope-soaring site it may be more economical to think in terms of powered flying.

towards the ridge, down elevator will increase the speed of the model and take it out and away from the ridge.

That's fine, we've got the model safely in the air, but how do we get it down again? (Ten to fifteen minutes is about as much concentration time as you will safely have in the initial stages.) We have to bring the model around and behind us, where there is no lift, to land it. You will probably find that the sink rate of the model is very high when it gets behind you. Though it varies from site to site, be prepared for the model 'falling out of the sky' at this point. Come round with plenty of height to spare, don't let the model go very far downwind and keep some down elevator on to keep it penetrating. If it carries on and flies past you at head height, or above, don't worry, just take it out, gain some height and try another circuit. When you are in the right position to land the model, keep it coming gently forward until it is a foot or two above the ground and then ease on a little up elevator. Be positive with the touch down, it is better to have the model

immediately, but you will then have to pull some up elevator to induce the turn. Where you are using rudder as your primary turning function, you will find that the model does not go into a turn immediately the rudder is applied; the model must first yaw (flat turn) before the wings start to bank and the model turns. Again, up elevator may be needed to stop the nose from dropping and to continue the turn. You must always try to avoid having the model turning back towards the slope, because if it gets into this position it will be flying downwind, the ground speed will be high and the model may reach the slope before you have time to make the corrective turning manoeuvre.

Your aim is to 'tack' the model up and down the slope, not too close, nor too far out where the lift will decline. Fly past yourself to the left, carry out a right-hand 180 degrees turn, fly past again, on to the right, now a 180 degrees left turn and horizontal with the ridge again. If you can keep to this extended horizontal '8' pattern you will soon learn how to handle the model. Remember that the elevator is your 'speed' control. If the model is climbing, but being blown back

There are some glorious moulded glass fibre and traditionally constructed sailplanes to be had as ARTF kits, requiring assembly only. Build qualities are exceptionally high in many cases, and with the 4,000mm (156in) and 5,000mm (195in) wingspan examples, this is reflected in the costs.

Many of the slope-soaring sites are located in beauty spots and the family will most likely be pleased to accompany you on such trips. Be aware, though, that the winds can be cold and it may be a long walk from the car park to the site.

land a little firmly than risk it being caught by a gust and flipped on its back. If you can obtain help it is to be recommended; an experienced flyer will know the wind and lift conditions, will be able to take the transmitter if you get into trouble – or, better still, may be able to teach you on a buddy-box system.

NOT JUST UP AND DOWN

Once you've become competent at slope-soaring simple rudder and elevator models and more advanced aerobatic types, there's a whole new world of flying open to you – and with no fuel costs. PSS (power scale soaring) allows you to fly model jets without the problems of ducted fans or gas turbine engines, WWII fighters and even Golden Era aircraft. You will be amazed at how good these scale models look as they fly along the valley below you and then climb away to height, all courtesy of the up currents of invisible air. Competitions for slope soaring include pylon racing and aerobatics and the latest adrenaline producer is combat. With the advent of the almost indestructible EPP models, especially the flying-wing designs, the idea of aerial combat was formed and this has proven to be great fun. There have to be

serious safety considerations when flying these models, ensuring that there are no members of the public in the areas where a model might be brought down, and keeping any heavy components, such as batteries and ballast, clear of the nose of the aircraft. A recent innovation is the Air Wars combat system which is a non-contact system that fires infrared 'bullets' and hits on the other models are recorded. Because it is possible to have an optional PC interface and software, up to thirty pilots can participate in aerial combat contests, adding another dimension to slope soaring.

FLAT FIELD FUN

Launching by Towing

Glider, or sailplane, flying is not restricted to hills and slopes; full-sized sailplanes are not totally reliant on lift from slopes and nor are RC model gliders. Flying from a normal flying site with gliders can take a number of forms. Although we rely on the up-going columns of air (thermals) to keep our models airborne, we need a method of getting to them, as they are rarely to be found down to ground level and the higher the model gets, the more chance there is of finding the thermal. The simplest method, but not necessarily the easiest to fly, is by towing the model to height on a line and releasing it by allowing the line to go slack and then slipping off the tow hook on the underside of the model. This method relies on a good understanding between the person towing, who should be reasonably conversant with model flying, and the pilot, speed of the two and the moment

Scale models of jet-powered prototypes are particularly suited to slope soaring as they are aerodynamically clean, with no propellers, can be flown without undercarriages and look great flying up and down the valleys.

57

of release are important for the safety of the model and for reaching a good launch height. The person towing continues to tow the aircraft to height, using his knowledge of glider towing, until the model reaches maximum release height, or the pilot calls for him to release.

When it comes to contest duration flying a system of pulleys is used to assist in towing the gliders to height, but these are not necessary for sports flying.

Bungee Launching

More popular, and allowing single-handed operation, is launching by bungee. For this a length of rubber, usually surgical tube, or cotton-covered rubber, is connected to a nylon monofilament line. The energy stored in the rubber, when it is stretched, is sufficient to 'catapult' the model to height. But, because the energy is gradually dissipated, the model is taken at the relatively comfortable speed of the line, with only the initial speed for the release being rapid. Surgical tube bungees will give a more gradual and controllable launch and are to be recommended. You will need about 30m (98ft) of the bungee and 100m (328ft) of the nylon monofilament line (20kg (44lb) breaking strain). The bungee and nylon line are joined, by a ring or swivel, and the opposite end of the bungee is secured to a special bungee spiral stake, which must be very firmly secured in the ground. The danger of this spike being accidentally pulled out of the ground, when the bungee is at full stretch, cannot be overemphasized; one person has already been killed through this happening. The security of the spiral stake will depend on finding suitable ground conditions where it can be screwed in to its full depth. At the opposite end of the monofilament line there is a drogue chute, or pennant, a fishing swivel (also 20kg strain) and a further 0.5m (20in) of nylon terminating in a release ring. The ring is attached to the hook on the glider underside (fitted in front of the centre of gravity; take a line at 20 degrees from the wing balance point and where it bisects the underside of the fuselage is where the hook should be located). A releasable hook is a sensible investment for larger models; particularly when they are flown in windier weather. These are operated from a spare radio channel and allow the glider to be released even when the model is under tension.

With the model in hand, the line and bungee are stretched until there is enough 'pull' on the line to take the model to height – the actual degree of stretch will depend on the wing loading of the model and how much wind is blowing, something that can only be gauged by experience. Obviously, you take one step at a time and don't go for broke on the first launch. The initial surge from the bungee will give the glider quite a high speed and speed creates lift and climb.

Directional control on the ascent is by rudder – not ailerons – and attempts should be made not to overcontrol, but to anticipate any weaving and give small rudder corrections in good time. Having a releasable tow hook can come in handy in moments of panic when the model has got into (or you have let it get into) a strong weaving pattern. In calm wind conditions you may have to weave the model purposely from side to side to increase the speed of the model on the line – in a similar way that water skiers tack from side to side to build up speed before carrying out a manoeuvre – and create more lift, but don't overdo the turning. Applying a little down elevator when the model is at maximum height should release the model. If it is difficult to get it off the hook it is probably in an area of strong lift, so persevere and you should be in for a good flight. Once released, the towline falls slowly to earth, retarded by the drogue chute (which also helps to maintain line tension during the tow). Away from the line, the glider will remain airborne as long as there are thermals about and dependent on the skill of the pilot.

For clubs specializing in gliders and sailplanes it is worthwhile them obtaining an electric-powered winch, which will take the place of the bungee and hand towing. The pilot can vary the speed of the winch by a foot switch, and the line is taken from the winch around a pulley and back to the pilot/glider. Winches can cope with a variety of models; the high-power competition types take the models to height in a very short time.

Lift and Separate

Two other forms of getting a glider to height involve the use of an IC powered model. Carrying the glider on the back of the powered model hasn't been too popular, probably because it is not easy to adapt the launch support mechanism to such a variety of models. By contrast, the aero-tow, as seen with full-sized aircraft, is becoming increasingly popular and meetings are held for this pastime, most of the gliders being scale sailplanes and the tug aircraft scale models of 'Wilgas', 'Cubs' and so on. Aero-towing is both exciting and effective and is equally suitable for non-scale gliders. Such is the power of some of the tugs that they can make multiple glider tows. The present unofficial world record is for towing ten gliders to height and successfully releasing them to make controlled flights back to the launch area. A certain degree of co-ordination between the tug and glider pilot is obviously required, the more so when you have a limited reserve of power with the tug. With a powerful tug the glider is virtually carried to height; the glider can even resort to rolling aerobatics on the climb to release height.

Hand Launches and Mini-Bungees

For those with a really strong right arm it is possible to have small, still radio-controlled, hand-launched gliders. The aim is to propel the model as high as possible, hopeful that it will get high enough to sniff a thermal. For those with flabby muscles, some of the competitions for this type of model allow a limited stretch bungee to be used.

A Bit of Both

For flat field flying there is a lot to be said for the powered glider approach. Using a small diesel or glow engine, mounted on the nose or on a power pod above the wing, the IC engine takes the model to height and when it cuts it reverts to being a glider. The alternative is to use electric power, which is more eco-friendly, and with a switch or speed controller installed, the power

An alternative to an IC-powered glider is to fit an electric motor to a conventional glider. It is cleaner and quieter, and you may be permitted to fly it at slope-soaring sites on days when there is no wind blowing.

can be applied as and when required. Many of the electric powered gliders, with folding propellers, are not far short of having the same efficiencies as the sailplanes, though admittedly they have a higher wing loading, but sometimes the non-powered models are ballasted to improve penetration in windy conditions.

Very long flights are to be had by going down the electric powered glider route, but do remember that when using a common battery for the motor and radio you only have a limited safe airborne time once the BEC (battery eliminator circuit) has cut out the motor. Although nearly quiet in operation, do not operate your powered glider on a slope-soaring site – the purists are unlikely to appreciate any sort of motorized model! Powered gliders do offer a good introduction to IC flying, providing you are prepared to wait for good weather conditions, but pure glider flying from flat fields is more problematic. Unless you are lucky enough to hook a thermal, your flight time is going to be quite limited, which will not give you much time to improve your model-control skills. Also, launch by towing or bungee requires quite a high degree of competence in reaching a safe height, something the raw beginner may not have. For the absolute beginner the slope soaring and electric powered sailplane routes will prove more fruitful.

Where no slope sites are easily available and if you wish to operate with a minimum of additional equipment, a motorized glider, powered by a diesel engine, is a good compromise between pure gliding and power flying.

COMPETITION MINDED

For thermal-soaring enthusiasts the competition element is very strong and the governing body will organize contests on a regular basis. Tasks of these competitions include combinations of speed, duration and spot landing, all within a single flight. Models for the highest echelons of thermal-soaring competitions are very sophisticated, using the most modern methods of moulded glass/carbon-fibre construction. The finishes on the wings of these models are as near perfect as possible, comparable to the flying surfaces on full-sized contest sailplanes. For the energetic and fit, cross-country contests will examine not only the flying skills of the contestant, but also his legs, as some of the flights will cover many miles.

Pylon racing, at slope sites, helps to increase the adrenaline levels. A pylon is erected at each end of the slope and the models have to complete a given number of laps in a minimum amount of time. It often becomes a battle between keeping in the air, but not wasting time leaving the slope to find lift, with the result that much of the flight is at low level. Aerobatics are also a compromise between having sufficient height to perform the manoeuvres, but not wasting too much time hunting for lift. Much will depend on the quality of lift at the time of the contest, and it may be a case of 'he who dares, wins'.

Scale competitions are not restricted to flat field sites; they are in fact more popular on the slope sites. As stated previously, almost any subject can be made to fly as a PSS model. As a result, there is usually a wide diversity of models at a PSS meeting, ranging from DH Comet racers, to Japanese WWII Zero fighters, Tiger Moth biplanes and enormous B-52 bombers. Perhaps it is the jet subjects that benefit most from this form of gliding, as they tend to have clean lines and low drag and simply 'grease' through the air. There is, of course, one thing missing from the scene and that is the sound of a jet engine. For these scale contests only, it might be permissible to allow electronic noise generators to simulate the noise of gas turbine engines; it would certainly add another dimension to the flying. You could even get completely carried away and include the sound of machine guns, rockets and bombs, but perhaps my flight of fantasy is going too far.

What more could you ask for than a beautiful seaside slope-soaring site, the sun shining, a gentle breeze blowing and the 'free as air' flying with a glider? Once you have overcome the fear of launching over the cliff, you are in for a wonderful experience.

BELOW: No worries about getting all eight engines started on this B-52 bomber – it is a glider and can be flown from a slope-soaring site, or towed to height by a powered tug and left to hunt for thermals.

CHAPTER 7

Whirlybirds

Autogyros and helicopters – what is the difference between these two types of machines, both of which rely on rotating blades for the lift to keep them airborne? It is a very simple difference, in that the autogyro relies on a propeller to give the forward momentum of the aircraft, the blades being freely rotating, while the helicopter has its blades driven by the engine. Once this *modus operandi* has been established we can look into the detail of design and control and how they are related to our radio-controlled models. One thing is certain, it took an enormous amount of research, experiment and sheer perseverance to get both types of aircraft models flying successfully, in particular with the mechanically more complicated helicopters.

AUTOGYROS

Unlike the helicopter, the autogyro has no tail rotor to counterbalance the effects of torque from the rotating blades. It does have the conventional tail surfaces of a tailplane/elevator and fin/rudder, but these are not ideal for countering torque effects. The problems to overcome are numerous and although fewer than those of a helicopter, their resolution is not simple.

The forward advancing rotor blades, in the direction of flight, are creating more lift than the retreating blades, that is, the forward speed of the model is added to the blade speed, whereas the retreating blade has the blade speed less the air speed. Allowing the rotor blades to flap up and down, providing less lift on the advancing blade, will, in theory, cure the imbalance of lift distribution; it should also cure the problems from gyroscopic effects from the rotor disc, resulting in a 90-degree reaction to a disturbance of the rotor. Also, allowing the rotor blades to lag as they advance and

slow down as they retreat should overcome the torque reaction. There are other possible methods of tilting the rotor head and fitting dihedral auxiliary wing tips, which do help to reduce the effects of torque and gyroscopic effects, but these tend to be effective at one flying (rotor) speed only. In addition, when the model is descending vertically, or near vertically, there is little airflow over the fin and rudder and this will not provide a directional corrective force. Because there will be some friction on the rotor bearing the effect of having no corrective force from the fin is to allow the autogyro to rotate in the same direction as the rotor.

Single-rotor autogyros have been developed to overcome these problems, and applying the same technology used in helicopters, with a fully articulated and remote-controlled rotor head, overcomes the torque and gyroscopic problems, but it is at a price. For one thing, it is no longer a simple, inexpensive answer to rotorized flight. Also, to have a degree of control and adequate lift from the rotors, they must be spinning at a reasonably high speed and to achieve this will either involve a very extended take-off run, or a mechanical means of spinning-up the rotor. It is possible to drive the rotors, via a clutch mechanism, from the engine, but the whole system is now becoming so complex that it would be as simple to construct a helicopter, which, in any case, would have a much greater degree of control.

There is, fortunately, one easy way of retaining the essential simplicity of the autogyro, although it may offend the purist. Attempts have been made to fit a second rotor, on a common shaft with the main rotor, rotating in the opposite direction to counteract the torque problems. However, because it is acting in the downwash from the main rotor it is less efficient and is only partially successful in causing the reactions necessary; it is also more effective at certain speeds than others. One simple way of overcoming the difficulties is to have a side by side twin rotor autogyro, with the rotors rotating in opposite directions. A stub wing, with sufficient span to give separation of the rotors, has the rotor bearings at each tip, angled back to ensure a vertical component of airflow as the model moves forward. Critics of the twin-rotor autogyro claim that the stub wing is providing part of the lift, but the rotors could be supported on a simple, non-aerodynamic beam and it would still fly satisfactorily; it is just that the stub wing is more convenient. In vertical flight, of course, the stub wing is not contributing any component of lift. Vertical flight, relative to the air, is possible, but because of the lack of airflow over the fin – and no tail rotor to compensate – it is likely to be directionally unstable. With a moderate wind it is certainly possible to carry out a vertical descent and landing relative to the ground.

The flying of these twin-rotor autogyros is extremely easy – they are near viceless and can be manoeuvred around like any conventional fixed-wing model, but with the added attraction of being able to include the ability to fly almost vertically up and down. A take-off requires the model to be directed into the wind and the take-off run continued until the rotor is providing adequate lift; lift-off is then essentially similar to a fixed-wing model. Hand launches are also possible, the model is held, slightly nose up, and the launcher runs with the autogyro until the rotors are spinning and then launches in the normal manner.

Basic aerobatics such as loops, rolls and stall turns are possible with most designs. It is with inverted flight that things get interesting. For inverted flight it is necessary to allow the rotors to stop, in the inverted position, and spin up in the opposite direction to achieve lift in a downward position. Naturally, this delay in the rotors slowing down, stopping and then spinning in the opposite direction sufficiently to create lift causes a fair degree of height loss, so it should not be attempted at low level. Equally needed is the height to revert to normal flight; the model may roll out quite quickly, but the rotor blades still have to reverse direction. During rolls and negative 'G' manoeuvres the blades will also stop momentarily, which is no problem when you are used to the phenomenon, but quite disturbing when it happens the first time.

Different landing techniques can be tried. A normal, forward speed landing presents no problems, a

Autogyros can offer a mechanically simpler and low-cost alternative to helicopters. They are more akin to fixed-wing model flying and cannot perform the manoeuvres of the 'copter, but can still be great fun.

Autogyros do not have powered rotors, they have a conventional motor and propeller in the nose and rely on the forward motion to spin-up the rotors and provide lift. Although true hovering flight is not possible, they get very close to this flying state.

more vertical continuous descent will result in a firm touch down, but not one that is likely to damage the model. Probably the favourite method is that used by the helicopter flyers with an 'auto-rotation'. Here the speed is maintained on the approach by the use of down elevator and the round-out is left until the autogyro is just clear of the ground, the energy and speed of the rotors allowing a soft touch down as up elevator is introduced.

Construction of the rotors, usually four-bladed, is extremely simple. The blades themselves are flat plate and glued to a hub of plywood plates and balsawood centre, set at angles of about 5 degrees negative pitch; the rotor shaft is inclined backwards by about the same amount. Accurate balancing is not critical, but will help with smooth operation. One of the most amazing features is that it is possible to lose one of the blades in flight and for the model to continue flying. This happens because the loss of lift on the rotor involved allows that side of the autogyro to tilt downwards, at the same time presenting that rotor at a higher angle of attack to the airflow. This, in turn, speeds up the damaged rotor and provides more lift, thus righting the model to level flight. A quite amazing spectacle.

There is still much research to be done on autogyros and the single rotor type is being developed with a more simplified solution to the problems mentioned.

HELICOPTERS

Over the past three decades or more, there have only been a couple of major technical breakthroughs in the field of radio-controlled model aircraft. One is the gas turbine engine, the other is the helicopter. It was quickly realized that the control functions of a model helicopter had to mirror, in miniature, those of the full-sized machine and anyone who has inspected the mechanics of the full size will know that these are very complex indeed. It took a great deal of experimentation, persistence, analysing and modifying, not to mention failures, before the first practical model helicopter was demonstrated to the world by Dieter Schluter, from Germany. As with many such achievements, once the invention was made and the problems resolved, it was a relatively simple matter for it to be duplicated and before too long other manufacturers were producing their own designs of radio-controlled helicopters.

Early helicopters were difficult to fly. They had fixed-pitch rotor heads that relied on an increase of power to gain lift, which meant that the inevitable lag between an input of throttle on the transmitter being translated to a speed-up of the rotor blades required very sensitive control. Rear rotor control, essential with any change of velocity, was also very sensitive and it was only with the advent of the gyro that this flight control was made easier. I wouldn't say that you had to be a genius to fly a model helicopter in those early days, but you certainly needed excellent flying skills and not a small amount of perseverance.

Now, the construction and flying of a radio-controlled model helicopter is within the realms of the average flyer. Yes, it is still more difficult to fly, comprehensively, than a fixed-wing model, but that only relates to taking a little longer to master the controls; it is a classic case of making haste slowly. An undoubted advantage of learning to fly a helicopter is that you are not committing to full flight from the beginning. You can gradually inch it off the ground, learn to hover it at a very low altitude, where it won't come to grief, before moving on to forwards and sidewards flight and, eventually, to carrying out a full circuit. Of course you may have a few 'happenings' along the way, but, if you choose a popular, well-tried helicopter kit it should be possible to obtain spares for the model at a reasonable cost.

As with fixed-wing flying it will be a great advantage if you can enlist the help of a qualified helicopter pilot and a buddy-box trainer lead. Also useful at the early stages of learning to fly, and later when attempting aerobatics, is a helicopter simulator. Orientation is one of the initial problems that will be encountered when flying a model helicopter (it's much easier when sitting in the cockpit of a full-sized 'chopper') and a simulator will help you to become familiar with the appearance of it from different angles. One thing is for sure, it is a whole lot less expensive crashing a simulated helicopter than it is the real thing.

HAVE I THE SKILLS TO BUILD A MODEL HELICOPTER?

Although they may be complex mechanical devices, the model helicopter kit comes either in the form of an ARTF, where a minimum of work is required to get it to a flyable condition, or as a bolt-together job.

Helicopter kits are all in the ARTF category and assembly is a case of bolting together, rather than gluing together, as with aeroplanes. No special tools or specialized engineering skills are required, just patience and care.

Unlike fixed-wing models, even the ARTF types, there is no cutting or gluing to do, and it is just a case of screwing and bolting together a series of metal and plastic subassemblies. Only basic tools such as spanners, screwdrivers and Allen keys are required, and adhesives are limited to the Loctite variety. Instructions for assembly are usually very thorough and include exploded diagrams, pictorial shots and written descriptions for both the mechanical parts and the radio installation. With a little care – and careful reading of the instructions – it should be within the capabilities of 90 per cent of model enthusiasts.

WHICH ONE AND WHICH RADIO?

Selecting the helicopter suitable for a beginner is not difficult, providing that you can get a bit of advice from an active helicopter flier or from an informed retailer. Certainly you should not consider any helicopter kit for an engine smaller than a '30' (0.30cu in) engine and the model should have the capability of being uprated to match your skill improvements. Look for a design that has been on the market for at least a year and check on the availability and price of spares. You will make the odd mistake in training and you

don't want to have to pay the earth for repairs. Some helicopter models reach the stage of becoming 'classics' and these are the kits to aim for if you can afford to go for the '60'-sized versions. Take note, too, of the starting methods used on the helicopter. Some kits are supplied complete with an engine incorporating a pull start, a system that has been in use on model cars for many years. Belt-drive starting, or electric starters with extension shafts, can be a little daunting to the beginner, particularly if he is trying to hold the model with one hand and start it with the other; a direct start system is much better in this respect.

It makes sense, if you are interested in flying helicopters, to concentrate on them at the expense of other types. Forget fixed-wing models for the time being; in fact, there are distinct advantages of going on to helicopter training without having any experience of flying fixed-wing models. If you already have, you will have to unlearn some of the natural reactions, not the least that in a panic situation you do not close the throttle, as you would for a fixed-wing model. Because the pitch and throttle functions are so interrelated with helicopters any assistance you can get from the transmitter to combine the action in a regulated manner is going to make life easier when flying the helicopter. Standard low-cost four- and five-channel radio systems

Learning to fly a model helicopter will depend on aptitude, conviction and the instruction you receive during the training period. There are training schools and if your local club does not have good training facilities it is worthwhile considering this option.

Get experienced advice before purchasing your first helicopter kit. It should be sufficiently large and have such elements as easy starting procedures. The cost of replacement parts should also be reasonable.

will not have these capabilities, whereas the computer outfits with helicopter specifications will have a host of features to assist with learning to fly, and later, when you become more experienced, for such events as auto-rotation landings. If you are thinking of flying both helicopters and fixed-wing models, then it is more important to purchase the radio outfit to suit the helicopter, as it will then have sufficient functions to cope with the fixed-wing designs.

I have mentioned the problems of torque and gyroscopic (precessional) effects earlier and with helicopters the rotors are relatively heavy and are spinning at high speeds, so these effects are magnified. Any pitch or throttle adjustment will require a correcting force by the tail rotor and as the pilot is already concentrating on the other three functions it is one additional control to worry about. This is where the tail rotor gyro comes into its own. These devices, originally mechanical, but now solid-state electronic, will sense any attempt at movement in the yaw axis (tail moving from side to side) and correct it immediately by increasing or decreasing the thrust of the tail rotor. For those modellers with super-quick reactions who may

think that they could outperform a gyro, forget it, the electronics win every time – and it does so automatically and without fuss, leaving you to concentrate on the other aspects of flying.

THE CONTROLS AND THE REACTIONS

With only two hands to control the transmitter functions, the principal controls being the two axis sticks, we have to combine the actions within these limitations.

Throttle, normally on the left-hand stick, controls the power from the engine, which is transferred to the rotor blades.

The drive to the tail rotor is taken from the engine and geared at a constant ratio to the main rotor speed. Yaw control is achieved by adjusting the pitch on the tail rotor blades, operated by moving the 'rudder' stick on the left-hand side of the transmitter.

Collective pitch of the main rotor blades provides the rise or descent of the helicopter. The pitch is mixed with the throttle so that the rotor head speed remains constant throughout the flight.

Designed for commercial applications, for example carrying video cameras, large helicopters, powered by spark-ignition engines, are virtually as complex as the full-sized examples, with costs in proportion.

Few full-sized helicopters are powered by petrol engines. Nearly all are gas-turbine-powered and the same may be true of RC models in the future. Gas turbines are already featuring in scale helicopter models, and they look and sound right.

Cyclic control allows the helicopter to be flown forwards or backwards, and banked turns to the left and right by transmitter control of the right-hand stick. The transmitted signal increases or decreases the pitch of the leading or trailing rotor blades, to provide more or less lift and move the helicopter in the desired direction. Hovering is when all of these forces are in balance.

SET-UP AND SAFETY

Although the instruction manual will explain how to prepare your newly assembled helicopter for flight, it is one thing to read about it and another thing to be sure of doing it correctly. A properly set-up helicopter will be easy to fly, relatively speaking; one out of balance, or with the controls incorrectly harmonized, will give the operator endless troubles. If you can get professional help with the setting-up at this stage it will save a lot of heartache – and quite a few pounds. The correct operation and setting of the engine is also an important factor, for example knowing how far to turn the main needle valve in, without the risk of the engine going too lean, getting too hot and cutting out, and obtaining a smooth, consistent transition throughout the throttle range is vital. This is why it is also important to have a first-rate engine, as poor throttle response will result in erratic flying and unreliability crashes!

Model helicopters get a hard life, as the engine is being run at high speeds for much of the time and the mechanical parts are whirring around at great rates. With the best balancing in the world there is bound to be a certain degree of vibration and with the control linkages going at sixteen to the dozen, there is always the risk of wear on the components and fixings coming loose. After every flying session you should check the helicopter thoroughly for any 'slop' in the control linkages, nuts and bolts for tightness and rotor blades for possible damage. Indeed, a quick check for security should be made after each flight. Fortunately most components are readily visible and the radio equipment is easily accessible by removing the body shell. If you have any doubts about the correct functioning of the mechanical or electronic components,

do not fly the helicopter again until the fault has been found and remedied. And if you do have to disassemble the helicopter, double-check that it is reassembled in the correct way. I had the task of acting as an advisor in an insurance claim where the modeller, preparing the helicopter for a public display, refitted the paddle blades the wrong way round – with near fatal results. (You have obtained insurance, haven't you?)

3D MASTERS

Nothing has illustrated the advances made in the design and flying of helicopters more than the 3D Masters contests. 3D helicopter flying is just a term to describe the extreme manoeuvres capable with the advanced models and incredible skills of the pilots. Inverted auto-rotations (engine stopped), manoeuvring the model to an upright state at the last minute and landing on the spot, featherlight, are a common occurrence – but not to be emulated by the inexperienced! World-class flyers demonstrate their craft in seemingly impossible positions. How can a helicopter stay on the knife edge, where the main rotor is in the vertical plane, while it performs endless circles and eights – where does the lift come from? The same applies to the astonishing vertical speeds from a standing start, the flicks, the snaps and the pirouettes; the manoeuvres are heart-stopping. Let

Helicopter competitions call for specific manoeuvres to be flown with a great deal of accuracy, similar to fixed-wing aerobatic contests. Long periods of practice and full knowledge of the helicopter's flight characteristics are necessary for competition success.

Jeff Barringer, organizer of the 3D Masters competitions, describe the flying of a Master Class winner, Curtis Youngblood, from his perch on the media stand:

Curtis still had a few tricks up his sleeve, one of which was an interesting manoeuvre that I think he calls a Whirlwind. It is an increasingly larger and faster inverted knife-edge circle flown at a VERY low level. Come the time the circuit had increased to 50m diameter, his machine was heard to crash through the tops of the trees and then disappear from sight. Now the crowd couldn't see it, Curtis couldn't see it, and, 10m above him, I couldn't see it either!

A brief moment when the world stood still and then suddenly the machine reappeared from behind the trees, still on knife-edge and still moving at an almighty rate of knots. The crowd went wild and justifiably so, we were witnessing the State of the Art. Curtis' flight ended with an inverted auto almost to ground level and then a roll erect to mighty approval

3D helicopter flying seems to defy the laws of gravity and the extraordinary manoeuvres performed, such as knife-edge flying and 'death spirals', really have to be seen to be believed. Flying inverted, inches off the ground, calls for immense skills and strong nerves.

from the crowd, and no one was left in any doubt whatsoever why he is the World's Number One – it just doesn't get any better.

At the 3D Masters events you will also have the opportunity of witnessing the latest gas turbine helicopters, surely the way forward with the high potential thrusts and smooth operation. Flying to music, be it Pink Floyd or Prokofiev, is also becoming more popular, and it diminishes the drone of the engines.

ABOVE: *Flying a radio-controlled model helicopter from a billiard table would have been unthinkable a few years ago, but, thanks to the miniaturization of electronics, it is now commonplace to watch indoor helicopter flying – and there is more miniaturization to come.*

CHAPTER 8

Instant Flying – Almost

With ARTF (almost ready to fly), RTG (ready to go) and ARTC (almost ready to cover) kits, instead of having to cut out numerous pieces of balsawood and plywood, glue them together, sand the model smooth and then cover and paint the model, the majority of the work is done for you. Just how much of the model is pre-built and how many hours you will have to expend before you can go flying will depend on the individual kit. With some, it will be a matter of minutes before the model is in a flyable condition; the biggest delay will be in waiting for the battery to be charged. Other kits require a greater commitment by the purchaser, but still only limited skills, and most should be ready for flying after a day's none-too-strenuous work.

Why has there been such a revolution towards the introduction of ARTF model aircraft and in particular fixed-wing models – helicopters have always been in the ARTF class – where most of the work is involved with bolting parts together? Undoubtedly there are more demands on our leisure time than ever before, but that is only one reason. For many model flyers the emphasis is on the pleasure of flying the models and not the building, so if that is the case and you can limit the amount of valuable time in the workshop and have more on the flying field, it would seem to be a sensible trade-off.

When you go into a modelling shop to buy a product the first thing that you see is the packaging, and there is no doubt that the full-colour box artwork on most of the ARTF kits is very seductive. Because the pre-covered examples have very fancy colour schemes, or are decorated with attractive decals, they have an immediate appeal, which is not dispelled when you open the box lid – the airframe really is covered in highly decorative colour schemes. Price is obviously another factor when

it comes to making the purchase; you will be looking for value for money. ARTF kits normally include such items as engine mounts, cowlings, canopies, fuel tank, wheels and all control linkages and accessories. When you are comparing costs of an ARTF with a traditional kit this fact has to be taken into consideration – if the conventional kit does not have all of these items, the costs of purchasing them has to be added to the basic kit cost. Covering, too, is a material that must not be overlooked, even if you do not count the labour involved in trying – and probably failing – to match the colour scheme of an ARTF.

GREAT VARIETY

Although the first ARTFs tended to be of the trainer and sports types, this is no longer the situation. While trainers still form the major part of the ARTF market, there is a growing demand for scale, aerobatics, glider and jet-powered aeroplanes. ('Scale' models are miniature flying replicas of full-size aircraft.) With scale, most manufacturers keep to the sport/scale standards and the limitations of manufacturing processes, for example straight lines where veneered foam components are incorporated. However, even these restrictions are now going by the board, with some of the scale ARTF offerings almost coming into the competition standard. Aerobatic models, scale and non-scale types, are popular ARTF subjects and it is not surprising to see why. Building accuracy is all-important and with serious aerobatic models, if they are constructed with twists and warps they will never fly accurately. Factory-produced airframes are virtually all built on jigs and this is more likely to produce true and accurate components than is possible by individuals

World Aerobatics Champion, Hanno Prettner, was one of the first to demonstrate ARTF models, and his skilled flying, plus the quality of the models, helped to popularize this type of model.

BELOW: Except for the lack of wing struts and the non-see-through glazing, this could be a full-size Cessna and not an injection-moulded ARTF radio-controlled model.

constructing their models on a building board. Even the top competition models, for example the huge specialist aerobatic designs, are mostly RTF types, admittedly constructed on a limited basis by professional model builders, but certainly not built by the pilot in lots of cases. Normal commercial aerobatic ARTF models are favoured by competition and sports flyers alike because of the consistency of build, which means that it is unlikely that one model will fly very differently to another from the same manufacturer.

Sailplanes are another area where the ARTF aspect is increasing rapidly. Whether you are talking about small 'fun' gliders, or the great majestic scale sailplanes of 3m (118in) wingspan or more, the kits tend to be of the type where the fuselage, wings and tail surfaces are ready constructed, covered and awaiting final assembly. Take a look at some of the medium-sized sailplanes and powered gliders, covered in transparent film – often manufactured in Czechoslovakia – the quality of the airframe and covering is stunning. Indeed, the standard of construction and finishing of the top of the range ARTFs is improving all the time and average aeromodellers would be hard-pushed to reach the levels of these factory-built examples. There will be an ongoing improvement of standards, and manufacturers will be finding new ways of producing 'identical' models with little or no variations, which will be, within the limits of the pilot, guaranteed to fly. ARTF models are increasingly becoming

RIGHT: ARTFs come in all shapes and sizes; this Piper Cub features a traditional built-up structure, with film covering (the inebriated pilot is an optional extra).

BELOW: Complex camouflage colour schemes, such as the one on this Bf 109, usually involve sticky-backed plastic covering, but printed heat-shrink films are being developed.

BELOW RIGHT: It may not be perfect scale, but this model will be instantly recognizable to any aviation enthusiast as a Tiger Moth and the ARTF kit offers a practical sports flying aeroplane.

BOTTOM: Manufacturers of ARTF kits keep up to date with new designs and follow the trends and patterns of competition models of all types.

more than factory-produced examples of conventional designs. We already have the ARC Ready 2, and two further designs in the range, where injection-moulding is used for the plastic airframe components and weight and quality repeatability are assured. In essence, these are like big Airfix kits, but designed and produced light and large enough to use as radio-controlled flying models. Providing there is sufficient demand, to defray the very considerable costs of producing the machine moulds, there is no reason why scale models of Spitfires, Focke-Wulfs, Mustangs and the like should not be manufactured in the same way.

EVEN MORE RTG

Another trend, with the smaller electric models, is for the model to be supplied complete with the motor, airborne battery pack and radio equipment (usually the basic two-function radio on 27mHz frequencies). Whether you consider these types as toys, the fact remains that they are flying models and should not be looked down upon, as many of them fly very well indeed. This trend will probably expand even more to the larger models, particularly trainers. As one famous

Ever inventive and experimental, manufacturers now often lead the way with innovative designs; this flexi-wing, microlight-style design is typical of the commercial introductions.

Smaller, all-moulded and pre-painted polystyrene foam models, such as this Corsair, are intended for free flight, but can be converted to RC, using micro radio systems.

RIGHT: Kit contents for ARTF models tend to include everything, except for the radio and engine, down to the last nut and bolt.

newspaper journalist, John Diamond, observed when he delved into aeromodelling via RC ARTFs, when you go to buy a car you don't expect to go back to the garage the next week and have to buy the engine, wheels and starter! Why should it be so with model aircraft? For the beginner, the idea of having a complete package makes a lot of sense.

NO 'ALMOST' PROBLEMS

We don't live in a perfect world and it would be wrong to give the impression that all you have to do is to purchase an ARTF model kit, spend a few hours gluing and screwing and you will have a model without blemish and be certain to fly perfectly. In common with most things in this life you tend to get what you pay for and some of the inexpensive kits may leave a little to be desired in the way of materials used and quality of construction. Price is not a complete guide, but if a model is from the lower price bracket you may find that the wood used is not balsawood. An alternative may have been substituted and the overall effect of this and other 'savings' will probably result in a heavier model – and lighter models fly better. There are no hard and fast rules for judging the quality of the ARTFs, except by inspecting the product, reading reviews in the modelling magazines and taking advice from your retailer or experienced modellers. Don't expect something for nothing, but you may well be delighted by the value for money of the modern ARTFs. Having been a kit manufacturer I am constantly amazed by the low cost of many, admittedly imported, kits on the market. I would not like to be in competition with them! However, improvements can certainly be made to ARTF models that will increase the longevity of the model.

GILDING THE LILY

You may think that suggestions for improving and modifying ARTF kits means that they are not very well produced in the first place. This is not so and the recommendations are simply to make the assembly easier, or to preserve the model better and give it a longer useful life. So here are a few ideas.

Fuel tanks are often supplied as two-pipe types, with one pipe for the fuel feed and the other for the vent/pressure feed. If there is no engine cowling and

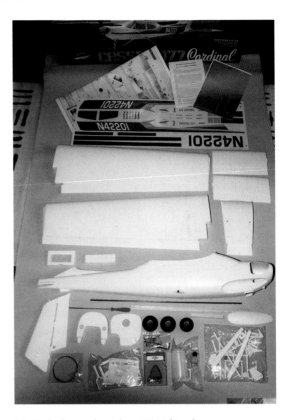

Typical of a good-quality ARTF kit, the wheels, fuel tank, spinner and all linkages are included, but do check the full contents when purchasing the kit.

it is easy to get at the fuel line on the engine carburettor, this is no problem, but if access to the fuel feed line is difficult you either need a third, filler, line or a commercial fuel filler that is fixed to the side of the cowling. It may be possible to drill a third hole through the fuel tank bung and caps, but it is probably easier to buy a replacement fuel tank. The brass or copper tubes that fit into the bung should be a tight fit, but if they are unduly tight they can be smeared with petroleum jelly (Vaseline), which will allow them to slip into the holes quite easily. Where the fuel tank neck has to project through the firewall any gap between the neck and plywood should be sealed with silicone bath sealant to prevent the ingress of fuel.

Metal clevises are occasionally supplied in the accessory pack, but, more often, they are the moulded type. The clevis should be a strong fit on the threaded

Fuel tanks are often supplied with only two pipes, one for the engine feed and one for filling. For cowled engines you will need a third pipe, or special filler.

pushrod end, but not so tight that the clevis cannot be turned for adjustment. If necessary, tap the hole in the clevis (or cut the thread by using the end of the pushrod) until it is adjustable. Should the clevis be too loose a fit on the threaded rod, and could be pulled away if force was used, it should be discarded. To ensure that the clevis will not accidentally uncouple a retaining ring, a short length of silicone fuel tubing should be slipped over the 'jaws' after it has been fitted to the control horn. Models having separate elevator halves and using a forked pushrod to link to the elevator horns can cause quite a lot of consternation on routing the two forked ends down the fuselage and out of the slots in the fuselage sides. There is an easy way to solve this conundrum. Take two pieces of control tube inners (snakes) long enough to extend from the servo location to the slots in the fuselage sides. Slip the tubes through the slots along to the servo area, fit each end of the forked rods in the tubes and pull, gently, the tubes out through the slots. The threaded rod ends will come out with the tubes.

Control horns are normally fixed by small bolts going through the control surface and securing the horn on one side and a flat plate on the opposite side. Where the control surface is unreinforced balsawood, a touch of cyanoacrylate adhesive in the holes will strengthen the wood.

Clear canopies may be held in position with small screws, or you may have to glue them to the fuselage. In the latter case it will usually entail gluing to a film covering, which will not give a secure joint. Mark the location of the canopy and either cut away a thin strip of film, or take a small-bit soldering iron and run it around the film where the canopy fits, which will seal the covering to the fuselage. The best adhesives for gluing clear canopies are RC Modellers Glue and Vortex canopy glue, both of which dry transparently clear. Do you have a separate pilot in the cockpit? Then make absolutely sure that he is well and truly fixed before the canopy is attached.

Wherever you have to glue one component to another, for example joining wing roots, you should not only make sure that any film covering is removed, but also that the edges of the film are sealed well to the framework.

Although general descriptions will be shown for the location of the radio-control equipment, every model will vary to some degree. Check the position of the engine and locate the route of the engine throttle pushrod, from the servo to the carburettor throttle arm. As the linkage may take the form of a solid wire pushrod in a tube, the linkage must take a direct route, with possible bends at each end. When the route is established you may have to drill holes through the bulkheads for

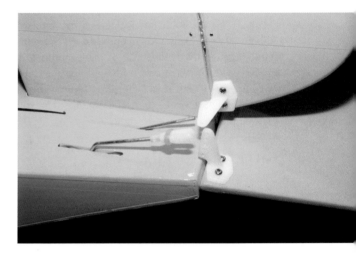

Clevises, for connecting to the control horns, are not always of the highest quality; if they are not easily and safely adjustable on the threaded rod, replace them.

Where components are to be glued on to a film-covered surface the film must be carefully cut away, or burnt away with a soldering iron, before gluing in position.

Any raw edges showing the wood structure, and there are usually quite a few, should be treated with fuelproofer before the fuel can soak into the wood.

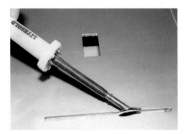

When cutting away the film covering for a servo opening or undercarriage slot, leave sufficient film to iron on to the return edges, then fuel-proof.

Engine and fuel-tank bays are areas where fuel ingress can rapidly cause deterioration of the wood, so fuel-proof thoroughly before fitting the engine or fuel tank.

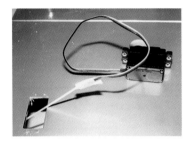

Where separate aileron servos are fitted in each wing panel you must be able to feed the servo lead to the wing centre area; often a thread is pre-fitted for the purpose.

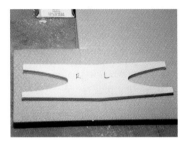

When carrying out a dry fit of components, such as a wing dihedral brace, mark the right-hand and left-hand sides so that it is glued in place in the same location.

Use all possible means to hold the wing panels together when they are being glued; masking tape and spring clips are useful, and be generous with the glue.

Adjustable clamps, available at stores and trade shows, help to hold wing panels tight together by holding the leading edge locators together and trailing edge by temporarily positioning lengths of dowel through the holes intended for the wing-fixing bolt.

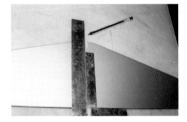

Measure for the centre line of the tailplane and use a set square to mark the line; a chinagraph pencil makes a good marker.

When you are certain that the marking for the seating on the fuselage is absolutely correct (measure twice, cut once) carefully cut away the film and iron down the edges.

the throttle linkage; if you don't have a long drill bit, a piece of 10 gauge piano wire, sharpened to a drill point, will do the job. Servo mounting plates are normally supplied to take standard-sized servos, although there may be methods of catering for smaller servos. If the plate is made only from Liteply reinforce the underside with pieces of 3mm (⅛in) plywood to give a better purchase for the fixing screws. Where the servo plate is supplied unfitted to the fuselage it is advisable to leave the fixing of it until the engine is in position and the wings and tail surfaces can be positioned. In this way, you can get a reasonable idea of how the balance will turn out and where the servos and battery will be best positioned to avoid the need for ballast to balance the model correctly.

Switch location is another consideration. If it is shown on the servo mounting board, fine, keep it there and fit an actuating rod to the outside of the fuselage. When it is fitted on the fuselage side, locate it on the opposite side to the engine silencer. While on the subject of planning and installing the radio-control equipment, plan a route for the aerial. An extra, lightweight tube down the fuselage will allow the aerial to exit the rear of the fuselage. If it is to route in front of the wing and extend to the top of the fin remember to fit a button, or short piece of dowel to the aerial, inside the fuselage, so that it cannot be accidentally pulled and strain the aerial connection on to the receiver.

Balance point limits and control surface movements will be stated on the instructions – do, please, abide by them and at least give the designers the benefit of any doubts!

With manufacturing processes and plastics technology developing all the time it is inevitable that new forms of modelling materials will come on to the market. EPP (expanded polypropylene) foam has been with us for some time and this requires different finishing techniques to other materials. Due to manufacturing limitations, when it arrives in kit form it may need trimming and sanding, particularly if it is for a semi-scale model. Be advised not to do this work in the sitting room, as the black waste gets everywhere! The standard finish is to apply coloured parcel tape, but for a more scale finish the surface may be sprayed with carpet adhesive, followed by brown parcel tape, followed by silver tape. For forming grooves or slots a piece of 1.5mm (⅟₁₆in) diameter wire should be bent to the shape of the slot, heated with a gas torch and pulled along the foam, using a plywood guide if needed.

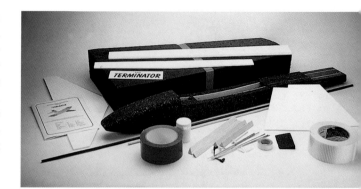

EPP foam, as used in car bumpers, is a relative newcomer to the model aircraft. It has great crashproof qualities, but needs different finishing techniques.

Tough expanded polystyrene foam models are also becoming very popular, with some of them essentially being one-piece models. Because the finish is often dark grey and the surface may be slightly open around the expanded granules, you may wish to apply another finish to the mouldings. Some of the non-cellulose spray paints can be used to colour the mouldings, but they may, if applied too thickly, start to eat away at the foam. To prevent this happening it is only necessary to brush on a coat of white PVA glue, thinned down to a milky consistency with water, before the paint is applied. You may also give a tissue covering, to smooth the surface further, before applying the paint. With these moulded models the locations for the servos are moulded into the surfaces, internally and, in the case of aileron servos, externally. Do not rely on a push fit only to retain the servos, as they may work loose; secure them with double-sided adhesive tape, having treated the foam surface with epoxy resin first.

Engine cowlings may be supplied as GRP (glass-reinforced plastic) or vacuum-formed mouldings. The latter are not as strong, and so will benefit from the application of epoxy resin and reinforcing cloth on the inside.

Whatever you do, take your time in assembling and finishing the ARTF model. Just because they are a quick build doesn't mean that you have to rush things. Always carry out 'dry fits' before committing yourself to gluing, use glue sparingly and keep a clean cloth and some methylated spirits to hand to clean off any excess.

Moulded expanded foam manufacturing techniques increase the scope of designs and also, for IC engine installations, call for new finishing systems.

Be particularly careful when applying the thin cyano-acrylate adhesive as this can easily run into unwanted areas, use a fine tube applicator for the tricky areas.

When the model is completed and radio installed, make a final check for the full and free movement of the control surfaces. Any catching of the control surfaces must be cleared, either with a sharp knife or a piece of abrasive paper.

DESPAIR OR REPAIR?

Accidents will happen. When learning to fly it is almost inevitable that you will crash a model, even when you have an instructor standing by to take control when you are in difficulties. There comes a time when you have to take control at the critical times of take-off and landing and even with the sharpest of reactions the instructor will not be able to save the model from a situation where the student has given an incorrect command. How badly the model is damaged will depend on the speed at which, and how, it hits the ground, and the hardness of the ground. You may be lucky and get away with a minor 'ding' on the airframe, or a tear on the covering; or the model may sustain more serious damage.

Any modeller who has served his apprenticeship in building model aircraft will have little problem in repairing such damage, but what about the enthusiast who has bought an ARTF kit and has no experience in constructing a model?

Very few damaged models can be considered as total write-offs; most can be repaired, if the owner knows how to go about the job. It may be that certain components, a wing for instance, can be obtained as a spare from the retailer, or distributor. However, you should not hold out too much hope in this respect, as the types of ARTF kits are constantly changing and your particular model may no longer be in production. Also, if you consider the number and variety of ARTF models on the market at any one time, it would be a difficult proposition for the distributor to keep spares of every component from these kits. Rather than thinking in terms of replacement, it would be more practical, and less expensive, to consider repairing a damaged model.

In essence, there are two types of damage likely to be sustained by a crashed model; that is, excluding damage to the engine and radio equipment. One is airframe damage, to the structure itself, the other is to the covering material. The first action to take is a non-action. When the model is broken on the flying field the temptation may be to carry out a quick repair with 'instant' glue and carry on flying. Don't, for two reasons. There may be more structural damage than you realize, and this could be a danger if you flew again. The other reason is that you will probably 'bodge' the repair and make it difficult, or impossible, to carry out an efficient repair at a later stage. Further, the radio equipment may have been affected and require treatment. Carefully collect all the pieces of wreckage, if they are strewn around, and take them back home with you.

Fortunately, good-quality balsawood is being used in more of the ARTF kits today. Some of the earlier, less expensive ARTFs, used woods that were prone to splitting when the model crashed or had a 'hard arrival'. Such woods are not easy to repair as there are frequently multiple splits, requiring considerable gluing and reinforcing. Incidentally, if you do purchase one of the ARTF kits with balsa-substitute-type wood (the retailer should be able to advise you in this matter), then you should go for the larger, simple models where the wing loading is still reasonably light. Scale models, with relatively small wings and quite a lot of detail, are a no-no when using the heavier woods for the structure as they will result in high wing loadings, a high stalling speed, often combined with a nasty wing drop. In other words, just the characteristics that you want to avoid in the early stages of your flight training.

Although it is impossible to give a blow by blow account of how to repair a built-up structure, there are a few pointers that can be given. First, the covering. You have to assess the type of covering used on the model, whether it is sticky-backed plastic, or the heat-shrink variety. If the model is highly decorative, or has printed-in insignia and markings, the chances are that it is of the sticky-backed variety. I say this somewhat charily as it is a fair bet that, as soon as this book is published, a manufacturer will come up with a process for printing decorations on heat-shrink covering. However, until that time, we will assume that these multi-coloured finishes are the sticky-backed variety. Run your fingers over the covering surface and if you don't feel any ridge when it comes to a colour change, then you can be pretty sure that it isn't a heat-shrink material, as with this type of material decoration is achieved by adding colour trims, or changing from one colour to another on various components.

I once had the misfortune to drop a spanner on to a wing covered with sticky-backed plastic, causing considerable damage. Reading the instructions of ARTF models so covered, you will probably find the advice that a warm iron (covering iron or domestic iron) can be run over the plastic film to tauten it, if it has gone slack. I must admit that I have not had great success with this proposed method, whether the iron temperature is critical I don't know, but it rarely seems to cause the covering to tighten. So I had to devise another method of repair. Eventually, I found that by applying a generous amount of white PVA glue to the edges of the gash and then covering the damaged area with cling film (as used in the kitchen), the edges would magically join. It is necessary to leave the cling film on the repaired area for a day or two, as the PVA glue is air-drying and there is not too much air under the cling film. Once dry, and the glue will dry clear, the cling film can be removed and the joints reinforced with cyanoacrylate adhesive. The joints should be almost invisible. Where the damage to the sticky-backed covering is more extensive, as in a crash, the problems are greater. You are unlikely to be able to purchase additional covering of this type, so you have to improvise. If you are not too worried about the appearance of the model you can glue fractured edges down with cyanoacrylate adhesives and then cover the repair with clear adhesive tape, although this may eventually come adrift when contaminated by fuel. Alternatively, you can use conventional plastic film covering, such as Solarfilm, to cover the damaged area.

Where a heat-shrink film has been used on the ARTF it is easier to repair damaged covering – another reason for opting in favour of this style of model in the first instance. The chances are that the film covering used will be of the polyester type and you should purchase this type for your repairs. Choose a colour as near to that used on the model; the manufacturer will probably have used one of the proprietary brands. Decide on the area you are re-covering, iron down the edges of the covering surrounding this area and then cut away the damaged material. Although film joins to film by means of the heat-sensitive adhesive backing, you can enhance the adhesion of the joint by first applying such products as Cover-Grip or Clearcote to the edges to be joined. Cut your piece of repair film to the size of the overlap joints, seal carefully with the iron around the joints and then heat-shrink with the iron over the area of the film. Instructions will tell you what temperatures to use.

Incredible detail can be incorporated in scale ARTF models; it would take many hours to achieve the same results conventionally. ARTF kits also generally have very colourful schemes.

But what of any structural damage? Where thin balsawood is damaged, for instance on a wing leading edge, it will be necessary to cut back to structural components, for example wing ribs and spars, and ensure that the existing balsawood leading-edge sheeting is well secured, leaving part of the component clear for attaching the replacement sheeting. It may be tempting to use one of the instant, cyanoacrylate glues to make this repair, but it is more sensible to use a slow-drying white glue that will give you ample time to make adjustments. For damaged spars, leading and trailing edges and fuselage longerons it will be necessary to splice in a new piece of strip to the same dimensions as the existing one. Cut out the damaged wood, angled on the ends to form a splice to increase the cutting area, and cut a new piece to fit the gap; dry-fit to be sure that it makes a close-fitting joint at both ends before committing to gluing. In some cases it may be possible to replace the broken part, particularly where the fracture is of a jagged nature and the ends will interlock again. Structural repairing is often similar to making a jigsaw puzzle, where pieces are matched up with the structural components and fitted back in with adhesives. Thick balsa sheets of block areas are easily dealt with by replacement of the damaged areas; minor dents and bruising can be filled with lightweight fillers and sanded smooth.

If you are unsure whether a joint in a spar or fuselage member has regained its original strength as a result of a repair, it can always be reinforced with a piece of thin plywood 0.8mm (1/32in) glued over the jointed area. One area where you might come across problems in repairing and covering is where the structure has become fuel-soaked through the fuel, or residues, having penetrated the surface of the wood. Before the adhesive or heat-shrink covering will take to these areas they must be cleaned of the contamination. Applying cellulose thinners with a rag will remove the surface oil, but to remove the ingrained oily substances you will have to resort to an iron and blotting paper. Place the blotting paper over the contaminated area and apply heat from the iron, which will draw out the fuel and oil, although it may take a number of attempts before it is acceptably clean. The area should then be treated with Clearcote or Covergrip before attempting to re-cover.

Repairing a damaged ARTF model is not only good economics, it will also give you a taste of building a model. You may find that you enjoy this aspect of aeromodelling and wish to extend it to building a model from a traditional-style kit or a plan. Whether or not you find the experience rewarding, one thing is certain, the vast majority of crashed models are repairable. It may be a 'throwaway' society, but financial considerations might dictate that we repair rather than reject.

Moulded foam, veneered foam and injection-moulded ARTF models will all require different repair techniques. With moulded foam it is often possible, because of the thickness of the foam components, simply to glue the parts together again using epoxy resin. Use a twenty-minute or one-hour epoxy and once the parts are accurately married together, tape them securely until the adhesive is set. For damage to veneered foam, usually limited to wing leading edges, the damaged area can be cut away and replaced with a piece of high-density foam. The surface can then be hardened with the application of PVA or epoxy adhesive.

As it seems likely that injection-moulded plastic ARTF models will increase in popularity, new techniques have had to be devised to repair these plastics. Epoxies are the answer to most repairs, but it is essential to experiment first, as it may be that the plastic used is not suited to epoxy repairs and an alternative, such as Deluxe Fusion, will have to be used. Crease marks and non-structural surface damage such as bruising and dents may be repaired by the careful application of heat, but, again, experiment on a piece of scrap plastic first.

No doubt there will be new materials and manufacturing techniques in the future, so don't be afraid of trying out repair methods – you can always subject the repairs to simple load tests. For example, wings can be supported on wood blocks and loaded with bags of sugar to a load factor of 5g (five times the weight of the model) spread over the wing structure. This will provide adequate strength for a trainer or sports model. For other airframe components a good pulling and pushing will give an indication of whether the repairs have been successful. The ultimate test will, of course, come with the flying of the model. Be sensible, don't try high 'G' aerobatics on the first flight, subject the model to modest manoeuvres, land, inspect the repairs and then fly again, gradually increasing the loads on the repaired parts. All very satisfying!

Engine and radio damage is another matter – any problems in these areas and you are advised to return the damaged item to the manufacturer or distributor.

CHAPTER 9

BIY – Build It Yourself

I cannot overemphasize the degree of enjoyment and satisfaction that designing and building my own model aircraft has given me. With over 500 designs, not all of them radio-controlled, you might think that I would have run out of new subjects. Far from it, I still have a list as long as my arm of different models I want to design and build. By the way, this is not boasting about numbers of designs, it is admitting to an addiction!

Not everyone will want to design their own models, but a large number will, at some time or other, be tempted to have a go at building, either from scratch or from a kit. It has to be admitted that the number of conventional, traditional kits on the market has seriously reduced in recent years, having been overtaken by ARTF types. On purely economic grounds it is virtually impossible to argue the case for traditional kits. By the time that you have bought the kit and the accessories and covering material, the cost is as much as, or even more than, an equivalent ARTF model. But this doesn't take into consideration that previously vaunted sense of personal

If you want to build and fly such oddball designs as this Henderson Steam Carriage, you will have to rely on your building skills, as there will never be ARTF kits for this prototype.

Can you imagine the immense sense of satisfaction when you have completed an intricate model of a Bristol Boxkite and then see it in the air?

satisfaction at seeing a model constructed with your own fair hands in flight. With the lack of traditional kits available, most BIY models will need to be built from scratch, that is, from plans and the raw materials. Ironically, although ARTF kits have taken the major share of the market, the sales of the modelling materials and accessories are remaining buoyant, with one distributor going as far as saying that they are on the increase.

Although the range of ARTF models is large, it can never match the variety of plans available for every conceivable type of radio-controlled model. Plans Services, where copies of the model plan drawings may be purchased, are still available through most of the aeromodelling magazine publishers, although an illustrated plans handbook may not always be accessible (except via long-established aeromodellers). You will find a wealth of plans in their lists, from vintage-style models to multi-engined bombers, autogyros to slope soarers, swing-wing jet fighters to pylon racers, all waiting to be built. It is also a truism to state that the construction and finishing of the model will be more pleasurable if you have the right tools for the job and the right working conditions. We can't all have the perfect workshop for modelling, or all the tools we

desire, but at least we can aspire to them. I have a friend who was divorced and eventually converted the bedroom to a workshop; not the spare bedroom, mind you, but the main bedroom. I am not suggesting that you should dispose of your partner simply so that you can have a good workroom, but it's worth bearing in mind!

If you are lucky enough to have an area where you can make a workshop, then it should be properly planned and laid out. For most it is likely to be the garage – with the less important car left outside – although the roof space can offer interesting possibilities. If you have sufficient headroom in the roof area and it is not all taken up with roof trusses, it is worth considering putting some flooring down, fitting a roof light and installing a loft ladder. You will be well out of anyone's way and as happy as the proverbial pig. Should there be any doubts about the structural considerations of making the conversion, do get professional advice.

Two essentials for making modelling comfortable and efficient are heat and light. The first requirement can be fulfilled by a combination of insulation and providing a heat source, such as an electric oil-filled radiator, which is safer than an open-element electric heater when combined with balsa dust or cellulose fumes. Insulation will depend on the location of the workroom. For a garage the application of heavy duty polystyrene blocks will do the trick, although a new skin of lightweight concrete blocks, leaving a gap between the outer walls and the blocks, is a better answer. This will give a more secure surface for installing benches, shelves and cupboards. You cannot have too much light on the subject and by light I mean artificial, electric light. If you do not suffer from claustrophobia, you can do without the rooflight, or you could block in a garage window. It is a warmer answer, and you will certainly be able to make use of the extra wall space; also an extractor fan is a more efficient way of dealing with air movements and removing smells – also better for cooling in the summer. Electric light is required in two forms, high-level background lighting from fluorescent strip lights and, if possible, spot lighting at critical areas such as machine tools. Locate the strip lights so that they will not be at your back and cause a shadow where you are working. High intensities of light are even more important as you get older and your eyes deteriorate.

An efficient workshop should be planned in the same way as a kitchen, where you have a storage area, a preparation area and a cooking area, although this, in our case, will be construction area. Also like a kitchen, if we can have an island unit for construction, this is ideal as it means that we can work on the model from all angles. The sizes of your work surfaces and benches will, of course, depend on the overall size of your work space – it is almost impossible for it to be too large. Nearly all model construction involves some parts being pinned to the work surface at some time. If we are to construct true and straight structures they must be built on an absolutely flat base. My favourite building board is an old 'double elephant'-sized drawing board, which has a true smooth surface from deal wood that allows pins to be stuck into the surface. With the arrival of computer drawing systems you may well be able to purchase one of these 'old-fashioned' drawing boards for a pound or two; it's certainly worth a free ad in the local paper to see if anything turns up. Alternatively, you will have to produce a flat plane and surface it with a material that will support building pins. Flush doors, now going out of fashion again, can be a source of a good size of flat surface and should be available as a second-hand object from a scrapyard. Get a good thick one and do check that it doesn't have

any twists, unless you want all of your models to have warped wings. Pins cannot be pushed into the surface of a door and you will have to cover it with a suitable material. The best I have found is the type of board used for pinboards in schools and colleges. This should be available from good builders merchants.

The bases for the benches need to be sound and strong and you can't really go wrong with kitchen floor unit bases, with or without the worktops. It surprises me how often some families discard their perfectly good kitchen units in favour of new ones. Again, an advertisement in the local newspaper may well give you a supply of units. While you are about it, you might as well pick up some wall cupboards, as you will certainly need some of these. For the remainder of the wall surface I have always favoured pegboard, a material that again seems to have gone out of fashion. It is ideal for holding all sorts of parts and pieces and there are hooks designed to fit the holes in the pegboard. You can fit the pegboard on battens (roofing battens are suitable) and fit insulating material, such as roofing insulation, between the battens. Shelves will also be needed; fix the tops of jars to the underside of shelves so that you can screw the jar in position. Interlocking plastic storage boxes are useful, and, for all the small screws, nuts and bolts and accessories, the racks with small drawers are ideal. Storing balsawood and plywood can present a few problems, particularly with the 1,200mm (4ft) lengths, but it may be possible to allow divisions at the end of an open workbench for slotting in the balsawood sheet and strip. Alternatively, you will have to arrange for vertical racking of woods, piano wire, covering materials, and so on.

Finally, before leaving the workshop layout, if you can avoid having to store the finished models in your workroom, do so. They will get covered in dust and paint spray and that is not good for the models, the radio equipment or the engines. If they must be stored there, place them in large plastic bags to protect them.

MORE POWER TO YOUR ELBOW

I used to think that you couldn't possess too many motorized tools to help you with your modelmaking activities, but now I'm not so sure. Certainly if you have plenty of bench space, and you do need a separate bench for many of the tools, then there are a lot of items that will speed up the preparation and construction of a

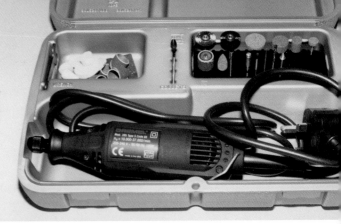

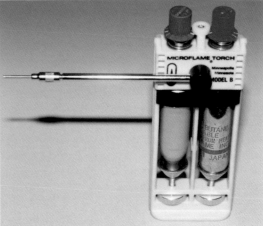

Five very useful motorized tools for the aeromodeller who builds his own models are clockwise from top left: a fretsaw; a Dremel Moto-Tool; a linisher/ sander; a miniature circular saw; and a bandsaw. The gas torch is also invaluable for silver soldering and brazing.

model. With the motorized tools becoming ever cheaper the temptation is to go and buy them all, but it is wiser to be selective and go for fewer but better quality machines. A pillar drill is highly desirable, one with a quality chuck that will not shudder and will hold the smallest of drill bits. A fretsaw (jigsaw) is a near essential and a band saw for the larger cutting jobs. Linishers will cut down the time taken to shape and sand wooden components and to smooth off metal parts. One of my favourite motorized tools is a small circular saw, not the 150mm (6in) diameter blade type, for household work, or the smallest 12V hobby type, which lacks power, but a purpose-designed, mains-operated fine blade saw. It has an amazing accuracy of cut, and is used almost exclusively for cutting wood strip, giving the advantage of having matched strip for the construction of wings and fuselage, and so on.

You must remember when locating the tools on the bench that you will need space around them for the material to be worked. So, for the circular saw you will need a minimum of 1m in front and at the rear of the saw; similar dimensions are required for a bandsaw, but less for the fretsaw, because of the restricted throat depth. Of course, it may be possible to achieve the same results with hand tools, although hand drilling can be a difficult operation, and I believe that I can still cut more precisely with a hand fretsaw – but my elbow aches more than it used to!

Of the hand tools, the one absolute essential is a vice, which must be firmly secured to a bench and have reasonable space around and should have both hard and soft jaws. Such items as spanners, screwdrivers, pliers, wire cutters, hacksaws, hammers, knives and set squares will be needed; many of these tools will already be part of the household kit. You will, however, need some specialist modelling items such as small Allen keys, nut spinners, razor planes and razor saws (very fine-toothed modelling saws) and modelling knives. The best knives are the surgical type, with interchangeable blades. One thing you will be doing plenty of is sanding and smoothing, and here two products have come on to the market that make our life a whole lot easier. Permagrit tools come in a wide range of sizes and types and are coated with abrasive materials that are as near permanent as you will get. If the surface gets clogged it can be cleaned with a caustic solution. There is even a coated hacksaw blade that will deal with spring-hard piano wire of the thicker diameters. For dealing with the

double curvature areas and final sanding, there are flexible sanding blocks that accept sanding sheets of various grades; they are fixed to the blocks with Velcro and can be easily discarded when worn.

What are the other tool essentials for our modelling activities? We will certainly need a stack of modelling pins, the variety with nylon or glass heads that won't puncture our thumbs when we press them into the building surface, and those little moulded spring clamps are endlessly useful. Clear adhesive tape, masking tape and double-sided tape will be used occasionally to hold things together temporarily. Pens and pencils will be needed for marking, including a chinagraph pencil for shiny surfaces.

Joining metal parts will require a soldering iron or a gas torch; the latter will also be useful for brazing work and some acid core solder, or the old-fashioned plumber's solder and a flux. For electrical work a smaller soldering iron and resin core solder will ensure that no corrosion of components takes place. When it comes to other portable electric motorized tools, one of the most used is the Dremel Moto-Tool; this is essentially a small hand drill with a chuck that takes drills and tools up to 3mm (⅛in) diameter and with a variable speed control. It is supplied with a wide range of abrasive and drill bits, cutting wheels, mops and wire brushes. For routing, cutting and shaping glass-reinforced plastic (GRP) mouldings it is indispensable. Another essential element for these motor tools is mains electric power outlets and you simply cannot have too many of these. Where you might think of fitting a single, or twin, power outlet, put a bank of three or four and have them situated all round the workshop. It is not only inconvenient to have power flexes from tools trailing all over the place, it can be positively dangerous.

Anything I've forgotten? I'm sure there is, but you can always buy extra tools as they become needed. Do invest in a vacuum cleaner; you are not going to be number one on the hit list if you drag all the dust and shavings into the house – unless it's a different form of hit list!

I haven't mentioned, in the list of motor and machine tools, the lathe. There is no doubt whatsoever that the lathe can be indispensable for producing certain specialist parts; there is also no doubt that a lathe can have a life in itself. More than one modeller has got so carried away with operating a lathe that he has succumbed to the temptation of making things purely for the sake of making them. You could argue

Desirable hand tools and equipment include: an assortment of Permagrit sanders and files (left and bottom left), as these virtually never wear out; a razor plane (middle left); clamps (two middle right pictures); and a flexible sanding block with changeable sanding sheets (bottom right).

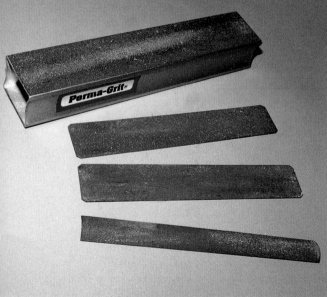

that, if it is giving pleasure and satisfaction, then it is fair enough; but it isn't aeromodelling. A good lathe is a costly item, it will also take up a lot of valuable workshop space, so you would probably be more sensible to find a friend or colleague with a lathe, who can make the rare item needing to be produced, rather than own one yourself. It may seem a selfish attitude, but perhaps you will be able to return the favour when it comes to cutting wood or some such thing.

CONSTRUCTION MATERIALS

Balsawood

Of all the materials we use for constructing our models, the most versatile remains balsawood. Although, botanically speaking, it is technically a hard wood, in purely weight terms it is a light material. It is not, by any means, the lightest of natural woods, but it does have the greatest weight/strength ratio of the lighter grades. It also has variations of texture, ranging from the 'carroty', easily snapped wood, to the stringy, tough variety. In colour, it can range from the near white to the orange hues of certain species. What will also affect the sheet wood is how it has been cut from the log; tangential cutting will give flexible sheets suitable for covering leading edges of wings and the like, while quarter-grain cuts provide a much stiffer sheet, which has its uses for wing ribs, fuselage formers, sheet trailing edges and items that do not require any bending. Model kits should be supplied with the balsawood components of the correct density and type, but where you are building from a plan you will have to make the selection of wood yourself. Experience is the main guide here, so try to enlist the help of a knowledgeable model-shop proprietor, or an experienced modeller. Plans and building instructions may give you a guide by stipulating medium- or hard-grade balsawood, but how hard is hard? Even experienced modellers will not agree on the density of wood to be used for particular components – there are 'light' builders and 'heavy' builders.

One of the most radical examples of this diversity that I have witnessed occurred with two Spitfire models, from the same design of 2,160mm (85in) wingspan. I happened to be commentating at the time and was worried about the flying of the first model, which weighed well in excess of 9kg (20lb) and looked likely to fall out of the sky at any moment. The second of the Spitfires took to the air slowly and gracefully, performing quietly and with authority. On checking with the owner after the flight, I was amazed to find out that this model weighed under 5kg (11lb). If proof was ever needed that a light model will fly better than a heavy version, this was a fine example. The builder had taken every opportunity to lighten components. He had made his own lightweight retracting undercarriage, had sprayed a very thin camouflage and had even scalloped out the already lightweight vac-formed pilot figure, to save an extra gram, and the results had been very worthwhile. Because of the low overall weight of the model, the 'G' forces were far less potentially destructive than they would be for a model of twice the weight.

But, back to the balsawood. Try to build up a stock of different densities and qualities of balsawood so that you have plenty of choice when it comes to selection for spars, longerons, wing-tip blocks, fairings and so on. In very general terms, the higher the stress area, the denser and tougher the wood needs to be. So, for wing spars you will need the strongest balsawood and if you are cutting your own strip you will find that the sheet wood needs to be harder than you might imagine, as when stripped it seems to be less hard. For fuselage longerons, uprights and cross pieces you can use a medium-hard grade, and for doublers, sheet control surfaces and ribs and formers, medium-quality wood is appropriate. The lightest grades of balsawood are only suitable for block fairings and cowlings, unless required for indoor free-flight models.

At one time plywood produced from balsawood was available, but it is rarely seen nowadays; perhaps the introduction of Liteply, which is probably as light, but not so rigid or torsionally strong, has taken its place. There are, though, times when balsa plywood has its uses, in large, light fuselage formers for example, and in those instances it is possible to make your own product. Take the sheet wood, say 1.5mm (1/16in) thick and laminate three thicknesses, with the grain going in alternate directions, using white PVA glue as the adhesive. The laminates must be thoroughly weighted or cramped down until the glue has set, but you will then have a very strong, tough material. It is also possible to produce an even tougher laminate, with a minimum weight increase, by using microply (0.4mm or 0.8mm thick) on the outside surfaces and a balsawood centre laminate.

Construction of this twin-engined Super Trouper is principally from balsawood and uses the same methods for the two sizes, powered by 25 and 07 engines, respectively. The basic structure is strong enough to allow film covering, which, in itself, does not add much to the strength of the airframe.

Obechi

Known as a balsawood substitute, obechi was available during the war years when balsawood was being used for full-size aircraft production and other purposes. It is still available from specialist outlets and is most used in the form of veneers for covering expanded polystyrene wing cores.

Spruce

Also know as hemlock, this wood is tough yet moderately light, and can be used to advantage for wing spars and trailing edge components where the available depth is at a premium. Spruce is also used for wing struts, elevator joiners and external fairings that may be subject to damage.

Ramin

Ramin is easily purchased from DIY stores and can be used as a substitute for spruce, but tends to be of shorter grain and less flexible. Other hardwoods may be obtained from the DIY stores, and it is always worthwhile experimenting with these materials, as they may have advantages over traditional modelling woods.

Beech

A really tough, hard wood, beech has its main use for engine bearers. In the days before aluminium and nylon engine mounts were manufactured, beech bearers, either on their own, or with a paxolin plate on top, were the standard means of mounting the engine on the model. Using beech engine bearers has good secondary effects, too, as they strengthen the nose area of the model and help to spread the engine vibrations through the structure in a more efficient way. Moulded engine mounts may be more convenient, but it doesn't follow that they are superior in a structural way. Small beech blocks are also good for securing the wood screws or screw-retaining cowlings, and so on. Dowels, for retaining rubber bands holding on the wings and tailsurfaces, can either be formed from beech or birch. Both woods are suitable and for further strength the dowels can be soaked in clear dope for a day or so.

Plywood

As mentioned above, there is a material called Liteply, which consists of laminates of lightweight wood, poplar or similar species. It is used effectively in ARTF models and has quite a few uses in the BIY field. For non-load-

Beech wooden engine bearers add to the strength of the nose area of the fuselage, but do not allow for alternative engines to be easily fitted. Captive nuts should be fitted to the rear of the bearers.

bearing areas, rear fuselage formers, some wing ribs, even fuselage sides if the rear ends have lightening holes cut in them, Liteply is a great material to use. For other, high-stress areas, we require the best-quality birch plywood that we can obtain. The best is actually aircraft-quality plywood, usually with a green 'approval' stamp on one corner, but this material is both expensive and not easily obtained. If you are going to a timber merchants to purchase the plywood you will want to ask for

Finnish birch plywood of BB grade. It is supplied in metric thicknesses of 3mm (just under ⅛in), 4mm (just over ⅛in), 5mm (³⁄₁₆in), 6 or 6.5mm (nominally ¼in) and 8mm (⅜in). It is also produced in 0.4mm (¹⁄₆₄in), 0.8mm (¹⁄₃₂in) and 1.5mm (¹⁄₁₆in), but these sizes are only likely to be found at specialist modelling outlets.

Regular plywood is used in model aircraft construction for the highest stress areas such as engine bulkheads, wing dihedral joiners, undercarriage plates and doublers, and so on. One thing to watch is that, in manufacture, release oil may be used on the metal mould plates and this may be transferred to the plywood. If you try to glue the surface of the plywood when traces of oil are present, the adhesion may be poor, so always give a light sanding to the surfaces before gluing.

Because plywood has odd numbers of laminations – three, five, and so on – it has greater strength in one direction compared with the other. Use this fact to your advantage, and if, for instance, you are cutting a dihedral brace, the outer wood laminations should have the grain running lengthways along the plywood.

Expanded Polystyrene (Styrofoam)

Used by the building industry for insulation purposes, expanded polystyrene is a lightweight foamed material that can be hot-wire cut (nichrome) and knife cut and sanded to shape. Produced in a number of densities, the lightest is suitable for unstressed components, such as fuselage top deckings and large section wings, while the higher density EP is more suited to thin wings where the smaller bead sizes produce a finer finish. Having little inherent strength, the cut foam components require veneering, the normal material being obechi. However, it is also possible to use the thinnest (0.4mm/¹⁄₆₄in) plywood for covering, which produces a very strong but relatively heavy structure. Depending on the radius of the leading edge and the overall chord of the wing, it may be possible to wrap the veneer completely around the wing. If the leading edge has a sharp radius, or the chord is too great for the veneer sheet width, a separate balsawood leading edge is fitted and shaped.

White polystyrene foam is easily cut by the hot-wire method and can be used for wing and tailplane cores (veneered with balsawood or obechi) or fuselage sections. The large pile shown here was a few sections for a flight of five very large Lancaster bombers.

Hot wire is adopted to cut the aerofoil of the wing panels. The wire is tensioned in a bow, a low-voltage current is applied to heat the wire and it is dragged across templates fitted at either end of the foam blank. It is only possible to cut parallel or tapered wings; shaped wing tips have to be added later. Curved leading and trailing edges can be formed by gluing and shaping thick balsa sheet, but this is something of a compromise. Balsa sheet veneers, well sanded, will give a smoother aerofoil, and the surface may be strengthened by applying glass-fibre cloth and resin, preferably by using a vacuum process. Once veneered, the panels are very resistant to twisting – for this reason, it is also important not to develop any accidental warps in the panels at the veneering stage. Joining the wing panels is by gluing the roots together with an epoxy for adhesive and then reinforcing the joint with a glass-fibre bandage and resin. Machines with automatic hot-wire cutting systems can be purchased, but are expensive and not economical unless a lot of foam units are to be produced. Epoxy can be used for adhering the veneer coverings to the foam, but it is more normal to use a water-based contact adhesive, as other contact adhesives may melt the polystyrene.

Modern moulding techniques and mass production of models, in the tens of thousands in some case, allow manufacturers to design radio-controlled model aircraft with all-moulded polystyrene foam construction. A slightly different constituency of foam to the building material may be used and it is possible to vary the density so that no veneering is required, as the finish from the metal mould will give a satisfactory finish and the airframe will only require localized reinforcement to add to the strength. With these moulding techniques it is possible to produce some very interesting and futuristic-looking designs – flying wings, deltas and twin-engined pushers all feature in manufacturers' catalogues. Most of the models are electric powered, but the methods are also suitable for smaller IC powered designs. If a pusher motor is incorporated it also keeps the engine exhaust wastes away from the fuselage.

Expanded Polypropylene (EPP)

EPP is similar to expanded polystyrene in that it is, for modelling purposes, normally hot-wire cut. It is popular for ARTF models, but is not a particularly easy material for the amateur to use. It is employed in the automobile industry using moulding techniques, but it seems reasonable to suppose that in time these techniques will follow for model subjects.

Carbon Fibre and Kevlar Composites

Here is a case of materials that were developed for the aero industry being adopted by aeromodellers. These incredibly strong materials are used to reinforce structures in the form of tows (strands of the material), woven sheeting and thin sheet laminates. Carbon fibre is also introduced into other plastic mouldings to strengthen and reinforce the components and also to GRP mouldings, resulting in very stiff, strong structures with a minimum of weight. To hold some of the moulded shells of large model fuselages is to give an idea of just how strong modern laminate techniques are.

Glass-Reinforced Plastic (GRP)

This is really the granddaddy of moulded plastic systems in aeromodelling terms. Polyester and epoxy resins have been available for many years and these have been used in combination with glass chopped strand mat or woven cloth, either to cover and strengthen a component, or to be used for moulding items such as engine cowlings and wheel spats. Strength for weight is good with GRP mouldings and is made even better when local reinforcement of carbon-fibre rovings or cloth is introduced. Moulding procedures can follow two routes. The shape can be cut from foam, filled with plaster, or similar filler, smoothed down, treated with a releasing agent and then coated with the resin and glass cloth or mat. This method has disadvantages, however, in that it leaves the smooth surface on the inside and not the outside and this has to be filled, filed and sanded to a smooth finish.

Although this is acceptable for one-off moulded subjects, a more satisfactory system is to make a wooden plug of the shape of the subject to be modelled, get a finish to the standard you require for the finished moulding, treat it with a PVA releasing agent and apply plenty of coats of resin and glass mat to produce a rigid female mould. Depending on the shape of the subject it may be necessary to split the mould into sections so that the final moulding can be released. When set, the female mould parts are released from the wooden plug and cleaned; they are then ready for forming the final mouldings. A good waxing and polishing follows, making certain that they will come out of the moulds cleanly. Using glass surface tissue, resin

EPP foam requires different techniques to the white and blue foams. It is less easy to cut with hot wire and is probably best left to the kit manufacturers. Covering also involves different methods, including covering with brown paper.

and layers of glass cloth or chopped mat, the moulding is developed to the strength and thickness required before it is left to set and then removed from the moulds. This method obviously has the advantage of providing repeatability – the moulds, carefully looked after, should last for many moulding sessions.

Moulding materials and techniques can be quite complex and there are specialist books on the subject. If you anticipate making many moulded components it would be worthwhile purchasing a technical book dealing with these methods, or visiting your local library to research the subject.

Synthetic Resin-Bonded Laminates

For modelling activities the two most familiar products are Paxolin and Tufnol, the former having a paper laminate and the latter, stronger, material having cloth as the reinforcing laminate. These materials are less used nowadays, but were once commonly used for engine 'break-away' plates, that is, engine mounting plates that would break in the event of a crash, thus

saving damage to the engine. Perhaps it is a sign that radio equipment has become more reliable and training procedures improved that the 'break-away' element is no longer so important.

One form of laminate that can occasionally be useful for making control horns, bellcranks, and so on, is ordinary household Formica, the tough laminate of about 1.5mm ($\frac{1}{16}$in) thick that is used for kitchen worktops.

Tubing

Aluminium and brass tubing comes in sizes with an internal diameter to match piano wire sizes. But, because we have imperial (from America), wire gauge (UK) and metric (Europe) sizes of wire diameters, we also have many sizes of tubing. One-foot lengths are the most common, but it may be possible to purchase lengths up to one metre for certain sizes. Round tube is the most frequently used, but other shapes are available. Rectangular hollow sections with matching steel flat bars are excellent for wing joining, and streamlined aluminium tubing can be made into wing struts. Copper tubing is much softer and more malleable and is useful for pipework in metal tanks. It is not only readily bendable, it is also easy to solder.

Carbon-fibre tubing comes in sizes from 4mm diameter upwards (0.5mm diameter in rod form) and this rigid, lightweight and strong material is increasingly being used for a number of modelling applications. Sailwing type ARTF electric models use tube or rod to act as the leading edges of the wings, built-up wing structures may feature carbon-fibre tube as a spar and it is also used to reinforce foam flying-wing gliders. Standard tubing has a consistent diameter and

wall thickness, and tubes specially produced as tail booms for helicopters will taper and reduce in wall thickness towards the tail. Another source of carbon-fibre tapering tube is from fishing rods, and arrow shafts are often made from carbon-fibre tubing.

Vac-Forming Plastic Sheet

In addition to the female mould techniques used for GRP, we can form thin plastic sheet, ABS or PVC, by vacuum-forming methods. Because the sheet is so thin we can adopt male mould techniques, unless a lot of

Carbon-fibre rod and tube are now commonplace in the construction of model aeroplanes and the material is extensively used in helicopters. Carbon tube can be used for wing joiners, either in conjunction with aluminium tube or piano wire.

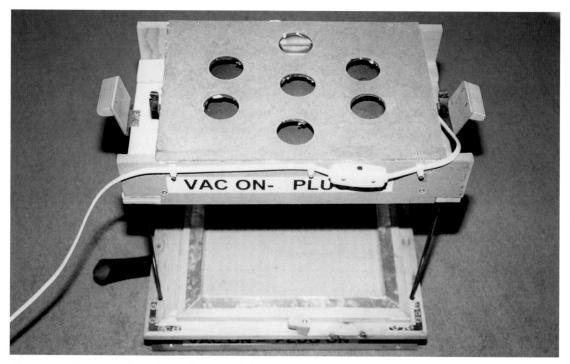

You may need some vac-formed parts for a scratch-built model and these are not likely to be available commercially. You can make your own vac-forming machine that will be capable of producing moderately sized canopies, wheel spats, engine cowlings and so on.

small surface detail is required, in which case the female mould is still to be preferred. Vac-forming relies on the thermic properties of the plastics; it will soften when heated and can then take up a new shape, which it will retain when it cools. By having the mould placed on a perforated base, the heated and softened plastic placed over it and the air evacuated through the base, the plastic sheet will form itself around the mould. Typical objects for moulding in this way are small radial cowls, lightweight wheels and spats, wing tips and, most commonly, windscreens and cockpit canopies. Clear PVC is used for canopies and special glues must be used to affix these in place. For very small objects it is possible to use a 'plunge' method of forming the moulding: the mould is fitted to a piece of dowel; a cut-out is made in a baseplate to the plan outline of the mould; then the plastic is pinned over the plate, heated and the mould pushed into the softened plastic. As with many of the modelling techniques you will need to experiment to obtain satisfactory results. Researching the subject through books and magazines will also help.

Clear Plastic Sheet

As stated above, PVC material is often used for vac-forming and this is available in a number of different thicknesses. Acetate sheet and butyrate clear sheet might also be on sale in model shops. The acetate is easier to glue, but is not fuel-proof to glow fuels and nitromethane. Whenever you use plastic sheeting of any type, test it for compatibility with adhesives, paints and fuels.

ADHESIVES

It is almost a case of not which glues and adhesives to use, but which, of the vast amount on the market, we can ignore. Both the range and efficiency of modern adhesives are superb, and it must be possible to glue virtually any one material to another. First, let us take a look at the principal types of adhesive we are likely to use in our aeromodelling pursuits. I am not including balsa cement because, although it has a few advantages in specialist areas, it has largely been superseded by newer types.

PVA White Glues

Probably the most useful and widely used of the wood to wood modelling adhesives, PVA glue is water-based and can be easily washed off the hands and other components. Developments of the standard white PVA adhesive include the quicker-drying varieties (but not so quick that you don't have plenty of time to readjust the position of the component) and waterproof versions, although a more correct term might be water-resistant. PVA is an air-drying glue, so it loses some weight during the drying process, but it is not a 'gap filler' – this means that the items to be glued together must be a tolerably good fit. It can be used for gluing sheeted areas together, but the surfaces have to be kept in close proximity, with weights, pins or clamps, until the glue has dried. PVA glue tends not to dry brittle hard and this gives it a certain flexibility for open structures that may flex slightly when a hard landing is made. This is preferable to a more rigid joint, which could fracture.

Good for pretty well all wood to wood joints, PVA is especially suited to areas where it takes time to pin and clamp everything together, such as wing leading-edge sheeting. The delayed drying time and tough eventual joint is a bonus, but the fact that the glue does not dry crisp and hard means that you must take care to use a sanding block when sanding down the joint. Using a loose piece of abrasive paper in the hand will only result in sanding down the balsawood on either side and leaving the joint proud. Don't be tempted to buy the cheapest bulk PVA glue used for building purposes, as it may have a high percentage of fillers and would not be as strong; stick to the well-known proprietary brands of glue.

Aliphatic Glues

These are usually yellow in colour (although I don't know why) and act in a similar way to PVA adhesives, except that the final joint dries a little more crisp and is easier to sand.

Epoxy Adhesives

Purpose-manufactured for modelling activities, these two-part adhesives are produced with drying times of four to five minutes, twenty minutes, thirty minutes, one hour, twenty-four hours and probably every time in-between! Consisting of an adhesive and a hardener, you should always read the instructions, as a different ratio of mixing is sometimes required. Heatproof epoxies and metal filler epoxies are also manufactured.

Putting it Together

However the model is constructed and irrespective of the materials used, the model will only fly as well as it is truly built. Twists, warps or misalignments in the airframe will certainly produce erratic flying and will present many additional problems when it comes to learning to fly. Build a good design true and light, and your chances of flying success are increased tenfold. This is where the ARTF models may have an advantage, as they are constructed under factory conditions with the aid of permanent building jigs and operators working on the same piece of construction day after day. Having said that, I have seen some poor examples of ARTF construction, with gaps between the wing ribs and spars and fuselage formers not touching the sides, so don't automatically assume that the model will be free of warps. Also, take care when assembling the model to keep everything square and correctly aligned – it will make a lot of difference to the flying characteristics.

Kit manufacturers increasingly use die cutting, or CNC laser cutting, for the sheet parts and this helps with providing accurate components. The way that the cut parts just fall away from a sheet of components never ceases to amaze me and the use of computers for drawings and for the automatic cutting ensures both accuracy and repeatability. However, even the best of designers and manufacturers make the occasional mistake and if you find an error in the kit do take the trouble to point it out, in the nicest possible way, to the manufacturer; it may prevent another modeller from having the same error.

The first thing to do when you get the model kit home is to examine all the parts carefully, check that they are all there and that none are damaged. Take the trouble to identify all the parts – for example, the strip wood may have similar cross-section dimensions, but have different lengths or densities. Try to identify the purpose for which each strip is intended and to pair, for equal strength and density, such items as wing spars and fuselage longerons. If there is a piece of wood that is substandard, perhaps a little too soft, then replace it rather than use it and regret it; unless there is a substantial amount of wood at fault, it is barely worth returning it to the manufacturer, although a local retailer should be able to rectify the problem. Writing about the matching of paired components reminds me of a manufacturing anecdote. A well-known British firm was producing control line model kits of a design with sheet wings, and a modeller purchasing one of the kits found that the starboard wing panel was heavy and rock hard and the port wing soft and light. When he complained to the company the supervisor went along to the packer (each kit would have a numbered slip indicating the identity of the packer) and asked why she had included one heavy and one light wing in the kit. 'Well,' she said, 'You told me that the wings had got to be of medium weight, so if one was heavy, I would put the other one with light wood to compensate.' Logical, but unfortunately wrong.

Obviously it will be quicker to build a model from a prefabricated kit, providing the parts are accurately cut, but you don't have the same degree of control over wood selection. It can be frustrating, for instance, if your kit contains some unduly heavy sheet tail surfaces and you know, or think you know, that the model is anyway likely to end up tail heavy. If you were building the model from scratch, you would have been careful to select a lighter grade of balsawood. Unless the manufacturer is a one-, or two-man band, operated by experienced aeromodellers, the selection of materials and packing will have been carried out by non-modelling types and they may not understand the importance of wood grading to the same extent as the hobbyist. Apart from the fact that the wood parts are cut out for you and that there will be more preformed and moulded components in a kit, the building and assembly will remain the same.

There are a few basic rules to bear in mind when constructing the model. They may seem obvious, but are worthy of emphasis.

Accuracy

The old adage of measure twice, cut once should be remembered. If a part is drawn accurately and cut accurately it will fit and will not require a great glob of glue to fill the gap between it and the adjacent part. Excessive glue equates to a weak joint, or more weight. It is equally bad to force-fit a component as this will put extra strain on the wood parts, causing twisting. If the part doesn't fit precisely, trim or sand it until it does and then glue it in position.

Alignment

When fitting wing ribs to spars, for instance, use a small metal square or special moulded tool to check that they are fitted vertically. Your eyes might tell you that they are upright, but your eyes can be very deceiving. Correct alignment for fuselages is equally important and sometimes more difficult to achieve. Making a pair of fuselage sides shouldn't create too many problems, but joining them, with formers and cross pieces, can result in some horrendous banana-shaped (on plan view) fuselages. This is where the use of building jigs comes in handy. Many wings are built directly over the plan drawing and a jig is not required; it is only when building wings with biconvex sections that a jig may be necessary, and even then the design often incorporates a means of propping up rear spars and trailing edges so that the wing panels can still be built directly over the building surface.

Fuselages, though, are a different matter and joining the sides will definitely benefit from the use of a jig. Fuselages rarely have a straight top or bottom and it is therefore difficult to assemble the sides over the plan view of the drawing. Using a building jig, with adjustable side supports, has a number of advantages, as the formers and cross pieces can be aligned over a centre line, so that the projections are equal on each side. Also, because the supports can be clamped in position, it holds the components together while the glue is drying. All you have to watch out for is that each paired component is of equal length, that they are fitted in the correct location and that they are at right angles to the centre line; a centre mark on the formers and cross pieces will also help with the side to side alignment. I cannot overemphasize the fact that, with a built-up structure, accurate, close-fitting glue joints will result in much greater strength of the finished airframe section.

Weight Watching

I also cannot emphasize enough the need to keep your eye on the weight of all parts of the model. As already stressed, light models fly better, so be vigilant and disciplined in keeping the weights to reasonable limits. When you inspect the plan of the model you may think that certain areas look rather weak and fragile. Many modellers decide that the design would benefit from 'beefing up' in certain places and proceed to increase the dimensions of some parts and reinforce others. All of this, of course, will result in a heavier model, sometimes to the extent of altering the flying characteristics to a disastrous extent. I have had modellers contact me and claim that a certain model does not fly properly, only to find out that the model, which should have weighed 4lb had finished up at 6.5lb. But, they explained, we thought that the tailplane looked rather weak, so we covered it with some hard ⅟₁₆in sheet, then we had to add three quarters of a pound of ballast in the nose. And, yes, the wings looked rather weak so we strengthened them – no wonder the model turned out heavy and flew like a brick! Please give the designer the benefit of the doubt and build the model according to the plan. Only later, when you have had more experience, should you start modifying designs; in those cases, if the model doesn't fly, be it on your own head – but not literally.

Preparing the Plan

Few plans come in a rolled state. They will usually be folded and the creases may be projecting. A domestic iron will generally get rid of the creases, but don't have the heat too high. When building from scratch we have to find a method of transferring the drawing of the components on the plan to the material being used for the component. There are numerous ways of achieving this end. For balsawood and plywood parts, there is the time-honoured method of placing the wood under the plan and 'pinning' the outline by pushing a pin through the plan into the wood. The part can then be cut, usually without having to mark the part any further. Alternatively, a piece of carbon paper, the pencil variety, can be placed between the plan and the material and the outline of the component traced around. This has the advantage of working on plastic and metal surfaces as well.

With photocopying facilities we have two further options for marking out the parts. With the standard photostat A4 and A3 copies (you may have to cut the plan to get to the component drawings), the copies can be used in two ways. You can glue the drawing part to the material with Spraymount adhesive, then cut out the part and the paper will peel off quite readily. The alternative, which works well on wood materials, is to place the photostat face down on the wood and then iron the surface of the paper with a hot iron. It will transfer the ink lines to the material, although the image will be in reverse. For photocopies, the larger

print machines, the heat-transfer system may not work and for these items the contact spray adhesive is the way to go.

Large areas, such as fuselage sides, can be 'papered' – place the pattern in the centre and allow it to fall in place. It is unlikely to crease and if it does, it can be repositioned. If you have a piece to mark out that is fairly critical regarding the size to the dimensions of the materials, cut with a long metal rule along one of the straight edges and glue this to a straight edge on the material. One further advantage of gluing the patterns to the wood is that it helps to prevent splitting of the wood in tricky areas; however, if you are using a stronger contact spray adhesive, such as Evostik, the paper pattern should be peeled away as soon as the cutting is complete. A similar system to prevent small areas of balsawood from splitting can be achieved by applying clear adhesive tape to the area to be cut.

Cutting

There is a whole host of methods for cutting the various materials employed in model building. For balsa strip and balsa sheet up to ⅟₈in (3mm) thickness, the hobby or surgical knives are the best instruments. Although we can cut the thinner sheets of wood in one cut, never attempt to cut right through in one go if it is hard going. It is much better to make a number of gentle pressure cuts and keep accuracy. One basic principle is worth remembering, and this applies whether you are cutting with a knife, with scissors or a saw. Always look at the line ahead of where you are cutting and not at the actual point of the cut. This even applies to curved cuts, although the sharper the curve the closer to the point of cut you must focus. It takes a bit of courage when you first make a cut with a fretsaw by looking ahead, as the natural temptation is to look at the point of cut to see whether it is on the line, but if you do you will have no indication of the precise direction the saw is making. The other temptation, with fret- and bandsawing, is to attempt to get in position by moving the material sideways – you mustn't, you have to rotate the material to take up a new direction.

Accurate cutting is important, but is not always achieved, and any errors in cutting should be corrected immediately, while you still remember them. With wood components it is usually a matter of a quick adjustment with a sanding block, but remember to

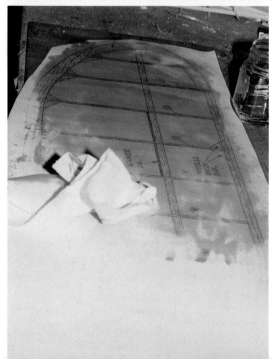

Vintage model designs (the Bulldozer is illustrated) show off traditional aeromodelling methods and materials at their best. Where only one wing panel is shown on a drawing the details can be shown on the reverse side by applying olive oil or similar. Use a set square to ensure verticality of wing ribs and a template for angled root ribs. Sheet balsawood can be more easily curved if a light spray of water is given to the outside. Use plenty of pins to hold the parts in place when gluing and check that all components are accurately positioned. Fuselage sides are built one on top of the other, with a layer of thin, clear film between. Curvaceous longerons should be formed from two or more laminations of strip. Build elevators and rudders integral with the tailplane or fin, as this will ensure that the correct outlines are followed.

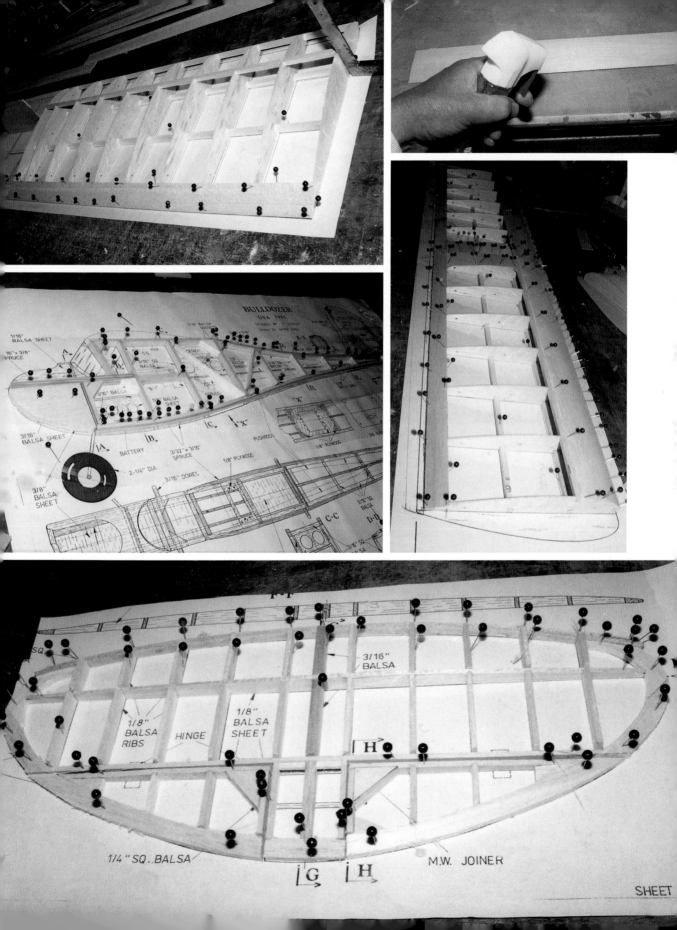

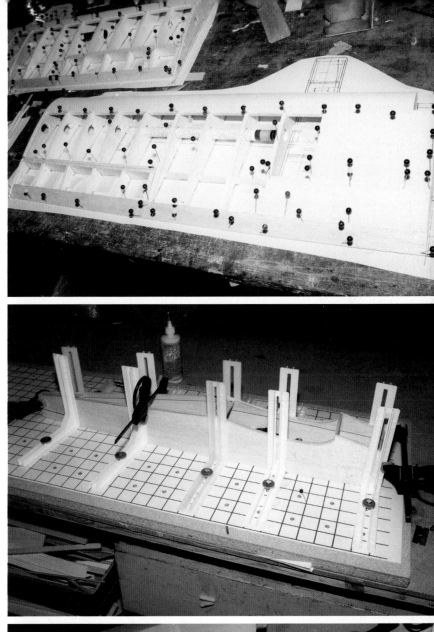

OPPOSITE PAGE:
Jedellsky wings, where the sheeted surface is on the top only, are built directly over the plan drawing; the thicker leading edge is contoured to a curved section on the upper surface. The wing ribs can be left extending below the lower surface, or they can be planed away and the underside covered with a film.

THIS PAGE:
Although built directly over the plan the wing, with a flat bottom section, will require the spars to be raised to the correct height with packing pieces. To avoid banana-shaped fuselages, looking in plan view, use a building jig when gluing formers to the sides and use clips and clamps to hold the formers firmly in place.

keep to the correct angle, for example at 90 degrees to the surface of the sheet. Cutting thicker strip materials is best done with a razor saw, which gives a cleaner, truer cut, but even here you must check that the saw blade is at the right angle for the cut. Thicker sheet materials require a fretsaw or bandsaw for easy cutting, as this will give a neat cut edge, whereas with a knife you are likely to finish up with a jagged cut. Don't forget, though, that the material is moved to the fretsaw blade and not the other way round.

One essential when cutting with a knife is to have a sharp blade. Many of the modelling and hobby knives have easily changeable or break-off blades, but the surgical knife blades are not exactly inexpensive. If you were a surgeon, of course you would replace the blade for each operation, but for the more impecunious modeller we do not want to throw them away so often. However, we still want a keen edge. A small oilstone for sharpening is the answer – a couple of strokes in each direction and the edge is as sharp as ever.

Sometimes, with block balsa, we have to carve seriously large lumps and the blades of our modelling and Stanley knives are not large enough for the job. A good-quality kitchen knife, suitably sharpened, will do the trick and we also have the razor plane to take off great shavings. Once the basic shape has been achieved, Permagrit tools and sanding blocks will do the rest. Sanding might be considered as a necessary evil – we have to remove the unwanted material and have a smooth finish, but it is sometimes a pain getting there. Anything that cuts down the time of reaching the desired finish is a bonus and motorized sanders, either bench-fixed or portable, will prove to be a great help in this. Also, it is a matter of starting with a good coarse abrasive paper to remove the bulk of the wood and then to go on to the finer grades for finishing. The only thing to watch is that you don't get too enthusiastic and over-sand with the coarse grit.

TRICKS OF THE TRADE

There are many 'short cuts' and ways of achieving boring or difficult modelling results. Take wing ribs, for instance. With a parallel chord wing, of equal depth, the wing ribs will be very similar. There may be a few slots for dihedral braces, or holes for wing joiners, but the outlines will be essentially the same. Now, we can cut these ribs individually, using a single template, or we can produce them by the 'sandwich' method where we have two identical templates, one at each end of the block of rib blanks, with the complete sandwich bolted together using lengths of screwed studding. The blanks are then planed and sanded away until the edges of the templates are reached, the slots are then cut for spars, and so on, with a razor saw. When the ribs are released, adjustments are made to any of the ribs where there are additional fittings or sheeting. By using the same wood for blanks in the respective port and starboard wing panels you can also ensure that the rib strengths are equal on both panels.

Tapered wing plan ribs can also be made by this method, but only as long as the rib stations have identical spacings.

What other methods do we have for cutting near-identical wing ribs? We can use a fretsaw or bandsaw, but remember to make the lower and upper cuts from the same end, for example the trailing edge, just in case the blade is not quite vertical. The ribs should then finish up at identical depths. After sawing to shape, the ribs will need a light sanding to smooth the surface. Finally, the ribs can be cut individually, around a template, preferably cut from metal or plastic. This is a more suitable method for thin and small wing ribs where it is difficult to locate the threaded rods needed for the sandwich method. It may also be more useful for wing ribs with an undercamber.

Wing structures vary from the fully sheeted, built-up or veneered foam types to the simple rib and spar style, without any extra sheeting. Most wings will have a built-up structure somewhere between the two extremes. Avoiding warps or twists when the wings are covered is one of the main aims and forming a 'D' box leading edge, with leading edge sheeting top and bottom and a full depth main spar (or two spars and some vertical webbing between the spars) goes a long way to achieving an anti-warp structure. Having a trailing edge consisting of top and lower sheet strips with webbing between would further add to the anti-warping structure and adding capping strips, the same thickness as the sheeting and about 8mm (⅜in) wide, to the ribs almost completes the wing rigidity; all that remains is to fully sheet the centre section. Joining wing panels, to given dihedral angles, is fairly critical as the strength of the centre joint relies on a good mating of the root wing ribs. These ribs should have been set to the required angle with a dihedral angle template during the construction, but the roots will require a final sanding to remove the spar nibs and any over-hanging sheeting before the wings are joined. Avoiding a curved action when sanding the root ribs is vital, otherwise the surfaces will not mate, and using a 'shooting block and board', where the sanding block is guided by a straight edge, for this purpose will give the best results.

Fuselages

Again, there are many forms of fuselage construction, from the simple slab-sided structure, to fully planked or GRP moulded examples. For built-up, planked scale fuselages it is normal to build half the fuselage, with the formers glued to a keel and the planking added; this half is then removed from the building board, the other fuselage halves added and the planking completed. The finished structure is light, probably lighter than a GRP moulded fuselage, but the latter has the advantage of being able to construct more fuselages from the same female mould and incorporating surface detail.

Undercarriages

Undercarriages also come under the heading of necessary evils. They are required for landings and take-offs, but are useless when the aircraft is in the air. It follows, therefore, that an undercarriage must stand up to the rigours that may be experienced in a hard landing, but we will want to keep its weight, plus that of the fixings and reinforcing, to a minimum. Many features that are included on models are directly related to the full-size arrangements, but this is less so for undercarriages. Piano wire is the most commonly used material for undercarriage legs, usually of a thickness around 10 gauge in diameter. How many full-size aircraft do we see with undercarriage legs of 13mm diameter piano wire?

There is also a significant difference when it comes to landing loads on undercarriage legs. On full-sized aeroplanes the main landing load is upwards and the pilot will be aiming to put the craft down as softly as possible. With the model, because of the approach and relatively hard landing, the loads on the undercarriage are more rearwards and the springiness of the piano wire helps to cope with this. However, when it comes to scale models and scale-type undercarriages we have to spring them in oleo type as would be found in the full-sized examples. Fixing of the oleo legs and undercarriage retracting systems calls for a lot of local reinforcement around the actual fixing point in the wing and there is always the danger that, with a high-speed landing on fairly rough ground, the leg will be pulled away from the wing structure.

Two arrangements of undercarriages are to be found on models, as with full-sized aeroplanes: 'tail-draggers' with two main wheels and a skid or tailwheel at the rear of the fuselage; and the tricycle undercarriage layout, where the two main wheels are augmented by a nosewheel. The legs and wheels may be fixed or, in scale subjects, retracting; aluminium alloy or GRP (with carbon-fibre reinforcement) can also be used for the main undercarriage legs. In practical terms, the tricycle undercarriage layout makes it easier to 'track' the model on take-off and there is less tendency for it to veer off course, but, with a small nosewheel, it may present problems of acceleration on rougher ground. With the two-wheel arrangement the pilot must be ready for some gyroscopic effects when the tail rises during the take-off run; it normally requires an input of right rudder to keep the model tacking straight. Also, the 'trike' is more likely to lift off itself when flying speed has been reached, while the 'taildragger' will need a gentle input of up elevator for the lift-off, unless it was being held tail down during the take-off run (and by so doing creating more drag and the risk of a premature take-off due to the increased angle of attack of the wings). Although it is more difficult to learn to take-off with a two-wheel undercarriage, it is good training and teaches you to use all four control functions. It is also extremely satisfying to carry out a fully stalled three-point landing from a few inches above the ground.

Positioning the main wheels relative to the balance point of the model is reasonably critical. With a tail-dragger they need to have an inch, or so, in front of the balance point on the average-sized model. Any further forward and it is more difficult to achieve a rotation, the tail rising to a horizontal position, and because the movement is more forced there is the possibility of a more sudden gyroscopic reaction. Similarly, the main wheels of a tricycle undercarriage should not be placed too far aft of the balance point, otherwise it might not be possible to generate sufficient elevator force to achieve a lift-off. You may notice that on vintage-style models (all taildraggers),

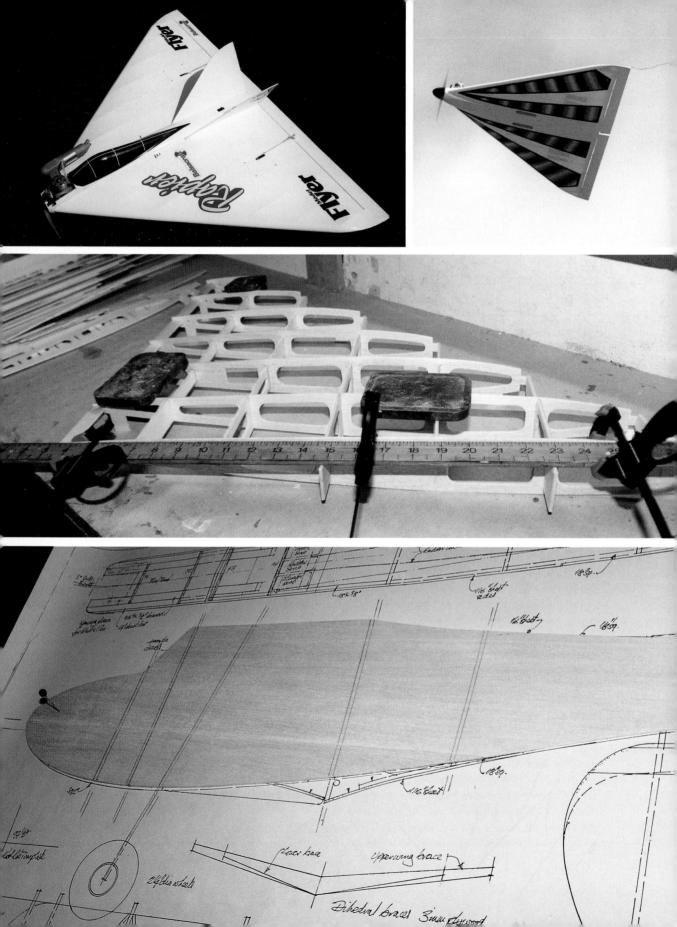

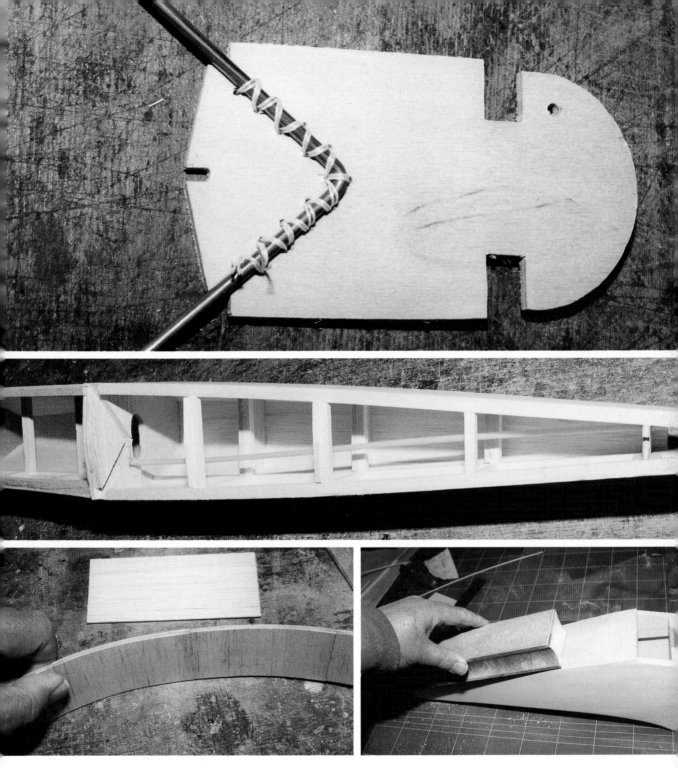

Now produced as an ARTF model, the Rapier was originally a kit with traditional-style construction. The long root rib was held straight by clamping a rule to the face of the rib. Visibility and orientation are helped with this fast model by adding reflective decoration on the underside of the wing. Positions of the formers on the fuselage sides are marked via the extended lines on the drawing. Binding undercarriage legs on to plywood formers, for smaller models, is a well established and reliable method; epoxy adhesive is spread over the joints. Do remember to fit any control-rod tubes in the fuselage before the lower sheeting is attached. Laminating sheet and strip balsawood both improves the 'bendability' and increases the strength. Use a Permagrit block to level the sheeted surfaces; sandpaper held in the hand will leave ridges at the glue and hard wood locations.

the wheels are well forward of the balance point. This is because they were originally designed as free-flight models and a good landing was more important than the take-off. Indeed, because of the light wing loadings on these types, the take-offs consisted of a very short take-off run, with barely time for the model to get off course. When these vintage types are fitted with radio control, and with a heavier wing loading, it can become quite tricky achieving a straight take-off – any potential turn must be anticipated and only moderate inputs of rudder control given.

Tail Surfaces

Tailplanes, fins, elevators and rudders are usually the easiest airframe structures to build. They often consist of flat sheet construction, or built-up and flat, constructed on the building board over the plan. It is important to make them warp-resistant and to this end the tailplane, normally the longest structure, may have anti-warp inserts on the sheet version, or diagonal struts inserted on the built-up type, with the possible addition of chordwise strips, top and bottom, to act like ribs. For larger models it is worthwhile constructing the tail surfaces with a fully developed aerodynamic symmetrical section (NACA 0012 or similar). Also, for large tailplanes, the incorporation of static balance elevators, where weights are used to counterbalance the elevators, and aerodynamic balancing, with areas of the elevator tips projecting in front of the hinge line, will assist in reducing the forces on the servo/s. But these considerations, and the possible need for supporting struts, are all probably future requirements.

Ailerons

Where fitted, these are of two types, the strip aileron and the inset aileron. The former, as the name suggests, is a thin strip at the rear of the wing, running near the length of the wing panel, operated by a centrally located servo linked to aileron horn cranks. This is the simplest form of aileron control, but quite effective. The second form is the inset aileron, forming a wider section of wing trailing edge and located inboard of the wing tips. These can be operated via bell cranks and pushrods, from a central servo, or, more normally these days, from individual servos in the wing panels, operated by a 'Y' lead from the servos to the receiver, and with direct linkages from the servo output to the aileron horn.

Inset, or inboard, ailerons can also follow the full-sized practice of having the surfaces balanced statically and aerodynamically and may incorporate the 'Frise' principle. This allows air to be diverted from the high pressure below the wing, through the aileron hinge gap to the upper aileron surface, to provide more efficient aileron control.

Wing and Tail Fixings

Securing the wings and tail-surfaces with rubber bands has largely gone out of fashion. This is understandable for tail-surfaces, where there are control linkages extending from the fuselage to the control horns on the elevators and rudder and the settings might be upset. For the wings, however, where the control linkages will not be affected (where ailerons are fitted the controls are all within the wing structure), there are distinct advantages to rubber-banding the wings in position on trainer models. On the final part of the landing approach it is all too easy to let a wing drop and the tip can easily catch the ground. If the wing is bolted to the fuselage there is every chance that the anchor nuts for the fixing bolts will be ripped out and other damage may occur. Where the wing is banded in position it will probably only skew round, or the rubber bands will be dislodged. This logic, incidentally, can also be applied to undercarriages.

COVERINGS AND FINISHES

Coverings and finishes are another subject that almost demands a separate book to do justice to the topic. With the introduction of heat-shrink films and fabrics the traditional forms of tissue, silk and nylon coverings all but disappeared. The latter involved the use of clear dopes for tautening and fitting the materials, and many wives and partners considered the dopes to be nasty and smelly (to modellers it was sheer perfume). Tissue can still be used on very small models and for decorating sheeted surfaces, although plastic film has also overtaken this form of covering. Nylon gives a tough, durable finish, which will survive for years, but you won't be popular if you dope it in the lounge – however, you can do that with the modern heat-shrink 'Tex' materials.

Before including information on covering with these materials it is important to point out that the final finish, whatever it may be, will only be as good as the preparation of the airframe. Lumps and bumps on the airframe wood will translate to lumps and bumps on the finished covering, the material may have a lovely shiny finish, but this will only show up flaws and imperfections even more. Use your sanding implements from coarse to finer grades until the wood finishes are as smooth as the proverbial baby's bottom. Then you must get rid of the specks of wood and dust. Use a small vacuum cleaner in the first instance and follow this up with a wipe down with a 'tack' rag (used by decorators for wiping surfaces before painting).

If it is at all possible you should carry out the covering processes away from the workshop, due to the possible problems caused by static electricity. I suffer from large build-ups of static electricity and this not only causes the plastic backing sheets from the covering materials to stick to me, but I also attract dust on to the film like nobody's business. Therefore, if I am working in a dusty environment it is almost impossible to stop the dust particles from inserting themselves between the airframe and the covering. I have similar problems when trying to paint cockpit canopies and cowlings, and so on.

Finding the Right Covering

The 'new' heat-shrink materials are not difficult to work with, but you must follow the basic rules. You will find a complete set of instructions with every roll of covering product – read, learn and inwardly digest.

There are a number of different manufacturers of the film and fabric covering materials, but the largest of these is Solarfilm, even if some of their products are sold under a different brand name. In the interests of simplicity I will only refer to the names of the Solarfilm products, although there may be equivalents manufactured in other countries. Take a look through the trade catalogues and you should find the products listed, with a short description of their purpose. For instance, under So-lite, the lightest of all the iron-on self-adhesive, heat-shrink covering materials, it states that it is designed specifically for indoor models and park flyers. So-lite is applied exactly as normal Solarfilm. On the other hand, Fibafilm might be described as being intended for models relying, in part, on the covering for torsional stiffness. With a weight of only 1?oz per sq yd (40–45gsm), Fibafilm is suited to small models and although it has heat-shrink properties, it does not have an adhesive backing. Adhesion is obtained by thinly brushing a coat of Balsaloc on to the airframe first, letting it dry and then ironing on the covering in the usual way. Airspan is similar as regards the means of application and is also suitable for small models. Although it does not have the same torsional attributes as Fibafilm, it might be considered as the modern equivalent to tissue.

Polyester films such as Solarfilm Polyester Super Shrink have one advantage over the original Solarfilm and Solarspan products, in that they are proof against diesel fuels and petrol. In the past all of the film materials have had a glossy exterior surface, but a recent innovation is the matt finish Polyester covering. For scale enthusiasts this is a real step forward, as few full-sized aircraft have a truly glossy surface and it means that they can use the matt covering and not have to worry about applying a matt fuel proofer to tone down the gloss finish. From a model photographic point of view it also has advantages, as the gloss finish sometimes produces highlights in the wrong places, making it look as though the covering is ripped and that the modeller has made a poor job of the covering – it also shows up fingermarks like crazy!

In addition to the covering materials there are also Balsaloc, a primer and adhesive for Fibafilm; Litespan and Clearcoat as a fuel proofer before applying iron-on covering and as a finish for Solartex; and Solarlac paints for use on Solarfilm coverings. The latter are resistant to moderate nitro content fuels, available in matching colours, and can be mixed with a flatting agent and brush or spray applied.

Areas where fuel spillage or exhaust residue may penetrate, for example the fuel tank bay and inside the engine compartment, should be liberally treated with Clearcoat. The only other areas requiring treatment are large plywood and hard smooth surfaces where the application of Balsaloc will improve adhesion and help prevent air bubbles forming between the covering and airframe.

Application

Solarfilm, Solarspan, Solartex and Glosstex all have one thing in common – they consist of two essential parts, the base material, that is, plastic film, synthetic fibre or a combination of these, and an adhesive backing. During application to the airframe heat is applied to the covering material and causes changes in both the base and adhesive. Some changes are reversible

The early de Havilland airliner was only intended for static display, but was covered with silver Solartex and sprayed with black Solarlac.

BELOW: Covered in red and white Polyester film with white spray-painted floats, the engine bay and other 'fuel sensitive' areas of the floatplane were painted with Solarlac, of a matching colour, first. Polyester film is available in gloss, matt and translucent types, Solartex in antique and vintage colours in addition to the standard colour range. Installing a …

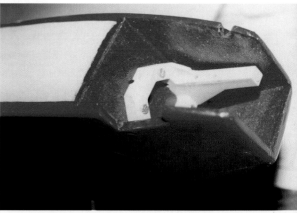

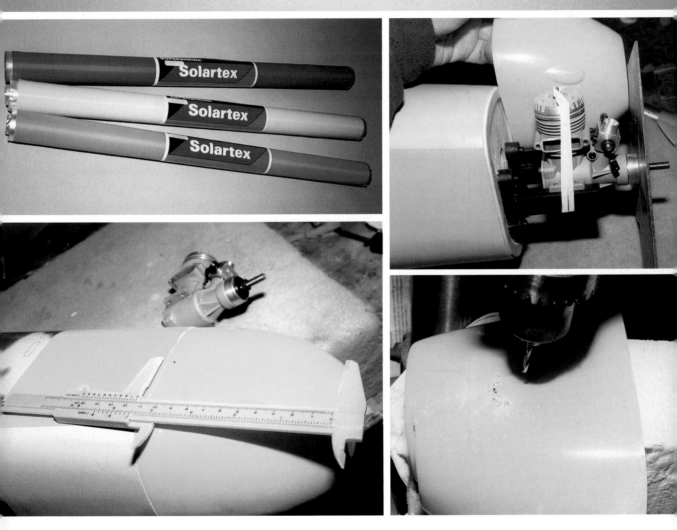

… *moulded engine cowling, in this case on an ARTF model, requires precise marking of the opening for the silencer manifold, glow-plug lead, needle valve and cooling air. Position the engine to give the correct propeller clearance, then measure the distances to the openings and mounting-block screw holes.*

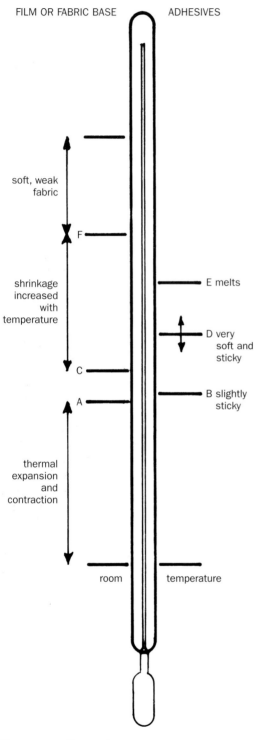

FILM OR FABRIC BASE   ADHESIVES

soft, weak
fabric

F

shrinkage
increased
with
temperature

E melts

D very
soft and
sticky

C

B slightly
sticky

A

thermal
expansion
and
contraction

room   temperature

*Temperatures for covering
with heatshrink film or fabric.*

and the material will return to its original condition on cooling, but in other cases the change is irreversible because of the temperature applied. It is the lack of understanding of the importance of keeping to these temperatures, or the failure even to acknowledge them, that causes some modellers to complain about the product – invariably the material is okay, it is the modeller who is at fault. If you need proof of this fact you only have to look at the many successful models covered with the products to realize that their builders must be doing something right – or you are doing something wrong.

Application, sealing and shrinking temperatures are quoted on all the instruction leaflets, but many modellers tend to ignore these and apply more and more heat (sometimes reaching the stage where the material melts) to tighten – and over-tighten. Neither the specialist covering iron nor a thermostatically controlled domestic iron will give accurate temperature readings. You will require a thermometer (typically a Coverite bi-metallic strip thermometer) and sit it on the sole of the iron to obtain an accurate reading.

What happens at the relative temperatures can be seen, left, in the diagram, where the base material is shown on the left and the adhesive on the right-hand side of the imaginary thermometer. Actual temperatures are not shown as these will vary for the types of covering (refer to instructions for actual temperatures).

- From room temperature to A – the film expands. This is normal thermal expansion that reverses on cooling.
- At B – the adhesive surface has softened and will stick slightly if pressed on to a surface.
- At C – the film just starts to shrink.
- From C to F – the shrinkage increases in temperature in a regular manner with increasing temperature, provided that it is not prevented by being attached to a frame.
- Around D – the adhesive is very soft and sticky and will adhere well if held in contact with a surface and allowed to cool (if the adhesive is compatible with the surface).
- Around E – the adhesive has melted and will penetrate into the grain of balsa if pressure is applied to the covering, for example by ironing.
- From F to melt – the shrinkage rate increases, but the film is weak and easily distorted or stretched so it would exert almost no 'pull' on a frame.

These guidelines should therefore be followed.

For attaching film neatly work at C. The adhesive is sticky, but the film will not wrinkle up due to shrinkage.

To shrink the covering work at D, where there is enough shrinkage to take out slackness but still leave spare shrinkage available at temperatures above D. If you go above E the adhesive penetrates into the wood grain, which makes it difficult to remove the film for repairs (it either tears or leaves the colour on the wood). Up to D the film will peel off cleanly – just taking a few fibres off the surface of the wood

Keep well below F when shrinking. Coverings that have been heated above F will slacken off and bubble or wrinkle later on in the life of the model. The covering will have been permanently degraded, although it appears unaffected. (It can be re-shrunk using higher temperatures but the bubbling will return. The period between re-shrinkings will get shorter – and the temperature needed gets higher every time.) Once a covering has been shrunk tight, then extra heat does not increase tightness. Most modellers use far too much heat when covering.

Watch out for the 'ratchet effect', in which the iron is turned up slightly to shrink a stubborn wrinkle and isn't turned back down. After a few tweaks of the thermostat the iron is a lot hotter than necessary. Mark the thermostat with T for tacking and S for shrinking – and glance at the setting occasionally. It is easy to find temperature C by ironing small strips of the material you are using on to a piece of clean balsa – lowering the iron temperature until the material just adheres to the balsa but pulls a few fibres away when peeled off after cooling. Do not be surprised if the setting is lower than expected. Invest in a decent modellers' iron. Domestic irons have less precise thermostats controlling more powerful elements, so the temperature swings as the thermostat switches power on and off will be much wider.

What about the finishes where the covering does not adhere well, such as glass fibre, epoxy resins and fuel proofers? The easiest solution is to find a material that will adhere to the substrate, such as thin masking tape, give this a brushing of Clearcoat and attach the covering to this.

Advantages

In case the obvious has been missed, the reasons for using the heat-shrink covering include: clean and virtually odourless application (can be done in front of the television); the material is self-coloured and only requires a contrasting colour trim; it is available in a multitude of colours (with some matching paints); is generally fuel proof; and compares favourably in weight and strength with traditional materials and methods.

You may need a few more hints and tips on covering that might not be included in the instructions. They are as follows.

Sometimes it is more convenient to cut to near the precise size of the parts to be covered, whereas at other times you need to be rather generous. If the area to be covered is relatively flat, say the underside of a wing, or a flat plate tailplane, the covering can be cut with just one side a little larger than the component. One edge can then be ironed precisely in position, with the other having a small overlap for securing and trimming. If, however, you are having to work over some double curvatures round a nose or a curved wing-tip, you need enough spare material to grab and pull over the surface as you iron it in position to avoid the wrinkles.

Heat guns are preferred for shrinking the covering by some modellers, but these lack the degree of heat control supplied by an iron. We even used to shrink a Solarfilm panel by holding it in front of an electric open element fire, often with spectacular results – the covering would get too hot and melt! Also, as mentioned previously, if the material is over-heated on application, it does not leave room to tauten it at a later stage.

Using contrasting colours of films for decorative effects can result in some very attractive schemes on model aircraft – and some pretty horrendous examples, too. I can never understand why modellers have always had the tendency to give one colour to the fuselage and another to the flying surfaces, as there are not too many full-sized examples that are finished in this way (except for Tiger Moths and these often have the fuselage colour as a trim around the flying surface edges). It can look good when proportions of the fuselage and the flying surfaces are given contrasting colours, but, with open structure airframes, you have a limited number of places where you can make the colour division. Attempting to use one colour to cover the whole of the airframe and then to over-cover with another film colour will probably end in failure. It may work for small sections and strips of trim, but attempting larger overlaid areas will probably result in trapping pockets of air (bubbles) under the top covering. The

ABOVE: Simple, but effective decoration on the 'El Forte', another build-from-the-plan model.
BELOW: Rivalling the ARTF designs for colour decoration, the 'Mean Machine' was conventionally built and film-covered.

The epitome of the scale builder's art. World Champion Peter McDermott not only includes every detail on his models, but he weathers the surfaces and they have the appearance of being handled by miniature pairs of hands.

only alternative is to select a joint line where there is some 'solid' structure underneath, such as sheeted wing leading edges, or a fuselage longeron. Small overlaps are acceptable at these joints, and are preferable to a butt joint, which will almost certainly part when heat is applied from the iron and you will then need to cover the gap with a piece of decorative trim.

When using contrasting colours of film for decorative effect, remember that if you are using it as 'handed' decoration, for example a left-hand and right-hand wing panel, the decorative pieces must also be 'handed'. Mark out the film or fabric with a Chinagraph pencil on the backing film protecting the rear of the material and cut two pieces, back to back. Although it may be difficult to cover film on film, it is easier when you get to the Solartex materials. These seem to take more kindly to overlapping without trapping air bubbles, providing that you work with the iron from the centre of the material to the outer edges.

You don't have to opt for the difficult decorative schemes. A single colour model can be made more attractive by the simple expedient of applying self-adhesive decorative stripes as used for automobiles. They come in a wide range of colours and combinations and are easy to apply. There are also decorative self-adhesive polyvinyl stickers that can be added and if you can't find any that are suitable your local supplier can possibly make some to your own specification.

PAINTS AND COLOURED DOPES

When you see an example of a superbly finished and decorated scale model, one of contest winning standard, you can be sure that it is the result of a painted finish, and a sprayed finish at that. For authentic scale finishes you really have no option but to do it the hard way, that is, quality construction, first-rate covering, careful preparation and immaculate application of decorations and markings. Another thing is certain, it hasn't been achieved in a couple of nights, or, probably, a couple of months. Serious competition scale models are more likely to take a couple of years to get to the standards now required to be competitive at the highest standards.

How are these superb finishes achieved? Blood, sweat and tears will be among the ingredients, and so

will a great deal of experience and knowledge of some of the traditional methods of covering and finishing. This is where tissue, silk, dope and talcum powder are still in evidence (the latter is used to mix with clear dope to act as a filler and to allow the finish to be rubbed down to a smooth finish). Like the specialist car industry, you may have a finish that comprises of eight base coats, all individually rubbed down before the colour is sprayed on. And spraying is the operative word here. The last thing that we want is a heavy build-up of colour finishes; weight, as I have said, is the modeller's enemy, so the paints and fuel-proof finishes have to be applied very thinly.

Not all of us wish to produce a national contest-winning finish on our scale-like models, but at least have them resembling a full-sized aircraft, which can be achieved by using dopes and paints, either sprayed or brushed on. Cellulose clear dopes must be used for the covering and tautening of the tissue or nylon covering, but the colour application can be in the form of cellulose, acrylic or enamel paints. Enamel paints are available from model hobby shops, either in gloss or matt finishes. They are resistant to diesel fuels, but only to glow fuels without any nitromethane content; for these fuels you will have to apply also a two-part fuel proofer, which is again available in gloss and matt finishes. Although enamels can safely be applied over cellulose finishes, the reverse is not true and attempting to paint a coloured dope trim line over an enamel base colour will result in the paint 'pickling'.

There are so many possibilities and alternatives when it comes to applying and creating finishes that the subject is too large to include in detail in this book. For instance, you do not have to cover the model in a traditional manner, with tissue, silk or nylon, to use a paint finish. It is possible to use Solarlac and other finishes over Solartex covering to simulate a fabric-covered full-sized aircraft. Either read specialist books on the subject, or consult aeromodelling magazines, or experiment yourself. It certainly makes sense to try out the combinations of coverings and finishes before committing yourself to an important project. There are few sights more depressing than to see the final application of, say, a fuel proofer completely ruin all the previous hard work of covering and preparation.

CHAPTER 10

Radio Installations and Linkages

Radio-control system manufacturers are very good at explaining, in the instruction manuals, how the radio equipment works, how to program it and how to install the component parts of the outfit. What they might not be so good at explaining is the complete overview of how the servos are linked to the control surfaces and how the control surfaces are hinged. The latter subjects will almost certainly be dealt with when you purchase an ARTF kit, but if you are building from scratch the hinging and linkages may be an unknown area. We will consider some of the alternatives available.

Many of the special bellcranks, horns and linkages, to give reduced movements and differential movements, have now disappeared; the transmitter functions or the use of individual servos have dispensed with their need. Other specialist tools have come on to the market to make life easier for installations. A particular type of pliers has been devised where a spigot is inserted in the output hole of the servo disc, the pushrod wire is gripped in the jaws and the pliers close to form a neat 'Z' bend at the correct location. For opening the jaws of a clevis, a small tool can be inserted, turned through 90 degrees and the clevis is then open and ready to fit into the control horn. Although by no means essential, such specialist devices are highly desirable for modellers who are likely to be building quite a few models.

HINGES

The two essentials for an efficient hinge are full freedom of movement and sufficient strength. Allied to these are a sound fixing of the hinge and a close coupling of the control surface to the flying surface. Also, because the control surfaces will have more than one hinge, the alignment of the hinges is important. Misalignment,

particularly of the more rigid, moulded hinges, will cause a lot of friction and may eventually lead to failure of the hinge. To be sure of the correct alignment it is necessary for the control surfaces to be both straight and to align with the surface to which they are to be attached. Always plan the hinge positions before covering the airframe components and, for the more substantial hinges, make the openings for the hinges, but remember to mark their positions as the covering is under way.

A non-commercial hinge, which is rarely seen nowadays, is the sewn hinge. Not the most sightly hinge, it has to be installed after covering; it is, none the less, a very free and efficient method of hinging and is virtually cost-free. It is of particular benefit with thin surfaces, up to 3mm (⅛in), where it is difficult safely to cut a slot to insert a strip hinge.

Mylar has been used as a strip-hinge material for long enough, but it is only fairly recently that the coated mylar hinges have become available. With a rough, furry surface, the coated mylar has much better adhesion qualities than the old shiny mylar ever had, even when the surface was roughened with abrasive paper. It took me quite a time to accept that 'wicking' thin cyano adhesive, where the adhesive is drawn into the slot by capillary action, was a sufficiently strong answer. I used to cyano them into the control surface and then epoxy the other end to the flying surface, giving me time to position accurately before the glue set. Having now completed a lot of models with the final joints being made by wicking the cyano between the hinge gap and down the hinge slot, I am satisfied that the hinges are secure. None of the control surfaces have fallen off in flight and the cyano hasn't glued the control surface to the flying surface. Whatever the hinge type to be used, the best form of testing the strength of the hinge fixing is to grab

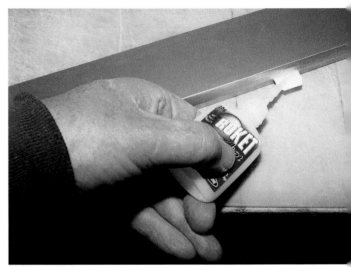

Round 'furry' mylar hinges make sense for ARTF models where the hinge slot is cut with a circular cutter.

Fit the hinges into the preformed slots in the control surfaces and wick thin cyano adhesive down both edges.

the control surface and pull as hard as you dare. Needless to say, it shouldn't come away in your hand.

Another form of hinge that I like is the barbed hinge. It has the advantage of only requiring holes drilling in the surfaces, opposite each other, to accept the hinge. Smaller barbed hinges will probably have the hinge section as a thin portion of the moulding material, while larger ones will be moulded in two parts and joined with a small metal pin. When gluing the first half to the surface you must make sure that the other half falls down at 90 degrees to the surface and that the hinge is central with the hinge line. Advice will be given with the hinges on the size of drill bit for drilling the holes – keep to this precisely and do not make a trial fit, as part of the security of the hinge is that it can be pushed into the hole but cannot be easily removed again. When the hinge is finally inserted it should be smeared, first, with slow-drying epoxy. When the

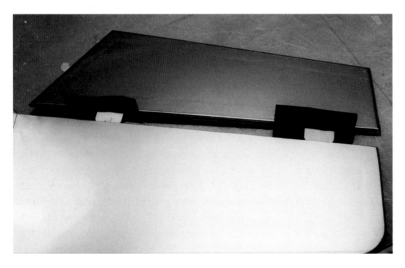

When fitting the control surface, with hinges glued in place, to the structure you can use epoxy adhesive, which gives time to position, but first protect the control surface from glue by slipping pieces of polythene over the hinge.

control surface is to be fitted, possibly with four or six hinges to fit, check that all hinges will match the holes by just inserting the tips of the hinges in the drilled holes. Heavy-duty barbed hinges are suitable for hinging Frise-style hinges where there is a substantial offset from the hinge line to the hinge pocket.

Leaf and pin hinges have also been around since Adam and they have their uses in larger scale and aerobatic models. Giving a strong and free hinge, providing that they are well aligned and kept free from glue (smearing with petroleum jelly, over the small hinge area only, will help to keep the hinge free from glue), they will benefit from being pinned in place as well as epoxied. Also, one end of the pin should be bent over and inserted with the hinge, to prevent it falling out.

Moulded polypropylene hinges are similar to the mylar versions except that the thickness of the body material is greater and the material is less easy to glue, so additional pinning is necessary. Many ways of cutting slots in the wood to be hinged have been tried – there are special slotting tools, and fine circular saw-blades (used in a Dremel Moto tool) and abrasive wheels have been used, but these would be better if the hinges had semicircular plan forms.

Top-hinging a control surface can present problems, although slots for the hinges can be made diagonally into the wood from the top corners of the wood. One suitable way of forming a top hinge with a sealed gap is to use the heat-shrink material used for covering. The bevelled cut on the faces of the control surface and flying surface are joined by folding back the control surface over the wing and then the first strip is glued to the faces. The top surface covering is then extended over the hinge line to the trailing edge of the aileron; the lower covering then stops at the flying-surface trailing edge and continues again for the underside of the aileron. The main point to watch here is that the joint doesn't tighten on the hinge line. To avoid this, place a piece of cardboard between the wing/tailplane and the control surface before the first strip of covering is attached.

LINKAGES

Do not wait until the airframe is complete before planning the route of the linkages, from the servos to the control surfaces, and deciding on what type of linkages to use. In many cases provisions will have to be made for

If cyano adhesive is used for the final hinge gluing, ensure that it wicks down the hinge slot and avoid getting the glue on to the covered surface. Protect the control surface with slotted pieces of polythene.

routing the linkages, and parts of the linkages may have to be inserted and glued as the airframe proceeds. We can lose a high degree of efficiency of a control surface or function if the linkage is poorly installed. Allowing a certain degree of lost movement (slop) to occur will result in poor control centralizing and jerky flying response, but stiff movements of the linkages will put extra strain on the servos and increased battery consumption. Flexing pushrods will also induce unwanted control-surface movement and heavy pushrods will have undesirable effects in a crash, tending to damage servo gears and pull away control surfaces due to the inertia.

There are many ways of linking the servo to the control-surface or function. We should select the method that will give us the most efficient results and then mark the routes on the plan drawings and determine the implications regarding holes in formers and ribs and when the linkages are to be installed.

Closed-loop control, where you have pull–pull cables from each side of the servo to a control horn on each side of the control surface, is one of the oldest and most efficient of all linkage systems. Used on the earliest of aeroplanes, it is a very positive system because the control action is always in the pulling mode and therefore has no lost movement in the action, providing that the

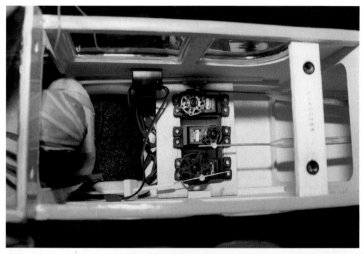

Most ARTF models have predetermined servo and receiver locations and pushrod lengths are made to suit those locations. When using screw-clamping servo to pushrod connectors ensure that the screws are really tight and check occasionally for security.

BELOW: Pushrods with a 'Z' bend at the servo connection and an adjustable clevis at the control surface end are the standard and safest linkage system.

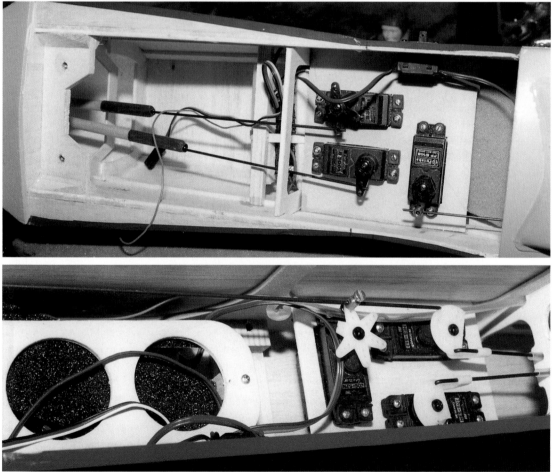

Swinging keepers can also be used for the pushrod linkage to the servo; note the guide tubes for the rods and the Liteply cover restraining the receiver.

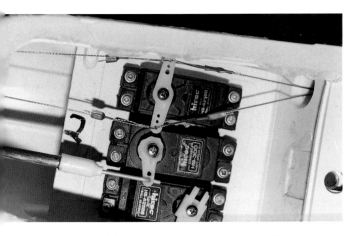

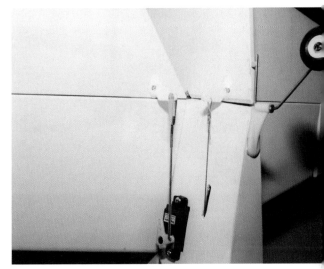

Closed-loop linkages are often used for rudder control and are also used here for the water rudder linkage on floats.

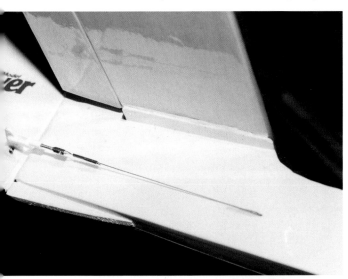

ABOVE: To reduce the linkage run lengths, servos are fitted in the rear of the fuselage for aerobatic aircraft; the closed-loop cables to the rudder give positive control.

LEFT: An adapter and adjustable clevis at the control surface horn allows the closed-loop cable to be tensioned.

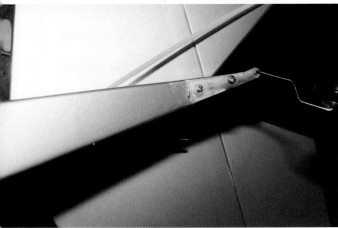

ABOVE: Preformed pushrods may use heat-shrink tubing to secure the wire ends; always check that they are sound.

LEFT: Use lengths of outer control tubing to route the forked ends of the elevator pushrod through the fuselage exit slots.

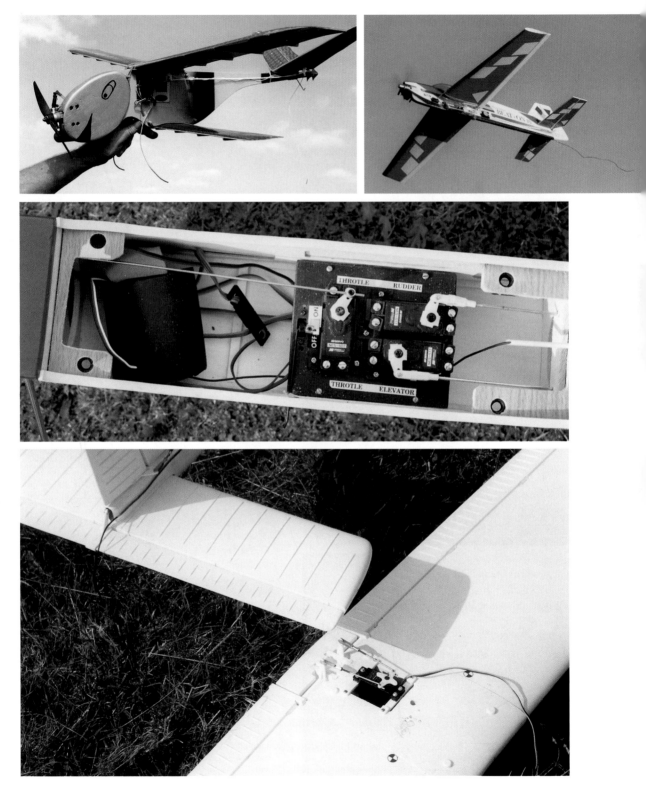

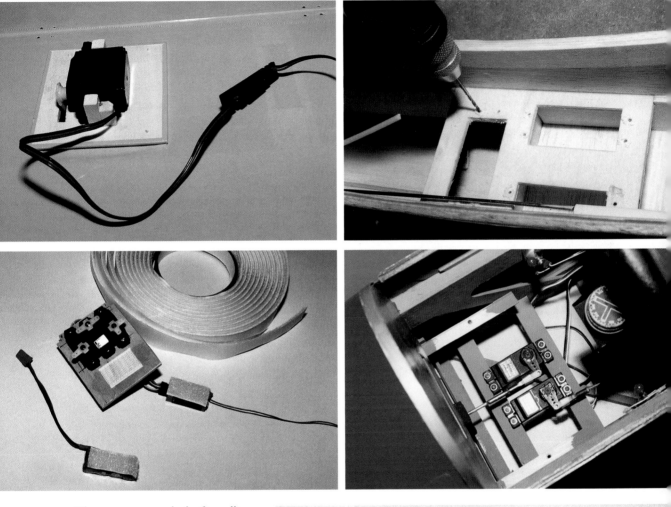

There are many methods of installing the radio equipment and linkages, from those externally mounted under clear plastic on small models and conventionally inside the fuselage. Wing-mounted aileron servos may operate both ailerons, via torque rods, or have independent servos for each aileron. With scale models it may be necessary to hide the servos out of sight, under the pilot's seat or elsewhere. For small models a removable radio unit, consisting of micro receiver and battery, held in position with hook and loop tape, and servos can be transferred from one model to another.

cables are taut around the neutral and the servo output take-off centres are at the same spacings as the rudder horn connections. When it is also considered that the extremely low weight of the cables provides little in the way of inertia, it can be understood why it is such a favourable choice of linkage. Nylon-covered fishing trace line may be used for the cables, and because these may eventually stretch, any slack, or original adjustments, can be made by having a screwed connector and clevis. With small models the cable connections, using small lengths of crimped tubing, can be direct to the servo output and the horns, using the transmitter trims for any small adjustments.

Although closed-loop control is used principally for rudder control, it can be adapted for elevator movements. Where it is impossible to obtain a direct line between the servo and control horns, the cables can be taken, in sinuous routes, through narrow bore PTFE tubing. This does create a little extra friction, but not enough to worry about. Similarly, full-sized aeroplanes using closed-loop linkage systems would have fairleads (over elevators, for instance) to change slightly the direction of the cables where a direct line is impossible. If you are building a scale subject with closed-loop controls you could do a lot worse than to imitate the system in miniature form.

'Snakes' is the generic name for linkages consisting of tubes in tubes and rods in tubes. For larger models the tube in tube system will be used; the outer surface of the inner tube may be ribbed to reduce the friction on the outer tube wall. The internal diameter of the inner tube will probably be suitable for inserting threaded rods that can then accept clevises or keepers. Rod in tubing is more suited to small models, for control-surface connections and throttle linkages. It is less strong than the larger diameter tube in tube snakes, but more flexible and can be taken around smaller radius bends before binding becomes a problem. The ends of the nylon rod will take, with a little scraping, a clevis at one end, and the servo end can be fitted in a servo connector, a device that fits into the servo output disc, or arm, can rotate and has a screw that clamps down on to the rod to hold it at the required length.

There is one smaller form of 'snake' and that consists of very thin (around 24swg) piano wire in small-bore nylon, or similar, tubing. This should only be used for very small models as it is difficult to incorporate any length adjustments for the rods, but it can be used to

good effect where small central aileron servos have to link, through arcs, with aileron control horns. A further application for the smaller-sized 'snakes' is for 'T' tail arrangements where the 'snake' has to follow the leading edge of the fin and curve quite sharply over the tailplane to access the elevator control horn.

Because of the need for minimum friction movement, the outer tubing used for the 'snakes' may be of a slightly greasy feel and will not accept glues readily. Where the tubing is to be glued to bulkheads and ribs, it should be wrapped with masking or draughting tape so that the joint will be made between that and the wood. 'Snakes' must be secured at their ends, and at frequent internal intervals; they should not have any latitude to flex.

Wooden pushrods with wire ends threaded to receive clevises are another time-honoured way of providing the linkage. With one end fixed at the servo end, with a 'Z' bend, adjustment can be made at the control horn with a clevis. If there is a clevis fitted at both ends of the pushrod they should be secured with a locknut or there is the risk that the pushrod will rotate and change the effective length of the pushrod. Also, to prevent the risk of the clevis from unclipping out of the horn, a small length of silicone tubing should be slipped over the clevis (from the rear end) to prevent this happening. The size of the pushrod dowel will depend on its length and the model size and power. For an average 1,270mm (50in) to 1,525mm (60in) wingspan model, with a '40' size engine, a 6mm (¼in) diameter birch dowel will suffice; smaller models should be satisfactory with a 5mm (³⁄₁₆in) diameter dowel. Any larger diameter beech dowel starts to give problems of weight and inertia, and it is then preferable to go to balsawood of treated cross section, round or square.

Also used for pushrods in fast aerobatic and large models, where the servos are still centrally mounted, is thin-walled alloy tubing and, more frequently, carbon-fibre tubing and fishing rod sections. Although the main body of the pushrod may be rigid, the wire ends are not and they have to be bent to extend through the fuselage sides and align with the control horn. It is vital to keep these angles as shallow as possible as there is always the risk of flexing with acute angles and for this reason the route from servo to horn should be as direct as possible. This will often entail the pushrod crossing diagonally from the servo on one side of the fuselage to the fuselage exit on the other side. No problem here except there may be two pushrods (rudder and elevator) traversing the fuselage and checks must be made at the planning stage that these will not clash.

How do we secure the threaded rod ends to the pushrod? If you look at those supplied with ARTF kits, you will often find that they are only held in place with a piece of heat-shrink tubing slipped over the rod and dowel. That is fine as long as the dowel is grooved to receive the rod and drilled for the 90-degree bend of the rod swinging on the dowel. A more secure method is to drill and groove the dowel, slip a piece of strong thread through the hole before inserting the bent end of the rod and then to bind the thread around the rod and dowel, finally coating it with epoxy adhesive.

Hinges and linkages are your passport to good controlled flying – among a dozen other things – so make sure that they are working smoothly and safely.

THE RADIO BITS

As stated at the beginning of this chapter, the manufacturers will give instructions on how to install their radio equipment. There are, however, a few generalities that they may not have included. For example, radio equipment and fuel don't mix very well, so if you can keep the fuel tank bay totally remote from the radio equipment, so much the better for safety – fuel tanks have been known to split or leak.

We sometimes have to position the battery in a pretty remote position. What we don't want to do, when we have to remove it, is to pull on the wire leads and risk pulling them away from the contacts. Place a loop of plastic material around the battery with the end extending to a position that can be reached from inside the fuselage and it can then be pulled clear without straining the leads.

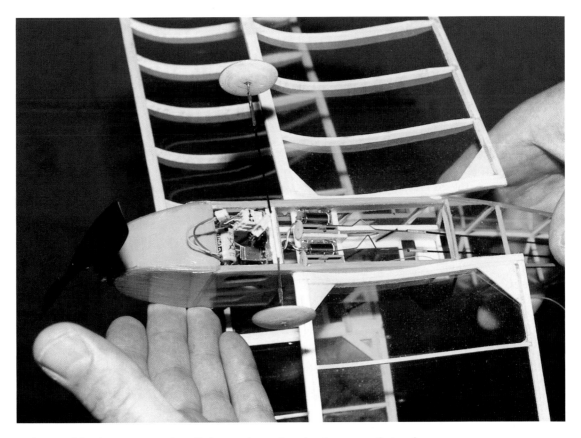

Indoor model radio systems require a little more ingenuity when it comes to fitting the equipment – weight is at a premium.

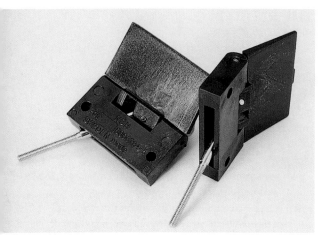

Special control linkages and hinges are commercially available. These 'Swingee' hinges operate ailerons from a horizontal control motion.

There are many ways of mounting servos. Servo trays may be provided with the radio outfit and they are a sound way of mounting the servos – you can make your own from a piece of plywood. Hardwood rails, well secured to the fuselage sides, are another good method of screwing the servos in position, but remember to cut a small arc where the servo grommet, protecting the wire leads, has to be located through the bearers. When it comes to individual aileron servos, these can be fitted in the wing, to hardwood bearers, or secured to the

cover plate so that when this is removed, the servo comes with it (once the rod from the servo output to the aileron horn has been removed).

Great care must be taken when mounting the servos in the aeroplanes. Use rubber grommets and brass eyelets so that the mounting screws do not over-tighten (the eyelet should always be fitted with the 'foot' locating on the bearer); this will also allow a little free movement for shock absorbing. What happens with servos installed in cars, and increasingly in helicopters? They are mounted solid, that is with no shock-absorbing rubber grommets or servo mounting tape! Who's right? I haven't found anybody to give me a believable explanation so far. Incidentally, if you do mount your servos with double-sided adhesive foam-backed tape, and it's not the most secure way ever of fixing the servo, do be certain to treat the airframe surface to which the tape is to be stuck with dope or epoxy, so that it has a non-porous surface for adhesion.

Always bear in mind the level of punishment likely to be inflicted on your model during the general rough and tumble of flight training. Ensure that you install the radio equipment carefully and check it frequently and thoroughly.

Servo arm connectors are held by a starlock washer, pushed on with a nut driver; the control pushrod is held by a screw.

'Magic foam'. Plastic foam material, ex-automobile industry, with a self-adhesive backing with numerous applications for providing protection and insulation to equipment.

CHAPTER 11

Into the Air

'Keep the model tracking straight, feed in some up elevator to get the model into the air, climb to a safe height and carry out a gentle turn to the left.' So might the instructions state, somewhat optimistically, for your take-off. But wouldn't it be easier if we first understood how a model flies and what effects the controls have on the flight patterns? There are two schools of thought here – one is that a little knowledge is a dangerous thing, the other is that you can't have too much knowledge. As aerodynamics is a very complex subject, it would be impossible to include a comprehensive course within a few pages. The real problem is to know just how much, or how little, to include, so that the reader has an elemental grasp of the causes and effects of operating the levers on our little black box.

THE FOUR FORCES

The forces acting on a model in flight are lift, drag, thrust and weight. In straight and level flight, with no acceleration or deceleration, the lift component will balance the weight and the thrust will equal the drag. Lift is created by the air flowing over the top of the wing surface, creating low pressure above and high pressure below. If you want a simple demonstration of lift being produced, take a piece of plain paper, bend the front edge through 90 degrees, let the paper take up a natural curve and then blow from the front edge. Note how the paper rises. Drag comes in a number of forms, but is essentially the resistance of the model travelling through the air, caused by the frontal area and the friction of airframe component junctions (this is why wing to fuselage joints are faired, to smooth out the airflow and reduce the drag). Thrust is normally produced by the rotating propeller fixed to the engine, or the jet efflux from a gas turbine engine and weight is simply the mass of the model and remains unaltered during flight except for a reducing fuel load, or if external loads are released.

We can now consider the effect of these forces on the model in various flight attitudes.

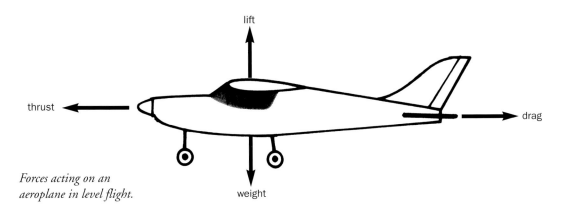

Forces acting on an aeroplane in level flight.

In a turn, with the model banked, the vertical component of lift is reduced. The model will therefore lose height unless the lift is increased by opening the throttle and going faster. To climb, with wings level, the throttle speed is increased, producing more speed and more lift. Because the angle of attack of the wing (its angle to the direction of flight) increases, it produces more lift. The opposite is true when the model is gliding – the nose of the model drops, the angle of attack decreases and there is a loss of lift, hence the model descends.

THE THREE AXES

The three axes through which an aeroplane can turn act through the centre of gravity. These axes are pitch, yaw and roll. For pitch control we operate the elevator, and by applying downward movement of the elevator

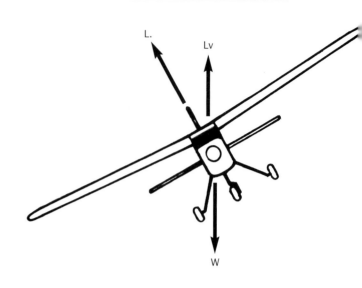

ABOVE: Forces acting on an aeroplane in a turn.

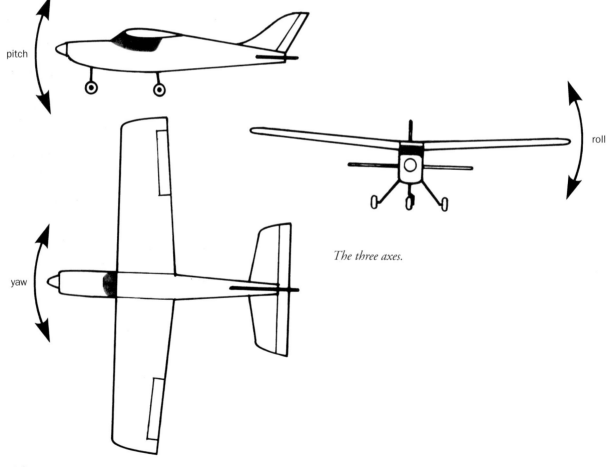

The three axes.

at the trailing edge, we are increasing the camber of the tailplane/elevator, creating more lift and causing the rear of the aeroplane to rise, pitching the nose downwards. A rudder operates in a similar fashion, only in a horizontal plane and causes the aeroplane to yaw to the left, or right. To roll the model we need to increase the lift on one side of the wing, by deflecting the aileron downwards, and decreasing the lift on the opposite wing by moving the aileron upwards. It is, of course, by a combination of operating the controls, including the throttle, that we persuade the model to fly in the directions and attitudes we wish.

STABILITY

Stability can be described as the ability of the aeroplane to right itself when it has been disturbed. How much inherent stability is designed into the model will depend on its purpose. A trainer model will require a high degree of in-built stability, so that it will recover itself from 'difficult' attitudes simply by the pilot returning the transmitter controls to neutral. Don't let me give you a false impression here – if the model is aiming vertically at the ground at a height of 6 metres, it will not recover itself and avoid crashing. For the inherent stability of the model to be effective you will have to input some controls from the transmitter to hasten the recovery.

Aerobatic models have the opposite stability requirements. Here we need the model to perform identically whether it is upright or inverted. We need it to react rapidly to control inputs and we even need it to stall as and when required. For these characteristics neutral stability is needed. Moving on to the violent form of flying exhibited in 3D aerobatics, here the need is for negative stability, that is, the model has to be controlled at all times. This, together with large control surface areas and movements, allows the models to perform near impossible manoeuvres, such as propeller hanging, continuous knife-edge flight and knife-edge loops. It is in these extreme manoeuvres that aerodynamics is almost stood on its head, whereas the wing is normally the provider of lift. When the 3D model is flying with the wing vertical, it is the fuselage that is providing the lift.

Without going too deeply into design considerations, for stability there are a few pointers that will indicate the degree of inherent stability of a particular design. The trainer model is likely to have a high mounted wing with good dihedral (the upward slope of the wing from root to tip). It will have generous nose and tail moments, that is, the distances from the wing to the nose and tail and relatively large areas of tail surfaces, but moderately sized control surfaces. It is likely that the wing will have a parallel chord, or only a slight taper on the planform, and the wing section will have an average thickness, not too thin and not too thick. In comparison, a highly manoeuvrable model will have close couples of nose and tail, no dihedral and large control surfaces. Intermediate trainers and sports models will come in-between the two extremes.

One concern to the beginner in radio-controlled model flying is when it is suggested that he might consider learning to fly with a model not incorporating ailerons, which means that the controls are limited to rudder, elevator and throttle (or, for a glider, rudder and elevator only). If there are no ailerons, how can we make the model bank and turn? To execute a roll to bank, the model must have wing dihedral, and what happens then is that rudder is applied, the model yaws and causes the outside wing of the yaw to go faster, increase its angle of attack and produce more lift than with the inside wing. It is this action that causes the bank.

One other confusion for beginners is the control of airspeed and height where it might seem that applying elevator to bring the model into a climbing attitude would be the way to gain height. But all is not as it might seem and we have to follow the logical, aerodynamic cause and effect to understand what actually happens. The effect of moving the elevator is to produce an upward and downward force on the tail, rotating the model around the centre of gravity and causing the angle of attack of the wing to increase or decrease. If the throttle setting is not changed, the end result will be to change the airspeed of the model, not the height. We therefore reach one of the fundamental principles of power flying – *elevator controls airspeed, throttle controls height.* As a simple example of the potential disaster if these principles are ignored, let us consider an approach for a landing. The model is too low on the approach to the landing strip, although it is at the correct speed. What do we do? Pull in up elevator to gain height, the model slows as a result, stalls and we have a broken model to collect. No, the correct action should have been to increase power.

The author's trainer design, for the RC Hotel in Corfu, is fairly large, powered by a 46 engine, covered in nylon and is in three- and four-function versions.

STALLING AND SPINNING

The two words stalling and spinning have struck terror in the hearts of pilots since time immemorial: for full-sized pilots they can spell death; for modellers, a heap of wreckage on the ground. However, once understood, recognized and the appropriate control action taken, they are no longer the fearsome duo of fable.

Stalling is caused by a sudden loss of lift and increase of drag when the normally smooth airflow over the top of the wing breaks away as a result of the angle of attack becoming excessive. At this sudden and dramatic loss of lift (the actual angle of attack at which it occurs will vary according to the aerofoil used), the model will lose flying speed and the nose will drop. Although a stall normally occurs at low speeds, where the angle of attack has been increased to obtain more lift, it can occur at high speeds if there is sufficient elevator force suddenly to increase the angle of attack. An example of the latter, with unfortunate fatal consequences, happened when a racing aeroplane reached the first turning pylon and although his speed was reasonably above normal stalling speed, the sudden application of elevator resulted in a 'high speed stall'. It must also be remembered that, in a banked turn, we are losing part of the vertical lift component.

Spinning occurs when the aircraft is stalled, but with one wing stalling before the opposite side. This will cause the outside wing, the one still producing some lift, to rotate the aircraft around its vertical axis. As it is in a stalled state the autorotation will continue, the yaw preventing the aircraft from increasing in speed and the lift on the wings being equalized. To recover from this autorotation (spin), the yaw must be removed, by centralizing the rudder, and the angle of attack must be decreased by introducing down elevator. Once the stalling point has been passed, control surfaces will be functioning again, the speed of the aircraft can be increased, the wings levelled and the elevator judiciously used to pull out of the diving attitude. Fortunately, most training models have sufficient natural stability to recover from a spin once the transmitter controls are centralized.

Enough of aerodynamics. Although there is plenty still to learn, it's time we did some flying.

PREPARATION

Did I say time to fly? Almost – first we must prepare both mentally and physically. The most prepared pilot of a radio-controlled model I have ever witnessed, demonstrating at a large public event, also happened to be a Boeing 747 Jumbo captain. He worked on the same principles for his models as he did with the giant airliner; in fact, with one additional checklist. Before leaving home for a day's model flying he would go through one checklist, to make sure that he would not forget any item and that all the batteries were charged. A second checklist was used during the assembly of the model and the final checklist prevented him from flying until all the controls were working correctly, the fuel tank was full, and the air cylinder for the undercarriage retracts had been pumped up. Over the top? Not a bit of it. He never made mistakes and as stand-

by pilot, to fly if another demonstration pilot had problems, he never failed to get airborne or make a classic flight.

Your DI (Daily Inspection – or before you go flying) should include a check of the airframe: for example no damage; hinges and linkages secure; radio installation not moved; receiver aerial in place; switch serviceable; batteries all charged; transmitter complete with aerial; engine fully secured; propeller free from nicks and cracks; propeller nut tight; wheels secure; and flying surfaces either in place or the fixings all there. You will also need your field box, complete with fuel and tools.

Flying field etiquette, how to behave and how not to behave, is mainly based on common sense and good manners, but here are a few dos and don'ts that will help you to become a welcomed and trusted member of a club or group of fliers.

Do

- Join the club and pay your fees as soon as possible. You may not be insured until you have paid your dues.
- Learn the club rules and observe them.
- Show your thanks for help and encouragement given by fellow members.
- Assist with the general club chores of grass cutting, maintaining equipment, cleaning the club room, and so on.
- Try not to waste the time of an instructor by not turning up for planned lessons, or by not having your model ready and prepared.
- Offer any particular skills you may have to help with the running of the club.

Do Not

- Walk up to someone and talk to them when they are flying their model.
- Walk heedlessly across the landing path of the models.
- Switch on without first obtaining your frequency clearance.
- Come with a model ill-prepared and take up valuable peg time, preventing others from flying.
- Hog the peg. When you have finished your flight return the peg to the frequency board.
- Start your engine or take the model out to the flight line when someone is test-flying a model, or is having trouble during a flight.

It is essential that you find a club or group when you are learning to fly. You will need the help and assistance of its members, and it also makes learning to fly a more pleasurable experience.

Training models tend to follow similar layouts, with high-mounted wings, a generous tail moment arm and reasonable dihedral. IC power has been used frequently in the past, but electric is gaining in popularity. Incidentally, the power lines are further away than they appear on the photo, which was taken with a telephoto lens.

- Never fly low near or over the pits area and avoid persistent beat-ups over the strip; someone else might be trying to learn to fly.

No doubt there will be someone to help you with the first training flights, but it is still important to get into a routine of checks. These engine-starting checks should be made after you have assembled and checked the model and obtained the appropriate frequency peg.

1. Check that the fuel tank is full, the pressure vent tube is connected to the silencer and a stopper is fitted to the filler tube.
2. Switch on the transmitter and receiver and open the throttle fully.
3. Prime the engine, either by placing the finger over the air intake and flicking the propeller until fuel reaches the carburettor, or by applying the electric starter and achieving the same results.
4. Return the throttle setting to one quarter open and check, with the starter, that the engine turns freely.
5. Check that the glow clip is live and connect it to the glow plug.
6. With the model properly restrained, either by a fellow modeller or a strap connected to a firmly implanted stake, apply the starter. It should fire within a few seconds.
7. Keeping clear of the propeller arc at all times, advance the throttle, via the transmitter, to about half revs and remove the glow clip.
8. Take the model away from the immediate pits area, get a colleague to hold it with the nose about 60 degrees in the air and check that the engine is at full throttle. If it starts to die (lean out), then open the needle valve a few clicks – from behind the engine!
9. If it is a first flight, or the model hasn't been flown for some time, carry out a range check, with the motor running, but please avoid causing a nuisance to other flyers, as they need to be able to hear their engine in flight.
10. Ensure that your transmitter aerial is fully extended again.

You should now be ready for take-off – almost! Just check that the engine is running smoothly throughout the speed range and that the throttle trim setting is right and the engine will not cut when the throttle stick is at the low setting. There should be no undue vibratory effects from the engine and all the controls should be moving freely (you should already, at the assembly stage, have checked for movements in the correct directions). All these checks should be made clear of the pits and the landing and take-off area; there should always be a safe area between the two. You are now ready to go, with your helper, on to the take-off area, providing that no one is on a landing circuit or approach. Never be frightened of calling out loud and clear that you are about to take off. Allow for the fact that the engines may be noisy and that your voice must be heard over the sound of the engine. This becomes even more important for landing, or if you have an emergency. All clear? Time for take-off – really!

CIRCUIT BASHING TO COMPETENCY

With a bit of luck you will have a qualified instructor with you and you will be training with the help of a buddy-box system, where the instructor has the master transmitter and can pass control, through an umbilical cord, to the pupil – and take back control when the student gets into difficulties. Or, you may have an instructor standing at your shoulder, giving you instructions and preparing to take the transmitter from your vice-like grip, if necessary. I am presuming that you are not attempting to learn the basics of flying on your own, but that the general control of the model and the effects of the controls have been learned with an instructor. You may, now, be in a position where you can fly the model, when it is in the air, but can't carry out the initial and final operations. Here is the remedy.

Before you can reach the all-important stage of flying a radio-controlled model aeroplane solo, it is essential that you become proficient on the circuit, that is take-offs and landings and the pattern to fly after, or before, these essential manoeuvres. Landing procedures, even for experienced pilots, should follow set patterns, where the model flies a downwind leg, base leg and approach (or final leg) before touchdown. It may be that it is unnecessary, from a skill point of view, for the trained pilot to follow these routines, as he is probably capable of making a straight-in approach without bothering to take a rectangular flight path. That is fine if he is the only flyer in the landing area but, when other planes are in the air, it gives them a chance to keep clear of the landing aircraft. For this and other disciplinary reasons, it makes sense to follow the set routines of flying a circuit and landing and to warn other modellers in the air by calling out 'landing'.

It is to be presumed that the student about to undergo 'pounding the circuit' is proficient in flying the model with regard to straight and level flight, turns in both directions, climbing and descending and flying away and towards himself. In other words, he is competent in the general handling of the model, without problems of orientation and that the cause and effects of operating the controls are understood. To my mind there are three other essential flight manoeuvres to practise ahead of circuit training – these are stalling, spinning and flying overhead. The former two are necessary because much of the circuit flying is at slow speeds, not far above the stall and it is necessary to recognize the behaviour of the model as it approaches stalling speed, both in straight flight and turns. Flying the model directly over your head should never, under normal circumstances, be carried out as this means that you are flying in a danger area – too close to the other pilots and the pits. However, there is the risk, during your initial solo stage, that you will inadvertently get into this state and it is important to be able to recognize the model's attitude and to steer it to safety. Only undertake overhead flying with the full knowledge of any other modellers on the field; better still, try the exercise when you are alone with your instructor.

EASING THE LOAD

Flying the circuit is one of the busiest and most demanding periods that you will experience during your RC flying at the pre-solo stage. Anything that can be done to make these training sessions easier is to be encouraged and this includes awareness of the surroundings of the flying site. You will need immediate visual references when you are flying the circuit. These will help you to fly a correct pattern, help you with deciding when to make turns and give you a general awareness of where you are positioned relative to the landing strip. This must come as second nature; you don't take your eyes off the model, the landmarks are seen in your peripheral vision and these give you the information you require for making heading corrections and, to a lesser degree, height adjustments. The more you fly from one particular flying site, the more you will become aware, unconsciously, of the landmarks – and as these can sometimes take the form of model-attracting trees, it is vital to get their locations firmly implanted in your mind.

With full-sized circuit bashing you are regularly trimming the plane so that it is flying hands-off, which makes accurate flying easier and less tiring. Although we may not use our transmitter trim facilities as constantly as those of a full-sized aircraft, they are there to help us and should not be ignored. In particular, the

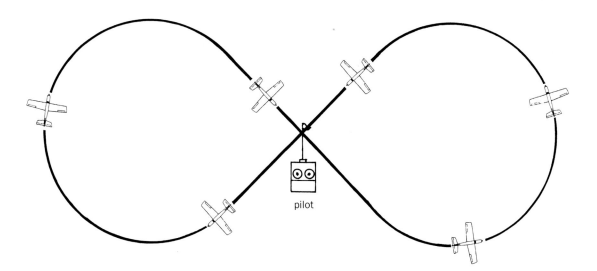

pilot

Overhead eights.

This is a hobby where father and son can participate, but be warned, it is only a matter of time before the son becomes a better pilot than the father – and grandfather.

elevator and throttle trims should be adjusted during the circuit training. To have a model correctly trimmed and not requiring continuous control inputs for maintaining heading, bank and climb and dive will leave you to concentrate on the basics. The engine should throttle smoothly throughout the range, hold a steady idle (low enough for the model to slow, in level flight, for landing) and only cut when the throttle trim is moved fully back. There is a tendency for modellers to power their trainers too heavily, which is not always their fault as the manufacturers/designers frequently give an engine range that is optimistically large on the upper limits. No problem, thinks the learner, I can keep throttled back to prevent excessive climbing. Unfortunately, pounding the circuit for minutes on end, all at low throttle, is not likely to be conducive to rapid throttle response if it is suddenly needed – you are more likely to get a spluttering and coughing, or the engine quitting, in these circumstances. Carburettors on model engines are not highly sophisticated when it comes to fuel metering and air mixtures, and too much should not be expected from them.

As I emphasized before, remember – *elevator controls airspeed, throttle controls height.*

Earlier in the chapter I stated that one of the hardest lessons for the beginner to learn is that height control

is not the function of the elevator, for example if the model is high on the approach for landing, you do not push the elevator stick forward to dive the aeroplane. Yes, it will go into a dive, but it will also build up speed and as soon as you level out the model will tend to 'balloon' upwards. Even with a neutrally stable model, where the model has no ballooning tendency, the model will overshoot the landing area because of the excess speed. The way to increase your rate of descent is to throttle back and vice versa. If the speed is decaying and the model moving towards the stall, then is the time you push the elevator stick forward, to get the nose of the model down and to increase the speed. If, as a result of this action, the model will not reach the landing area, this is the time you increase the throttle to maintain height. A 'draggy' model also gives the benefit of having the engine slipstream flowing over the tailsurfaces, giving better response from the elevator and rudder controls.

FINAL PREPS

Ready to go? Not quite – just a few final considerations, such as where to stand. Increasingly, clubs are positioning the pilot's box at right angles to the take-off strip, as this is the safest and most convenient location. While

A qualified instructor will save you time and money during the training stages. A buddy-box training system is to be recommended and where better to learn to fly than on holiday on Corfu?

this is fine for the experienced pilot, for the beginner on the circuit it is less easy during the initial take-off phases. During the take-off run the model is likely to veer to one side or the other, but if you are standing directly behind the model you can see immediately when the direction changes and make the necessary rudder correction in good time. When standing at the side, the swing of the model may be substantial before it is realized by the pilot. This leads to excessive correction movements and, usually, a continuing over-correction situation. For the first few take-offs I would recommend standing behind the model and, once familiar with the ground handling and rudder/nosewheel steering, take up the position of the pilot's box for take-off.

Although left-hand (anticlockwise) circuits tend to be the norm, there will be times when right-hand cir-cuits will have to be flown, because of the prevailing wind direction. It is important to be comfortable with either circuit direction and to familiarize yourself with the surrounding landmarks – and areas and obstacles to avoid.

Try to choose a time when there isn't too much other flying going on. This may be difficult, but it is easier to concentrate when there is little other activity. Your instructor will be standing-by all the time, up to your first solo, and he should be there to give you advice, practical assistance if required and confidence.

CLEAR FOR THAT TAKE-OFF

Having done all the pre-flight checks, you can carry out the model to the take-off position, ensuring that there are no models on the landing approach. Then follow the procedure below:

1. Choose a landmark at least 90m (100yd) directly upwind as an Upwind Marker.
2. Position the model dead into wind, held back by a helper.
3. Run up the engine, check the controls at full throttle, return to idle, and ask the helper to stand clear. You should be standing well back from the model yourself – this gives a better perception of the initial direction.
4. Open the throttle firmly. As the aircraft moves away, there may be an initial swing, probably to the left. Correct this with rudder; it will need more movement than you've been accustomed to using in the air. Once this is corrected, the aircraft will be picking up speed and will become much more sensitive to rudder.
5. Chop throttle immediately if a bad swing develops (if you get more than, say, 10 degrees away from the line of the Marker), or if the motor falters or loses revs (it is too lean).
6. Once she's moving smartly along (you'll have seen her take off enough times by now, to be able to judge the moment), come back very gently on the stick until she breaks ground. Watch the attitude carefully, and if the nose comes up too high (that is, if you continue to see the top of the wing), let the elevator return gently to neutral. Keep her climbing straight towards the Marker. If she climbs steeply, don't start pumping elevator. Your instructor will have checked her out, and at full throttle a trainer has a wide choice of climbing attitudes. You shouldn't need any down elevator – at neutral she will soon sort herself out.

If you have to clear an obstacle, the best way is to let her pick up speed before you try to climb steeply or to turn. Hanging on the prop is no good; the aircraft won't climb, the drag is increased and you may well get a disastrous stall.

ONE LEVEL CIRCUITRY

The next exercise will be to fly the course of the circuit, but not to descend for a landing approach, simply to maintain a steady circuit height.

The novice will naturally tend to fly rather too high at first, but should try to come down as the exercise becomes more familiar, to a comfortable circuit height. Higher circuits are of course safer, but they are much more difficult to fly accurately – and accuracy is now the name of the game.

The diagram is self-explanatory. About six or eight circuits; one or, perhaps, two sessions should be enough to achieve a fair degree of accuracy.

Points to watch are these:

- make sure you have clearly identified your Markers
- make your turns without gaining or losing height don't drift inwards coming downwind
- check your base-leg turn against the Marker, and regulate the turn so that you arrive above the threshold flying straight and in line with the Base Marker. When you can do this every time, you're ready for the next stage.

PRACTICE APPROACHES

Make sure the motor is running well, and will pick up reliably from idling revs after a prolonged slow run with the nose held slightly down.

Make a circuit as before, but as you go into the base-leg turn throttle back to a fast tickover. Let the nose drop to maintain air-speed, but try to make this turn very smooth in order to settle the aircraft in a steady gliding attitude. Make your turn as before, looking out for the Base Marker.

Once you are in line with the Marker, or have got down to about 6m (20ft), open the throttle and climb away, lining up in due course with the Upwind Marker. On reaching circuit height, throttle back to cruising revs and try again.

After a few attempts, you should be able to achieve a correct position over the threshold: in line with the Marker; wings level; 4.5–7.5m (15–25ft) up (the more wind, the higher); attitude steady; slightly nose down. When you can do this three times out of three, it's time to try a landing.

LANDING

Make up your mind that you are only going to land if you achieve a good final approach; if the approach is at all dodgy, you're going to open the throttle fully and go round again. If all is well over the threshold, nothing much can go wrong; in fact, if you chopped the throttle and did nothing more, in all probability she'd get down without damage on her own. So the watchword is, don't over control. The instructor will expect you to round-out with a little up elevator, but remember:

too little is safer than too much; too late is safer than too soon. As the aircraft passes the threshold she's in her nose-down gliding attitude, with a modicum of throttle, which is now cut. Keep her straight and let her come on down. When the aircraft is about 1m (3.3ft) off the ground, gently ease on a little up elevator for the round-out.

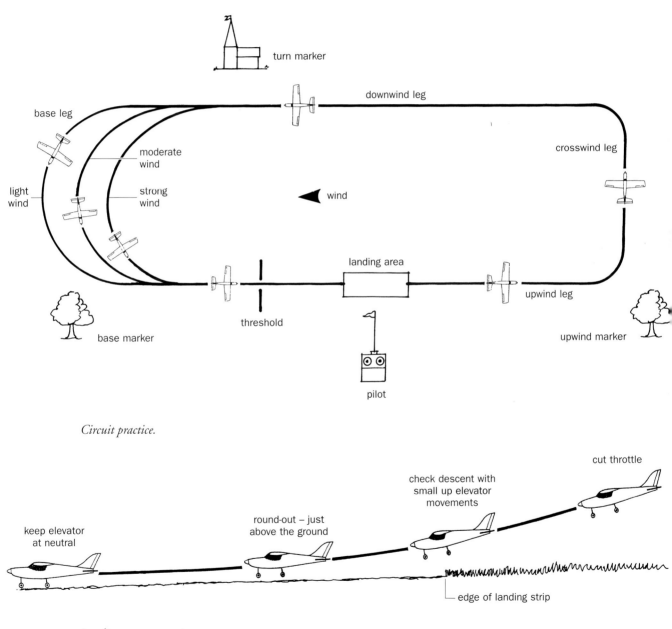

Circuit practice.

Landing.

If the nose lifts easily she's too fast – hold the stick where it is, and wait. If the nose is reluctant to come up, she's close to stalling speed, and you can add more up elevator. But remember – if you use too little elevator, nothing much can go wrong. If you use too much and balloon her, you can do a lot of damage. In a perfect landing, she'll touch down just on the stall, main wheels first – but we don't need a perfect landing; just a safe one.

When she touches, let the stick go to neutral. If there's a little bounce, do nothing, and let her sort it out. If there's a big bounce (more than 1m high), open the throttle and climb away, but not too steeply.

When she comes to rest, use the throttle trim to cut the motor, hand the transmitter to the instructor, and very calmly retrieve the model. This is the finest moment in all flying, so savour it. Afterwards, you may thank your instructor and celebrate appropriately!

If I had to select the most important factors in flying a landing circuit they would be the correct alignment, speed and height on the final approach; all the other circuit flying leads up to this position. Late changes of any of these three states will make a good touchdown unlikely; getting in the right position in good time is all important.

AEROBATICS FOR ASSURANCE

With the first flush of solo success you will be feeling great and ready to take on the radio-control flying world. However, you may have learned to take off, fly a reasonably accurate circuit pattern and land without breaking the model, but this is only the first stage of a lengthy learning curve. In fact, you never stop learning; there is always a different model, with different flying characteristics and new manoeuvres to master. It is something akin to driving a car – just because you have passed your driving test, it doesn't mean that you know how to drive safely on the motorway or deal with accidental skids. Such skills come with experience.

The more flying you do, the more experience you will gain, but it is not sufficient to just take off, meander around the sky and then come in for a landing. You will not gain *useful* experience in this way. It is necessary to have discipline and to practise specific manoeuvres. Our principal aim must be to be able to recover a model from all potentially dangerous situations – within reason, of course. To achieve this aim and save

the model crashing, we must also be able to recognize these dangerous model attitudes and this is where practising aerobatics comes into its own. In full-sized aircraft training, aerobatics are an end in themselves – they certainly have little practical application in transport or bomber aeroplanes and not many uses with fighter aircraft. Their aim is to teach the limits of the flight envelope of the aeroplane and how – if these limits are exceeded – to recover from the situation. The same principles should apply to RC models.

FORCED LANDINGS

While we set up our model engines to be as reliable as possible, an engine can still stop unexpectedly. Obviously, when this happens, you have no alternative but to glide in for a landing. You should practise power-off landings from various positions and heights, with the engine at low idle so that you can open up and gain height if the approach is incorrect. In theory, you should constantly be aware of your location in the sky and the proximity of the landing area so that, if your engine does quit, you can make the best approach without hesitation. Again, experience helps with these situations and the more you practise and fly, the better your chances of recovery from such a situation.

With a forced landing, getting to the normal take-off/landing strip is not, automatically, the highest priority. Missing obstacles, persons and landing into wind may be more important than actually getting back to the patch. Safety, for public and property, remains the principal consideration; the model is of secondary importance.

Immediate Action

When you experience an engine failure, you must decide upon your plan of action as soon as possible and then act positively – and stick with your decisions. Changing your mind halfway through the landing approach is more likely to result in problems than sticking with your original plan.

Make your initial turn, towards the landing area or base-leg position, as soon as you have trimmed out the model on a safe glide. Keep up the airspeed, comfortably above the stall, throughout the glide and add a few knots for turns, when you have less lift from the wings. Whatever else you do, keep clear of the pit area and spectators.

To practise forced landings, you should climb reasonably high, at least twice the normal circuit height and throttle back to a safe engine idle speed. The aim is to get from where you are to the base-leg turn position, arriving from the downwind leg at a little above circuit height. Circle overhead until you are at about twice circuit height and then carry out a normal (though descending) circuit. Make your base-leg turn so that you feel you'll overshoot, if anything. The illustration on page 137 shows how you can vary your approach path, to give you the correct threshold position. Open up when you arrive there; or before if you get into a mess.

Of course, your engine can cut when you are too low to make it to base-leg turn position at a decent height. Alas, there are too many possible positions to be itemized here – most of them are unpleasant, and it is not recommended that you practise them. Try, however, to keep in mind the precepts set out above. Whenever you get such a low cut, you need a little luck, as well as judgement, to get down safely. Don't continue any turn below 6m (20ft) height. If that means you have to land downwind or crosswind, do so; it's safer than putting in a wingtip. To reduce the chances of engine cuts, two points to bear in mind: always aim to land with fuel to spare; and don't run your engine lean – after tweaking up to maximum revs, always open the needle valve a few notches to be on the safe side. When you get a genuine cut, call out 'Landing dead stick!' to warn other fliers.

PRIMARY AEROBATICS

The manoeuvres suggested here are all within the repertoire of a three- or four-channel primary trainer; though some only just! Before you start, make sure the aircraft is in good fettle, and that you have plenty of bands on the wing. Get some tips, and, if possible, a demonstration on your model from your instructor. As to the model:

- increase the control throws, especially the rudder, but just a little at a time
- make small adjustments to the CG back (6mm/¼in) and the wing incidence (1.5mm (¹⁄₁₆in) packing under the trailing edge); you might find you could increase these later, but always go a little at a time

- make sure the motor is in good form, and won't cut when you shake the model about, point it straight up or down, or invert it.

Before you take off, identify your aerobatic area. Some clubs do not regard the use of an aerobatic area as compulsory, but there are good reasons for using one:

- 'aimless' flying does not encourage one to develop well-formed manoeuvres; a constant frame of reference is needed
- it is good form when flying aerobatics to keep well clear of the circuit and the pit area.

Wing Over

This is an easy manoeuvre with which to begin your aerobatic training. It can be described as a steeply banked climb and dive turn, which turns the aeroplane through 180 degrees. Originally devised in WWI either to get away from an enemy aircraft after an attack from the rear, or to be able to meet it head-on, the manoeuvre allows the aeroplane to be flown at a safe, above stall, speed throughout the turn.

With full power, introduce some rudder to start an arc to, say, the left. Keeping power on allow the model to come over the top of the arc, with the wings nearly vertical and then continue the arc until the nose is pointing fully down. At this point you can ease back on the throttle and apply up elevator to recover from the dive. You should have completed the wing over with the model flying in the opposite direction to that started, at approximately the same height.

A similar manoeuvre, but where it is completed at a higher level than that commenced, is known as a 'Chandelle'. Max Immelman, the WWI German fighter ace, used the wing over as a tactical manoeuvre and it was named the 'Immelman Turn'. However, the name has now become, incorrectly, associated with a half loop, with a half roll at the top. The low-powered Fokker monoplane, with wing warping, would not have been able to achieve the low-speed half roll at the top of the half loop. A common fault is holding on too much up elevator over the top of the arc, causing the model to pull over into inverted.

Loop

Loops are also easy to do, but difficult to do well. A good loop is as large as the aircraft can manage, and of perfect

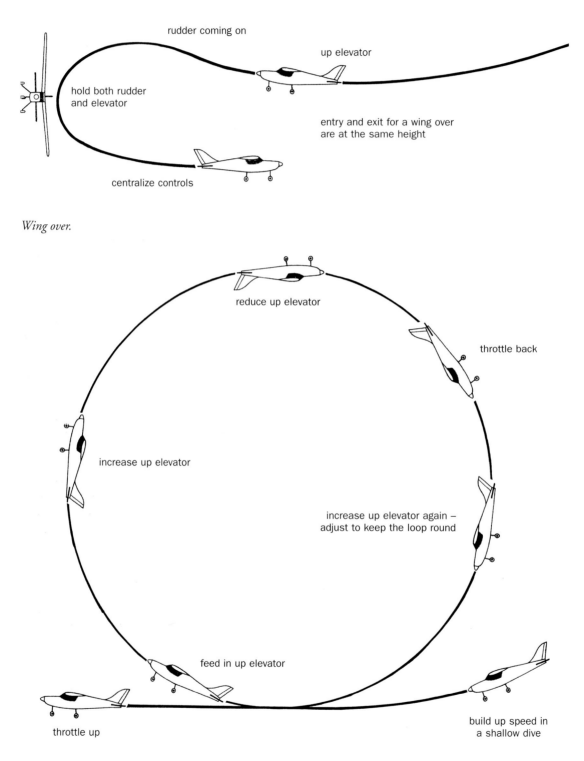

rudder coming on

up elevator

hold both rudder
and elevator

entry and exit for a wing over
are at the same height

centralize controls

Wing over.

reduce up elevator

throttle back

increase up elevator

increase up elevator again –
adjust to keep the loop round

feed in up elevator

throttle up

build up speed in
a shallow dive

Loop.

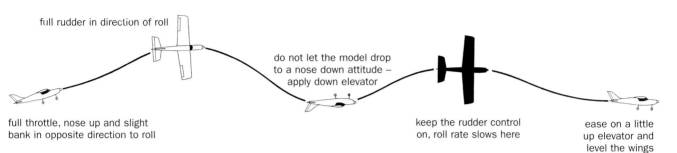

full rudder in direction of roll

do not let the model drop
to a nose down attitude –
apply down elevator

full throttle, nose up and slight
bank in opposite direction to roll

keep the rudder control
on, roll rate slows here

ease on a little
up elevator and
level the wings

Roll – using rudder control.

circular shape. Because of the large variation in speed, a trainer will tend to wander off course; concentration will be needed to keep the wings level. Start with a shallow dive at full throttle to gain maximum speed, and pull up smoothly. To maintain the radius, you will probably find you need a little more elevator as she goes through the vertical position, and a little less as she goes over the top. Once you are well over, throttle back and, halfway down, ease back further on the up elevator stick, aiming to keep a constant radius. When the model is straight and level again, increase the engine power.

As power and speed increase, so do the torque effects from the engine and you may need a little right rudder to keep the model tracking straight. Entering the loop when the wings aren't level will result in a 'corkscrew' loop – the wings must be kept level throughout the manoeuvre. If you fail to give enough elevator throughout the first 180 degrees, your model may be at the top of the loop with little speed. Don't panic – take off the up elevator, let the nose drop and when the speed has increased, half roll the model and ease back on the elevator to pull out of the dive. Conversely, if you apply too much elevator during the loop and tighten the radius excessively, the model may 'snap out' at the top, performing a half 'flick roll' to the upright position. Although the aim is to perform a perfect circle, it takes an aerobatic model, with a good reserve of power, to do this. A trainer will actually produce a vertically extended circle.

Rolls

There are a number of different types of roll, ranging from the 'aileron roll', which is, in essence, an extended corkscrew loop. Aileron rolls are only possible with

higher-speed aerobatic models, as they rely on powerfully acting ailerons to give a high roll rate, allowing a 360-degree roll without the need for an elevator or rudder input. Barrel rolls can be performed by rudder/elevator models. Start with the model banking about 30 degrees in the opposite direction of the proposed roll, feed in up elevator and opposite rudder, and the model – if your co-ordination of elevator and rudder is correct – will fly a round, not axial, roll.

Stall Turn

From straight and level, power on, pull through 90 degrees, neutralize the elevator to keep the model climbing vertically and reduce the throttle to about one-third open. As the speed decays to near the stalling point, introduce full rudder, yawing the model through 180 degrees. Centralize the rudder as the model dives vertically, ease back on the elevator and bring the model to the horizontal. It should now be flying in the opposite direction to that started.

For a true stall turn, not practical with a training model, the aeroplane should reach the stall speed vertically and pivot about its own axis, turning in its own length. We will find it easier to keep a little extra speed on and some throttle to maintain an airflow over the rudder. Because our trainer has wing dihedral, there will also be a rolling force resulting from the yaw – if we have ailerons fitted, we can combat that rolling tendency – if not, we must accept a slight roll into the turn. Usually, it is easier to stall turn to the left, with engine torque, but turns in both directions should be practised. Stall turns are pretty to watch and very satisfying when performed correctly – well worth the effort of conquering.

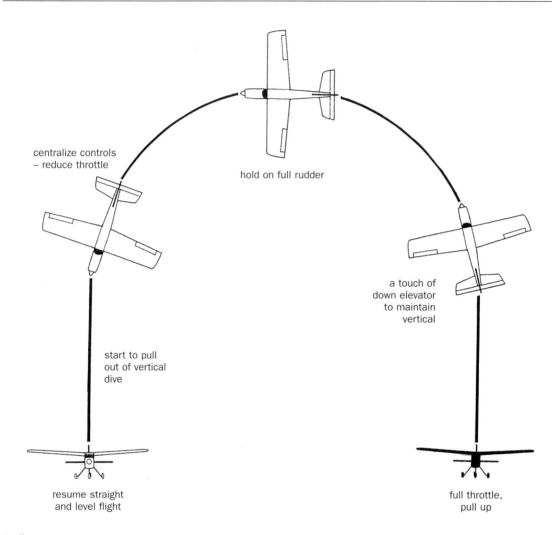

centralize controls
– reduce throttle

hold on full rudder

a touch of
down elevator
to maintain
vertical

start to pull
out of vertical
dive

resume straight
and level flight

full throttle,
pull up

Stall turn.

Spinning

The first importance is to be able to differentiate between a spin and spiral dive – the latter is a tight descending turn, but the speed is always above the stall. With a truly developed spin, the model is stalled and performing an auto-rotation. The fear of spinning comes about because the condition can be entered into accidentally. Always remember that a spin can only occur if the model is in a stalled condition, although the stall can be reached in straight flight, in a banked turn and with the engine on or off. It also follows that to get out of a spin, we must un-stall the aeroplane – and this is the function of the elevator. It will break the

stall and reduce the spin rate when down elevator is introduced. Because many spins are accidentally entered into during a slow turn (a final landing turn being the most dangerous), it may not be necessary to introduce down elevator for a spin recovery – just centralizing the controls will be sufficient – but you must have sufficient height to complete the recovery.

Whether or not your trainer model will spin will depend on the design, the centre of gravity and the control surface movements and areas. Take the model up to a good height, throttle back, pull the elevator up and when the model reaches the stall (nose drops), apply full rudder movement (left) and the model will start to rotate around its own axis, with the nose down. If it fails to auto-rotate, you can try entering the stall with some power on, to make the rudder and elevator more effective, and introduce some in-turn aileron (if fitted) to help it into the spin.

To maintain a stabilized spin, you must hold on full elevator and rudder – after a couple of turns, release the transmitter sticks – and the chances are that, after a turn or less, the model will cease rotating and build up speed in the dive. From here, you can ease on up elevator to bring the model to straight and level, increasing the engine speed as you go.

It may be no good trying to stop the spin rotation simply by applying opposite rudder, as this control may be blanketed during the spin. Also, too violent application of rudder and elevator during the spin recovery may cause the model to enter a spin rapidly in the opposite direction. Remember, the airspeed will be low after recovery. For most models, however, spin recovery is attained by centralizing controls, although with some it may be necessary to apply opposite rudder and down elevator.

Inverted Flight

Flying a model consistently upside down will be difficult if it has a fair degree of dihedral on the wings. In the inverted position the inherent stability will be trying to right the model all the time and you will have to be making constant corrections to keep it on a level, inverted, keel. Inverted flight is much easier to achieve with a model that has little dihedral and should be equally easy as flying upright when no dihedral is present. However, it is possible to keep a non-aileron-controlled model flying inverted, even with considerable dihedral, but it does need rapid reactions on the rudder control. Apart from the model looking odd when it is upside down, you will find one other difference when flying a trainer, in that it will need quite a lot of down elevator to keep the nose high so as to prevent it losing height. This is for two reasons: the model has a positive wing incidence to help with longitudinal stability, that is, automatically pulling out of a dive; and there will probably be engine down-thrust incorporated to prevent the model nosing up as a result of the incidence giving a greater angle of attack. Both of these desirable features, for normal upright flying, are working against us with the model inverted. To counter these conditions, we must give more power and

increase the angle of attack of the wing by giving more down elevator.

When the model is inverted the ailerons will work in the same sense, for example if the model is going away from you and you want to turn to the left, you give left aileron control. However, if no ailerons are fitted and you wish to maintain inverted flight you must remember that the rudder control is reversed, for example if the model is going away from you and you wish to turn it to the left, you have to give it right rudder. Hence, it is even more difficult to keep a non-aileron model, with pronounced dihedral, straight and level in the inverted position.

Problems with flying inverted are often associated with mental difficulties rather than pure flying abilities. There can be a tendency to panic when the model is upside down and starts to dive. Instead of taking the safe option and rolling the model from inverted to upright, the automatic reaction may be to pull in full up elevator. This can be disastrous in two ways: if you don't have enough height when you command up elevator the model may hit the ground before it completes 180 degrees; and during the dive, unless the engine is throttled back, there may be unacceptable loads and forces placed on the airframe. These fears and false reactions must be overcome, however, and, as with spins, the right corrective controls must be learnt. Start your inverted flying at a safe height, roll the model into the inverted, feeding some down elevator in as the model gets on to its back, and hold it there for a short period. Gradually increase the length of time flying inverted and then practise turns in that state. You will find that you will need even more power and down elevator to prevent the model sinking during the inverted turn. When you can maintain steep turns inverted, without losing height, you will feel even more confident about your flying capabilities.

Although you can go out on your own and experiment with aerobatic manoeuvres, it will be more productive if you have an experienced pilot standing by. He will recognize what mistakes you are making and help you to avoid them. This is the safe, non-traumatic way of learning to fly 'close to the edge'.

Once you have learned to fly all of these basic aerobatic manoeuvres you can practise linking them together to produce a series of complex patterns. What is even more important is that these aerobatics will tell you what the full flight envelope of the model is, and in making mistakes along the way you will have found out how to correct them. When you know how to get a model into any situation – and to recover from it safely – then you are a competent pilot.

Thought you'd finished with the checklists? Not quite – there are still the post-flight ones to make and these include:

- remove the model promptly and safely from the landing area
- switch off the receiver first, followed by the transmitter, and collapse the transmitter aerial
- return the frequency peg to the board
- clean down the airframe
- check for any damage and repairs that may be needed
- thank the modellers who have been helping you
- go home with a sense of satisfaction of a job well done – or to cry in your beer.

Solo stage having been reached, where do we go from here? Before inspecting the wider canvas we should take a while to hone our general skills and take a few tests to prove that we have reached certain levels of competency. Clubs will probably have rules stating that you cannot fly without a qualified pilot standing with you until you have obtained a given skill level. This may be to the club's own devising, although the most common levels are those accepted by the governing body, the British

If you wish to progress to sophisticated scale models, such as these Bf 109 and NA Harvard designs, you must first become competent on basic, intermediate and advanced trainers.

Model Flying Association (BMFA), and are classed as 'A' and 'B' certificates. The latter is a level where the pilot is competent at flying and capable of aerobatic manoeuvres and, therefore, safe to fly on his own. You may think that these tests are an imposition; indeed, older modellers often take the attitude of 'I've been flying for umpteen years, why should I bother to take a test?' However, they are important, never more so than when we have to prove to others that we are a well-governed and responsible body of hobby/sports enthusiasts.

HEALTH WARNING

The number of RC flyers has been increasing rapidly in recent times and this encouraging trend also can bring problems and dangers. As the vast majority of sales of models come into the ARTF category, the model can literally be flyable in a matter of a day. Hopefully, the retailer will have pointed the purchaser in the direction of the nearest club or group, where it is possible to obtain some help and assistance with learning to fly the newly acquired model. But what if the club has a full membership or, as some misguided clubs rule, they do not take in beginners and pilots who have not reached the solo flying stage? There will be a temptation to take the model to a local park or open common ground and attempt to fly it on your own. Under no circumstances should you take this action; for one thing it would probably be illegal and even more importantly you could be putting other people at risk – and without having insurance cover. Although it may involve travelling greater distances, you must find a club that will help you. If you cannot find a local club, give a call to the BMFA (*see* Appendices) for details.

CHAPTER 12

Indoors and Out
of the Weather

Who would have ever dreamed, in those far-off days of radio-control equipment weighing pounds, rather than ounces, that we would be able to fly radio-controlled models indoors? The possibilities became apparent when the annual Model Engineer Exhibition was held at Olympia, London, in 1992, and one of the main halls was set aside for model flying. After the first tentative flights, using small models powered by IC engines, the professionals came along with their 3D models to show how it should really be done; and not only with fixed-wing models, as helicopters were put

Go into your local model shop in the morning, buy an ARTF Bleriot-style electric-powered indoor model, and you can be flying it at one of the many sports hall sites that evening.

through their paces, too. My admiration for some of these exceptional pilots knows no bounds and to watch a pilot fly a model, from one side of the Grand Hall, in and out of columns on the opposite side of the hall, just leaves me flabbergasted. Regrettably Olympia is no longer the venue for the MEE.

With the possibilities of radio-controlled indoor models being established it then became a challenge to fly them in more moderate surroundings. With the availability of dozens, even hundreds, of sports halls built in the past score of years, there was the potential of indoor radio-controlled flying throughout the length and breadth of the country. It didn't take long for the experimenters, rapidly followed by commercial interests, to rise to the challenge. Because of the cleanliness of electric power (owners of sports halls take exception to fuel being spilt over the polished floors of the badminton courts), this was the obvious way to go, especially as it also offered a flexible range of motors and batteries. Demand dictates supply, and before too long specialized indoor equipment and kits were becoming available, although it was thanks to individuals who were prepared to experiment and evaluate that these products became commercially available.

It is the proliferation of sports halls and miniaturization of radio-control equipment that has made indoor flying one of the largest growth areas of all aeromodelling interests. You only need to take a look at the diaries of events, published in the modelling magazines, for modelling activities through the winter months to realize just how many indoor flying meetings there are. At one time the winter signified a cessation of flying for many modellers, although the hardy of us continued to fly in the cold, but with indoor meetings it now means that we can continue to fly the year round.

Miniaturization has come at a steady rate. Receivers on 35mHz, as are the outdoor receivers, came down in weight from a typical 25 to 30g (0.9 to 1oz), to 12g (0.4oz), then to 9g (0.3oz), and, at the time of writing, commercial radio receivers of 4g are on the market. Servos, too, have reduced in size and weight. Regular manufacturers are producing 5g (0.2oz) servos and the specialists in indoor products sell a servo of half that weight. Rechargeable nickel cadmium and nickel metal hydride cells of 50mAh capacity helped with the overall airborne package weight. The four 1.2V cells, with a total weight of 17g (0.6oz), typically gave twenty to thirty minutes of flying with a two- or three-channel lightweight system. With these systems it became possible to fly smallish models in moderate-sized halls. But this was still only the beginning.

Some of the small electric ARTF designs are equally suited to outdoor and indoor flying. With the use of some of the new generation of lithium batteries, flight times in excess of thirty minutes are possible.

RIGHT: Micro-receivers and servos have transformed indoor RC flying, and if the US military is to be believed we are only at the beginning of true miniaturization, spin-offs from which should allow us to have lounge flying in the near future.

BELOW: Because of the small size and low weights, indoor RC flying encourages modellers to design and build their own models, using both modern and traditional materials. Costs of materials are minimal and the time to complete a simple model is short.

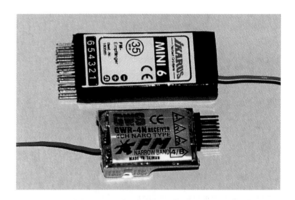

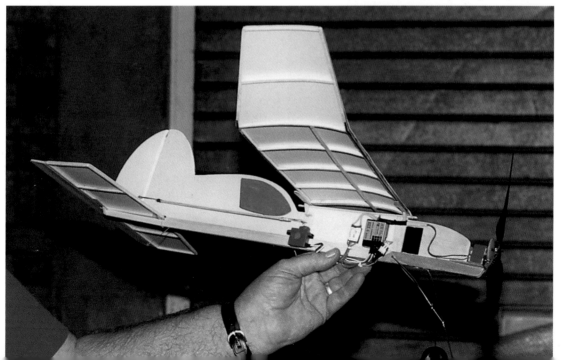

In addition to controlling the models with conventional radio-control equipment, the use of infrared control was developed, similar to the method of using a remote controller for the television. With the limitation of only being able to use one IR transmitter at a time, it also had a number of advantages. For a club, or a group, it was only necessary to have one infrared transmitter and the cost of this, and the airborne outfit, was at a very reasonable price, the equipment

essentially being home-made. Furthermore, with small magnetic actuators to operate the rudder and a micro speed controller, weight levels for the airborne equipment got seriously low. Again, I can only speak of the time of writing this book, but I recently saw, at the Leicester Aeronutz meeting (one of the foremost groups for innovation in indoor radio-controlled models), a commercial moulded-foam profile model of a Japanese Zero fighter, with rudder and motor control, weighing a grand total of just 10.5g. If there had been a wind in the hall, it would have blown away. It is not only the developments in infrared model technology that have allowed the reductions in weight, another important breakthrough is the wafer-thin lithium polymer rechargeable cells with voltages of up to 4V and output weight ratios far greater than the normal nickel metal hydride cells.

What will happen in the future is anybody's guess, but the American military is working on equipment so mind-boggling that almost anything seems possible. For instance, can you imagine gas turbine engines of ⅛in (3mm) diameter, operating at half a million rpm – and with a generator on the end? Or of miniature insect-like robots capable of landing and regenerating their fuel cells from plants? It all sounds very Sci-Fi, but if only a small percentage of the projects come to fruition there will be spin-offs for the aeromodelling sphere that will make our activities ever more exciting.

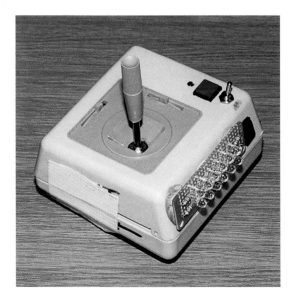

ABOVE: Infrared offers further possibilities of low-cost indoor flying. Although only suitable for flying one model at a time, it does mean that the inexpensive infrared emitter can be shared by club members.

Weighing only 10.5g ready to fly, this expanded polystyrene foam flying-wing model is controlled, through ailerons and motor speed control, by infrared – similar to the controls you use with your television remote controller.

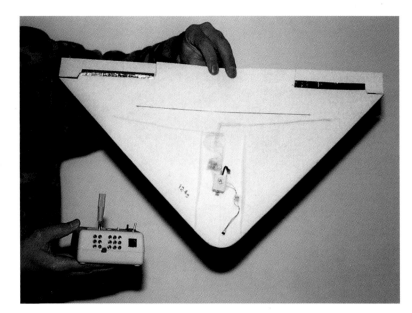

Personally, I can't wait for the time when we are flying miniature jet-powered models, with full control functions and weighing no more than a standard-size servo.

But back to the present. There are many excellent commercial introductions to indoor flying, most of them taking the form of moulded polystyrene airframes with lightweight moulded plastic fittings. Radio equipment consists of standard, off the shelf receivers and servos and the total all-up weight is likely to be in the region of 60g (2oz). Electric motors, typically of the 280 size, are normally geared to allow a larger propeller, of greater efficiency, to be used. Clever designs of flying-wing types, using a plastic rod frame and plastic film covering, can be highly aerobatic, so you don't want more than two of these flying at a time. Perhaps this is the time to remind prospective radio-control indoor fliers that indoor flying first started with free-flight models and a number of the clubs still fly these types. Free-

This Zero model is converted from a ready to fly 'toy' and, complete with electric motor, battery and infrared control system weighs an amazing 10.5g, little more than the weight of a one pound coin.

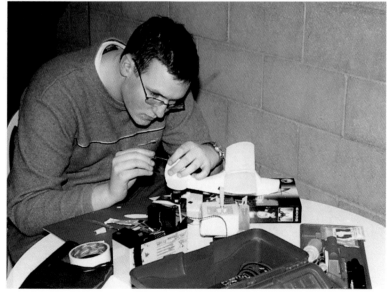

Indoor RC model aircraft (including rotary-wing types) brings out the experimenters, both those interested in the electronics and those keen to improve flying capabilities and characteristics.

Let your imagination fly – it doesn't take long to make these balsawood and film models and they use the innards from the inexpensive toy cars and motorcycles for their power source and control systems.

flight models and heavier, faster radio-controlled indoor models don't always get on well together, as the radio models can be a bit intimidating. However, with common sense and reasonable discipline the two styles can be flown at the same meeting. The only ones that won't mix are the ultra-light, microfilm-covered models, which are disturbed by the smallest air current.

One of the big advantages of indoor flying is that the models are small and very cheap to make. With modern foam and film materials they are also quick to produce and therefore it gives more encouragement to make a whole range of model types, experimenting to your heart's content. If the model doesn't fly, or doesn't perform to expectations, there is very little lost; you will have learned something and the next one will be better! Some of the developments of indoor radio-controlled models include ducted fan designs, with the fans made

from the plastic of yoghurt cups, and even rubber-powered models being controlled. Steering with twin-engined models can be achieved by independent control of the motors, the model yawing into the slower motor and the yaw being converted into a bank.

Regarding the variety in model types, I have seen a Canberra with twin ducted fan engines using homemade fan units, Tiger Moths, Spitfires and non-scale aerobatic biplanes all flying at the same meeting; certainly as big, and probably a larger variety of models than you will find at a typical outdoor meeting. Capacitors are now also being used as a power source for electric motors and the improving standards of power make these a potential power source, although they are not yet suitable for powering the motor and the radio-control system. Also being tried, with increasing degrees of success, is muscle wire, which expands and contracts

Here's an opportunity to have a fleet of scale model aircraft without the need to own a hangar in which to keep them. Minimum cost outlay, except for the control equipment within the model, and an almost limitless choice of prototypes to model, will make the winter months vanish rapidly. With no-wind conditions indoors, you can fly models that would crash in tough conditions outdoors.

according to the electric current applied: a direct connection to the control surface allows it to be used. It is used to replace the servo or magnetic actuator, and relies on a variation of electric current to either stretch or shorten the wire, which is connected to a control-surface horn. By having a lightly spring-loaded control surface, the muscle wire can give controls in both directions.

We first benefited from the space age for improvements to small electric motors, although these are not small by present-day standards. Now we look to such devices as pagers. The electric motors in these (used for vibrating, and so on) are truly sub-miniature and although the torque levels are low, they are perfectly adequate for the small model when they are geared down.

The future for radio-controlled indoor flying is fabulous, and it won't be too long before we are flying models around our sitting rooms, never mind the school and sports halls. Smallness just for the sake of smallness, however, should not be the only aim. Where there is a reasonably large hall and a meeting specifically for radio-controlled models, the sight of a scale biplane, of around 60cm (24in) wingspan flying slowly and sedately around can be more satisfying, and certainly more scale-like, than a little 20cm (8in) WWII fighter flitting around in a barely controlled manner. Yes, there will those who will be hell-bent on making the equipment and models ever smaller, but if they continue on these ever decreasing circles we know where they will end up!

CHAPTER 13

The Sky's the Limit

For the fledging pilot there are so many exciting prospects and possibilities where the sky really is the limit. It would, indeed, take a very large book to describe them all, but I can at least give a flavour of some of the types and varieties of radio-controlled model aircraft that are waiting in the wings.

Before moving on to these, though, a heart-warming story about one of our less fortunate colleagues. Ken and his wife came to the realization, through some of his more bizarre actions, that he had Alzheimer's disease. Ken used to be an aeromodeller in previous years, and so his wife suggested that he might consider taking up the hobby again, although she insisted that she would be at the sharp end – starting the motor. Funds were at a premium, but an advertisement in the local paper brought forth an excellent response of equipment and help from local club members. Having completed the model (and been rejected for flying by one misguided group), he rejoined a club of which he had been a founder member many years before and was welcomed with enthusiasm and assistance. Ken progressed very well, learned to fly the model, had a few setbacks, one or two accidents, but improved in mind and spirit. On cold, rainy days Ken gets a little dispirited (don't we all), but knows that he has got the warm, sunny days to look forward to, and most of all, the friendship and companionship of his fellow modellers. Life is truly more than building and flying model aeroplanes, it is about people and understanding.

BACK TO THE FUTURE

Probably, for the majority of model aircraft enthusiasts, their endeavours will be leading to making a fabulous scale model, a precise replica of a full-sized aircraft and seeing it performing in the air in a convincing manner. It gives us the opportunity to 'fly' a whole range of aeroplanes that we would never have the chance of flying in 'real' life. Indeed, we can recreate aircraft that are extinct as far as flying examples are concerned. Go along to one of LMA (Large Model Association) public displays and you will see a wide variety of scale models, some of them as large as half scale, from the earliest wood, wire and fabric types to the most modern aircraft. Where else could you see World War I air battles being flown again, or four B-17 'Flying Fortress' bombers with 5.5m (18ft) wingspans being formatted around the sky? No prototype is now out of bounds for the RC scale modeller. Helicopters, even twin rotor types, can be reproduced and flown, and now that gas turbine engines are a commercial proposition, the replication of F-16 fighters or the BAe Concorde is not only feasible, they have been successfully flown. Nor are gas turbines the only way to go for powering 'jet' aircraft. Improvements in battery technology, allied to efficient motors and ducted fan units mean that large Antonov transport jets can be modelled, complete with retracting undercarriage, flaps and landing lights – all very majestic. There will always be a desire to emulate the full-sized aeroplanes; it is as basic a desire as little girls wanting dolls, young boys wanting 'Action Man' and model cars and trains.

Would Your First Solo be on a Tornado Jet Fighter?

Once you are a competent RC flyer, have flown high wing and low wing sports models, can fly aerobatic routines, can cope with flight emergencies and can carry out a good landing nine times out of ten, then you are ready for the more challenging scale types. Is it impossible to learn to fly with a scale model? No, if you choose a Piper Cub, Cessna Skyhawk or similar high-wing cabin models, they will fly in a predictable, trainer-like way. The disadvantages lie in the areas of glazing (unless painted on), wing struts and other vulnerable parts, which are likely to be damaged in one of your unplanned 'arrivals'.

Is the Colour of the Pilot's Socks Correct?

The meaning of a scale model will not be the same to all modellers. To some, if you can watch a model in the air and recognize it as a Mustang or a Fokker triplane, then it is a scale model. In truth, the Mustang may have a fixed undercarriage and no extended areas at the wing roots and the other model may only have three wings, a round cowl and semicircular fin and rudder, but to the observer they are recognizable and therefore scale models. For the competition scale modeller it is important that the scale outlines are accurate and that the finish

and markings copy the original as accurately as possible. Scale purists will be looking for a structure to represent accurately the full-sized aircraft and then for the flying characteristics to mimic the larger version; if the prototype is a competition aerobatic aircraft the model should be capable of performing the same manoeuvres (they usually do, and a few more that the full-sized cannot manage). For the slow-flying early types of aircraft, the model must also stagger around the sky, and a replica of a WWII ground-attack aeroplane should look equally menacing. Where we still lag behind the 'real' aeroplanes is in the area of jet aircraft. With the first generation of gas turbine engines it is possible to put on a convincing demonstration of early jet flight, with models of Sabre, Vampire, MiG-15 and T-33 Shooting Star prototypes. What we cannot, at present, do is to emulate the power, noise and earth-shaking qualities of the modern fighter jets; for one thing, we don't have reheat mechanisms for after-burning our jets. It will come.

Scale modelling is probably the ultimate aim of most RC model aircraft enthusiasts. Two totally different examples are the Vickers Vimy, the first aircraft to cross the Atlantic non-stop, and the American F-18 Hornet jet, fantastically detailed.

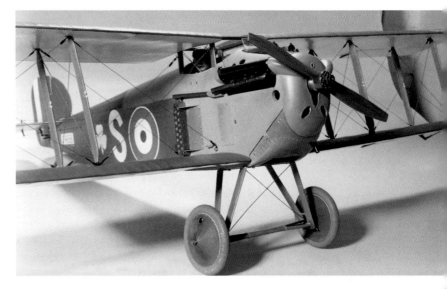

Examples of the scale modellers' art, from the small Sopwith Dolphin biplane, to the giant Fokker triplane and the highly unusual COW-gun fighter with the engine mounted amidships.

What's the Build Time?

We have to be honest with ourselves; we may not have as much leisure time to spend on our hobby as we would wish. Building and finishing flying-scale models can be very time-consuming, and that is where the modern generation of ARTF models comes into its own. There is now a range of scale ARTF models to suit all tastes. You can buy a kit for an Extra 300 aerobatic ship that will fly every bit as well as anything you can build yourself, or a twin-engined DC3 Dakota that, in the air, really looks the part. Scale ARTF RC model kits are available for as little as £70, or, if you want a really super scale Bristol Fighter biplane, for instance, it could set you back £700.

Many dyed-in-the-wool scale modellers have succumbed to the charms of the scale ARTFs and it is not difficult to understand why. Produced in countries where labour costs are low, it is economic to have the airframes constructed in a traditional built-up manner, and they are then covered with pre-printed covering material that has all the markings and details in full colour. It would take the skilled scale modeller a very long time to paint the model to achieve equal results. And they fly; in fact, it is almost disheartening when some of them fly as well as they do. Here we are, having spent hours and hours building and painting a scale model, only for Joe Bloggs to come along with his ARTF of the same prototype, having spent a day or so assembling the model, and it flies as well as ours, and, if we are honest, looks even better in the air. Is nothing sacred? But, as I have said elsewhere, nothing can really compare with the satisfaction of having built the model yourself.

To build a scale model from scratch involves many skills, those of woodworker, metalworker, painter and decorator, as well as being a historian in researching the project, and a pilot when it comes to flying the model. To involve ourselves in such a comprehensive project brings with it many rewards when we watch the model take to the air – or heartbreak if it crashes. Which brings me on to a piece of advice that is not always easy to accept. If you have been totally absorbed, for hundreds of hours, in the building of a top-class scale model you might well be the wrong person to carry out the maiden test flight. You have been so involved in its completion that you are 'too close to it' to be totally focused when it comes to the flying. If you can bear to hand over the transmitter to an experienced friend, do so. It will not only give a better chance for a successful conclusion to the flight, it will also give you the opportunity to look properly at the model and see its beauty. Surely you see it when you are flying the model? Yes, but not in the same way. You are concentrating so hard on the flying aspect that you don't have time to concentrate on the appearance of your pride and joy.

Having included chapters on gliders, helicopters, electric and indoor model aircraft, I won't dwell further on these subjects, although they may become your primary interests.

AEROBATICS

Considered by some as the purest form of competition flying, aerobatics has fascinated pilots since the days when a Bleriot monoplane was first looped, by a Frenchman, before World War One. Gradually, over the years, the aircraft were designed to be more aerobatic, the importance of high manoeuvrability was realized when aerial warfare started, and more powerful engines were developed to pull these aircraft through ever increasingly complex evolutions. For years the radio-control modeller struggled to emulate his full-size compatriot, but here, too, there were developments, not only with engines and airframe design, but with the radio-control equipment. We have now reached the stage where we can make the models perform antics

that, a few years ago, could only be dreamed about. With such advances in composite materials, resulting in ultra-lightweight structures and engines with highly impressive power outputs, we have models of great reserves of power and giving vertical performances that are truly outstanding. Now the boot is on the other foot and it is the full-size pilot who envies the modeller. They will watch a half-scale model of a Pitts Special biplane literally hanging vertically on its propeller, but being moved from side to side, rather like a helicopter. The full-size aerobatic pilots would give their eye teeth to be able to do that. Yes, modern jet fighters have awesome power, but they don't have the slow speed aerobatic potential to match our models. On the other hand, we have yet to fully emulate the incredible 'Harrier' jump jet; we must wait until the second generation of model gas turbine engines, so that we have sufficient thrust to compensate for the somewhat basic control systems we use on our radio-control models.

Non-competitive aerobatic models do not have to be large. They can be powered by '20' or '40' engines and they will be able to fly most of the manoeuvres of the larger and more powerful designs; they also take up less airspace. Where they have limitations is for serious competition, as they do not have the same authority and they are certainly not so easy for judges to see and mark. In fact, competition aerobatic models have been increasing in size over the years, partly because more powerful engines have become available and the radio equipment has been able to cope with the higher flight control loads, but mainly because the larger models look more majestic and have a larger flight envelope. Competition schedules have needed to be changed to reflect the increased capability of the models and the degree of difficulty for some manoeuvres will test even the most competent of pilots. There is no theoretical limit to the size and power of competition or display aerobatic models – they could finish up with the same dimensions as full-sized aeroplanes, but with the reduced weight of not requiring an onboard pilot. The limits become self-imposed, by the specialist body, in the interest of practicality and convenience, and to give an equal opportunity to all participants of the competitions – although the wallet does figure in the equation.

Aerobatic competitions do not just take place at the highest level. Clubs will organize lower skill competitions and then it is possible, through the Aerobatic

Associations, to enter intermediate levels of competition, before reaching World Championship standard. What is most important is that participating at any level of aerobatic competition will improve your overall flying skills and your flying confidence. It is all too easy to fall into the rut of going to the flying field, having a chat with your colleagues, having a couple of aimless flights and returning home. It is only by having specific aims in your flights that your skills will improve. This will allow you to broaden your interests and achieve higher aims. Aerobatics is one of your gateways to the wider horizons of model aircraft flying.

VINTAGE

At the other end of the spectrum of flying is the subject of vintage models. What is a vintage model? The definition will vary from one country to another. In the UK it is reckoned to be a design of the pre-1950 period, whereas in the USA the date is rather earlier. Why should anybody want to build models of yesteryear, when we have made all of these technical advances? Nostalgia is a very powerful emotion and the far-off days seem to be imbued with a more gentle, but glamorous aura. In truth, of course, when they were building and flying the models a half century ago, there were the same frustrations and heartbreaks that we have today – only more so! Engines were less messy to operate pre-1950, as most of them were still spark-ignition types, with all of the paraphernalia of batteries, coils and condensers that was entailed. Radio was in its infancy and one controlled flight in a day was considered good, two a miracle. Yet, we still yearn for the magic of yesterday. And we can get it, as never before, in the sense that we can fit modern engines and modern radios to these, arguably, beautiful designs.

Not for the vintage purist the modern engines; he will keep to the original motors used at that period and the thought of fitting radio to control the model is considered heresy. However, for the less of a perfectionist, there are a whole lot of lovely designs in the archives that are just waiting to be built and flown. If you class yourself as a builder, with the added attraction of flying the model after you have built it, then vintage designs offer many rewards. The building of model aeroplanes was, in many ways, more of an art in earlier days. Where we might use one sheet of balsawood for a fuselage side, the

3D aerobatics is nothing short of amazing. Imagine hanging this £2,000 model just a few centimetres above the tarmac, blowing away the dust with a flick of the rudder.

RIGHT: RC models do not have to be highly sophisticated. This sports low winger was based, by the author, on a vintage design.

vintage aircraft would have a complex structure of wood strip, gussets, cross braces and plywood reinforcing. And, as these models were covered with tissue or silk, it was possible to see the structure through the covering, and a beautiful sight it often was.

Slow flying and stable, the vintage models were designed for free flight and therefore mostly had a high degree of inherent stability; the exceptions were the competition duration models, which were developed for a maximum time glide. The sports models of that era often make good trainer designs for those with slower reactions, although it is important to limit the size and movements of the control surfaces. These are the type of model aeroplanes to nudge around the sky, interfering with the natural flight pattern as little as possible. For those prepared to wait for the halcyon days of sun, warmth and gentle breezes, there are few more enjoyable and relaxing pastimes than flying a vintage model, sitting in a deckchair, with a glass of your favourite beverage at your side. For the keen competitive modeller there are still contests to enter in the vintage section, mainly related to a limited-power time climb, followed by a thermal-searching maximum duration glide. Great fun, but also keenly contested.

PYLON RACING

Fancy some speed flying? Pylon racing takes place around a triangular course with up to four aircraft taking part in each heat. With speeds in excess of 100mph, pylon racing is for the experienced flyer wishing to have an adrenaline rush and undergo wingtip to wing-tip flying in competition with like-minded speed freaks. In common with most other competitive classes of radio-controlled model flying, there are classes for smaller and less expensive racers, such as Club 2000 and Sport 40. Fortunately, these junior classes are no less exciting as regards the actual racing. In fact, the opposite is true, as, being more evenly matched, the models tend to be closer together. What they may lack in straight-line speed, they make up for in competitiveness, both of the models and the pilots. FAI pylon racing is the top international standard and the '40' engines are specially tuned so that the propellers are turning at over 20,000rpm. You will be hard pushed to find a more exciting sound than three or four of these motors screaming in unison. You will at least have to attend an F1 car race to equal the 'buzz'.

The sports classes are different in that they can be operated from grass strips. The Club 2000 models have no undercarriages and are hand-launched, a fine sight as four models get away at the drop of the starter's flag. Because the engine choice is limited to certain types and manufacturers and the airframe sizes are specified, the models tend to be very equal in speed, so when you get a group of equally matched pilots you are in for quite a race. No pilot is prepared to give way at the pylon turns and mid-air collisions are by no means uncommon. However, engines are rarely badly damaged, flying over grass, the radio equipment should also survive if it has been well installed with good insulation, and the airframes are not expensive to repair, or rebuild.

Sports racers with size '40' engines come somewhere in-between the Club 2000 and FAI racers. The airframes are similar in areas to the FAI class, but more powerful engines are forbidden. Take-offs are the norm and the course flown is identical to the FAI course; it is, therefore, a good stepping stone to the ultimate class. One of the major differences between Sport 40 classes and the FAI class is the cost differential. Sport 40 airframes can still be made by the competitor, although they are normally purchased in a semi-ARTF state. By contrast, the FAI airframes are glass-moulded fuselages with glass-covered wings and the cost, including a competitive, tuned engine, will be in the region of £1,000 – and you will need at least two of them. If you don't know whether pylon racing will suit you or not, try to persuade a few members of the local club to take part in an impromptu race. You will very rapidly know whether you are likely to get hooked on racing. If someone goes past you on the circuit and you then try to out-turn him at the next pylon, you're pretty certain to become embroiled in the race circuit.

WATERPLANES

Forgive me if I eulogize again, but one of the finest sensations you will experience is to carry out a touch and go with a floatplane. As the floats of the model kiss in the water there is a gently hissing sound and the model slows down and begins to sink lower on the floats. Open up the throttle, the model builds up speed, gradually rises on the step and then, with a touch of up elevator, breaks free of the water and climbs away with a sparkling stream of water droplets falling from the

Waterplane flying adds another dimension to take-offs and landings, or, more correctly, alightings. There is something special about a floatplane slipping out of the water and leaving a stream of water droplets gleaming in the sun.

underside of the floats. This is heady stuff indeed and it can be performed by flying boats as well as float-planes.

There is no shortage of waterplane types to build and fly. You can fit twin floats to most conventional land models, although they may require a slight increase in fin area, to compensate for the side area of the floats, but you only have to realize the different types of air-craft during WWII that were equipped with floats to realize that 'almost anything goes'. Spitfires, Austers, DC3 Dakotas and Blenheims all were flown at some time or other with floats fitted. At the planning stages it is not difficult to allow for the fitting of floats at some time in the life of the model. A little extra plywood here, a bit of reinforcing there is all that is required to make the model have an amphibious potential. Floats are not difficult to make from balsawood and plywood, and commercial floats, vac-formed, injection-moulded or veneered foam, are available for various types and sizes of models.

One aspect of floats that I am not over-enamoured with is the fitting of the linkages to operate the water rudders. For the largest models it is possible to bury the steering servo in the float itself and have the servo extension lead routed conveniently up one of the float supports, into the fuselage and to the receiver. The link-age in the rudder can then be by direct closed-loop cables. It is possible to use closed-loop cables from the servo, round the fuselage to the top of the float, through another 90-degree tubing bend and back to the water rudder horn. A form of closed loop can also be used to

go from the air rudder horns, down to the outsides of the water rudder horns and a link made between the water rudder horns. All these systems are rather convo-luted, but do work.

I came to question why aeroplanes have their fins and rudders sticking up in the air. So that they don't hit the runway when the model is landing or taking off is the obvious answer. But, with a floatplane this is not a problem; in fact, it would be an asset because it would put the air rudder into the water and it could also act as a water rudder and steer the model when it was sit-ting on the water. That was the theory, but would it be backed up in practice? I converted one of my regular shoulder wing floatplanes to a high tailplane, under-slung fin and rudder set up and went flying, hopefully. Sure enough, the model took off and flew around with the same flying characteristic as the conventionally arranged fin and rudder model. True, it looked odd, but that was only because we weren't used to seeing such configurations. The landing was equally placid; it could only be faulted in not having sufficient rudder area actually in the water to give adequate steering. That was an easy problem to solve and the next model featured a larger rudder tip area (shortening the float struts would have caused the propeller to have created too much spray being thrown up during the take-off run).

Incidentally, if the clearance between the prop tips and the water is marginal, as it often is in rough water conditions, fitting a smaller diameter propeller is a sim-ple answer – a three-bladed propeller will certainly achieve this purpose. Unlike land-based aeroplanes, where wheel and undercarriage shock absorbing is highly desirable, the opposite is true of floatplanes. Supports for the floats, normally one ahead of the balance point and one behind, need to be rigid in both the fore and aft and side to side restraints. GRP undercarriage-style mouldings are ideal and you can use piano-wire supports, but they must be adequately cross-braced. Cross pieces, from float to float, can be in the form of glass-fibre tubes, which are strong and light. Locations of floats can be critical. The top of the float needs to be about parallel with the wing aerofoil mean chord (from centre of leading edge to centre of trailing edge). Float steps, the small vertical rise on the under-surface of the float, need to be about 13mm (½in) behind the balance point. If you are fitting floats in an unknown combination with a model, try to leave room for adjustment with the float locations, as this may prevent the model simply becoming a high-speed boat. Very approximately, the floats should be 75 per cent the length of the fuselage and the spacing between the floats, 25 per cent of the wingspan. There have been articles written about the design and fitting of floats. There is also the British Waterplane Association to contact, which will be able to give you advice.

Flying boats have not been as popular as floatplanes, probably because they are more specialized, although they also be adapted to amphibious operation. A couple of brass tubes fitted ahead of the main step, for undercarriage legs to be plugged in, and a tailwheel/water-rudder combination, will allow the flying boat to take off from the land. ARTF kits of flying boats are available and there are plenty of plans for the BIY enthusiast. Flying boats and floatplanes are no more difficult to fly than landplanes, but they do need to be landed and taken off directly into the wind. There are obviously fewer places to stand when flying the model, unless you have a very shallow lake and can wear waders, so you may have occasion to take off directly towards yourself – not an everyday occurrence with a landplane, but good flying experience.

So where do you find these idyllic areas of water? Look at an Ordnance Survey map of your area and you may well be amazed at how much of your area is covered by water. You won't be able to get permission to use all of it; fishermen will have rights on some stretches and the water boards may own other sections, but other lakes and ponds might be available for flying and asking costs nothing! What are the downsides of water-

plane flying? Well, water is wet and water and radio equipment don't mix. We can do all possible to water-proof our models, but a good dunking will probably result in the model getting wet, both outside and inside. No problem with the engine, just empty out any water, give a good turnover with the electric starter, fuel up and away you go again. For the radio, the servos will probably not have suffered, but the receiver, battery and switch need removing, putting in the airing cupboard and drying out slowly, followed by a spray with WD40.

SKIS

Not quite in the same class as floatplanes, ski-equipped models can be great fun and, like water, the snow tends to be nice and flat and fairly forgiving. Skis will not be readily available commercially, but it is simple enough to make them from laminations of plywood, with the noses turned upwards, the remainder of them flat. Give them a good coat of fuel proofer, fit them directly in place of the wheels, put a sprung (rubber band) connection from the top front of the skid to the top of the undercarriage leg and a strong nylon chord attachment at the rear. To hear the hiss of the ski on the snow, as you touch down for another 'greaser' landing, is yet another of those rewarding moments.

COMBAT

Are you of a combative nature? Do you like the idea of shooting down an enemy aircraft in flames? Well, we haven't quite got to that stage with radio-controlled model aircraft, but we do have great fun with ½ scale WWII models. What we do with these '20' to '25' powered models is to have paper streamers, of stipulated lengths, tied to the tails of the models with the object of opposing aircraft cutting the streamer. With six of these models, Spitfires, Mustangs, Fw 190s, Bf 109s, and so on, wheeling and turning around the sky the fun is fast and furious. Although the aim is to cut the ribbon of another model, with many models rolling and looping in the same small airspace collisions are bound to happen. You learn quickly not to call 'landing', if your engine cuts out (a normal reaction for flying at the club field) as you are certainly a dead duck if someone sees you. Models are generally constructed from EPP foam, as used on flying-wing gliders, and they are not built to exact scale standards, nor is a lot of time lavished on them to get a good finish and decoration. More important is the fact that they can be involved in a mid-air collision, glued together again with quick-drying epoxy and flying again in the next heat.

SPORTS CONTESTS AND DEMONSTRATIONS

Sports contests and demonstrations cover a wide range of models. They simply imply something a little out of the ordinary. It may be a 'spot landing' competition where the object is to land as near to a predetermined spot as possible and as near to a specified flight time. Simple, but great fun and one of the oldest competitions around. Fun-fly models have been specially designed for the 3D style of flying required to compete in contests where there are multiple tasks, including the most limbo passes within a given time, upright and inverted, touch and goes, and a duration element, too. Again, a contest for quick reactions and strong nerves.

Parachute dropping can be in the form of releasing a number of dummy parachutes, or a radio-controlled parachutist can be dropped, operated by pulling on lines in the same way that a real parachutist would guide himself down for a gentle landing. This is a popular demonstration for the children, but nowhere near as popular as a 'toffee bomber drop'. Here a specially converted model, one capable of carrying a good payload, has a hopper full of sweets, which, at the right strategic moment, is released and the sweets, each with a little ribbon attached, fall to the ground and are chased after by the children. You would think that sweets had only just been invented! Naturally, this has to be carefully planned, so that the model is not flown dangerously over the public and the sweets also fall in a safe area.

I mentioned, in Chapter 6, that a glider can be carried to height on the back of a power model and then released. Similarly, it is possible to carry a power model to height on a larger model, then release it and let the two aeroplanes fly independently. The released model may have an IC engine, in which case it is started before the flight, or powered by an electric motor, which can be started at the release. One of the most impressive flying demonstrations I have seen involved a giant B-29 bomber releasing a rocket-powered Bell X-1 model, exactly as was done by the Americans when they were first experimenting with reaching the speed of sound.

A few years ago, some carrier-deck landing competitions were organized. These were for control-line models, complete with a dummy flight deck, and the radio-control events were also good fun. All that it involved was stretching some cables across the runway, fitting a simple hook on the rear of the model and aiming to pick up one of the cables with the hook. Together with a timed slow and fast run of a section of the runway and you had an interesting competition that did not require a lot of effort or equipment for organizing.

Youngsters should be encouraged to participate, either by trying their skills on a buddy box, or chasing toffees dropped from a model.

We are in danger of losing the fun element of our flying. Yes, the training has to be taken seriously and the safety element must always be to the fore, but it is a hobby and it should be fun.

EYE IN THE SKY

Aerial photography can produce some fascinating results. It can be as simple and cheap or as sophisticated and expensive as you wish. Take an inexpensive 'throwaway' camera, as long as it has an automatic motorized rewind, tape a servo to it, rubber-band the camera to the side of the fuselage, plug the servo in a spare channel and off you go for an aerial photo session. It is a simple matter to shape a servo output disc into a cam so that it will trigger the shutter release button each time it moves through a 90-degree arc. Experience and experimentation will tell you how much anti-vibration packing you will require to get a steady picture and which camera angles will give the most interesting pictures, but try to avoid facing the lens vertically down.

A step up from the instant camera is to install a 35mm SLR (single lens reflex) camera, which will give you a wider selection of exposure programs and lens options. You will be able to set the focus permanently to infinity as the distance from the camera to the ground will never be close. How high do you need to fly for the best results? Only experimentation will tell. On your first flights make a series of adjustments to camera angles, heights, lens settings and shutter speeds and check the results, but do make a written record of each run and occasionally check that the lens shutter is working. You will need to be able to see the film wind-on window. For shutter operation you can mount the servo, with double-sided tape and rubber bands, to the top of the camera, or you can use an electronic remote release and mount the servo in any suitable location. With some SLR cameras it is necessary to block off, with a piece of masking tape, the viewfinder window at the rear of the camera. In the past, I have designed models with a pannier arrangement under the wing so that cameras were interchangeable by changing the pannier. Such a model was the first in the UK to transmit video pictures direct from the plane to the ground. The cameras developed for the onboard F1 car installations were used for the purpose.

Commercial live-link airborne video transmission systems are available at moderate cost, and consist of the airborne camera (colour or mono), transmitter, aerial and battery pack. On the ground you have the antenna to receive the transmissions, a standard portable television or a smaller screen that can be attached directly to the radio transmitter (for instant visual reference) operating through a VCR. With low all-up weights, in the region of 200g (7oz), the airborne equipment can be fitted to moderately sized models. It does not have to be purpose-designed, and can also be fitted to helicopters and boats. Ranges of up to 1km are normal, but the receiving antenna must be in line of sight with the model. Obviously this type of equipment has commercial applications and although the transmitted frequency is licence exempt, you may require permission to overfly certain areas and take pictures; prisons and nudist colonies are particular no-go areas!

COMMERCIAL INTERESTS

I have been fortunate to have been involved in a number of television drama series and films where radio-controlled scale models have been used to represent full-sized aircraft. It may be that there are no flying examples left of the aircraft that they want to portray on the screen, and building full-sized replicas would be too expensive. In such instances the producer has limited options remaining. He can try to recreate the sequences with small, solid models being slid down wires in a studio, which is not very convincing, or he can simulate the aircraft in flight by electronic graphic systems, as you might see on some of the computer games and video films. The standards of these graphics are improving rapidly and may be the way to go in the future, but it hasn't quite reached a stage of complete acceptance yet. Combining the flying sequences of large radio-controlled scale models with non-flying full-sized mock-ups, where the actors can be sitting in the cockpits and walking around the aircraft, is probably the most convincing way of recreating flying activities.

Other commercial projects I have been involved in are banner towing for television adverts, with the manufacturer's product name painted on the model, not to mention editing magazines, writing books and manufacturing model aircraft kits. Never assume that other people know what your hobby is all about, as we do not get much public exposure and our flying fields are usually well distant from general areas of population. It is only at special modelling public events that they may

When the author organized Barnstormer Air Displays he included an act where an RC Tiger Moth was flown in formation with the full size.

get a chance to witness our activities so, if you know a newspaper editor or a television news person, why not let them know what radio-controlled model aircraft are all about and see if we can get some more publicity.

DEMONSTRATION TEAMS

Flying our models before the public is good PR, and it gives a sense of purpose. Whether it is at a local club level, where the members have been asked to participate at a fête or gala, or an open day has been organized, the flying display should be thoroughly planned. Why not develop a display team where three or four identical models are flown in formation? You don't have to be the Red Arrows – as long as you can all keep in the same patch of the sky and the aerobatics are performed together, it will be pretty convincing. When forming a demonstration or display team remember that you will be performing before an audience that will include lots of children and they will also need to be entertained. I have already mentioned dropping sweets, but there are

other things that can be done to keep the young amused. Television programmes have a profound effect on young people, so why not introduce some of these characters into your models. The Woodvale meeting, which has been entertaining tens of thousands of visitors for well over thirty years, has had model flying as its core event from the beginning. Novelty items are introduced from time to time, a recent duo being 'Noddy' and 'Mr Plod the Policeman'. Balloon bursting and limbo are other crown pleasers, and pyrotechnics, the more spectacular the better, never fail to grab the public's attention. The first properly controlled power flight of Wilbur Wright occurred on 17 December 1903. This provided a wonderful opportunity to use radio-controlled modelling expertise to entertain the public to recreating aviation history.

RECORD BREAKING

Man has always been fascinated with records or the breaking of records, and there are plenty of records,

The last frontier! When the model gas turbine became a practical proposition it allowed the prototypes of the past fifty years to be modelled. With the costs of the gas turbines becoming more reasonable we can expect to see more jet-style models, although it would be a shame if too many of these motors found their way into non-scale models. We must also be vigilant in respect of the safety aspects involved with these miniature flame throwers. Shown here are, clockwise from top left: a BAe Hawk, a non-scale 'Hot Spot' trainer, a pair of Gloster Javelins and a Supermarine Swift.

national and international, for the model aircraft enthusiast to attempt to beat. With the straight-linc speed record standing at over 400km/h (250mph), you will need a powerful gas turbine-powered model to take this record, but there are lesser mountains to climb. It has to be said that world records for height, speed, endurance and distances are quite staggering and it would take a lot of time, patience and probably the assistance of the military to challenge them – in August 2003 an RC model made a non-stop crossing of the Atlantic! But, records are there for the taking and few of them will last for ever.

GAS TURBINES

I have left the subject of 'jet' engines, and other specialist engines, to the last in this chapter because they represent the most recent developments in our sport. Before practical and commercial gas turbine engines were developed we had few ways in which we could represent a jet aeroplane. The power slope soarer was one possibility, but it lacked the sound and excitement of IC engine power. The ducted fan approach, where the IC is internally mounted in the fuselage or nacelle and drives a small diameter multi-bladed fan was a more realistic answer, except for the noise. A glow engine, turning at 20,000rpm and fitted with a tuned pipe exhaust system, may give the operator a great thrill, but the sound is not fully representational of a full-sized aircraft. However, ducted fan models are practical and reasonably priced and should not be written off just because an alternative has come along. There are several scale models with these propulsion systems regularly performing at public displays and thrilling the assembled guests with their flying.

Because of the newness of the gas turbine engines and the rapid development of the type (plus, it has to be said, the equally rapid entry and departure of some manufacturers), it is not possible to state, with real authority, what the present development of the gas turbine design will be when you read this book. Reference to the current model magazines will give a better idea of how far the design and production of these motors have progressed: whether they have got larger or smaller; whether they have become more or less expensive; whether, even, they are still legal to operate, or that insurance cover can still be obtained. Sensibly operated by responsible persons the gas turbine engines are safe; few are now made completely from

scratch and the kit versions have all the critical components preformed, so the risks of operating the self-assembly kit should be no greater than with the fully finished units.

My guess is that in, say, five years from now it is likely that the fully prepared, ready to install, press the button and go turbine engines will head the commercial market. These would be started by small electric motors, on gas with an automatic changeover to kerosene; in fact, the only difference with the present generation may be that two-stage compressors and axial flow designs, replicating full-sized developments, may be introduced. Fuel consumptions are high on our existing model gas turbine engines; with two of the more powerful gas turbines fitted to a full-sized, piloted Cri-Cri aeroplane, flight time is strictly limited. There will always be modellers who want to build at least part of the engine themselves and the smaller, specialist manufacturer will be able to cater for these enthusiasts. They may also be the ones who produce the turbo-prop and geared output gas turbines; these will certainly be in demand for scale models of turbo-prop prototypes and for the gas turbine-powered helicopters of the future.

There are other specialist IC engines that will fascinate and enthral the engineering-minded aeromodellers. The thought of a five-cylinder radial motor is enough to start some modellers drooling, and as for a working model of a seven-cylinder rotary engine, well, that is almost too much to contemplate. But, such engines do exist – multi-cylinder radial and inline engines are commercially available. They aren't cheap, but also are not impossibly expensive; just start saving your pocket money now. Four-stroke engines are commonplace, but not those with sleeve valve operation and these, too, are being produced in model sizes.

It is, though, in the field of electric power that we should expect the greatest advances and innovations. The electric revolution is only just beginning.

ULTIMATE SIMULATION

The nearest I have got to virtual reality in simulators is in a South African Airways Boeing 747 simulator, where you are on a full flight deck with 3D visuals around all the cockpit windows. These awesome commercial airline simulators, costing many millions of pounds, are so good that they can be used for all training procedures of the real aircraft. Model aircraft simulators have not quite reached these exalted states, but they are becoming ever more realistic and versatile. For instance, the AeroFly Professional system allows you to select a specific model or design your own, and view the aeroplane form all angles. You can adjust the proportions of the flying surfaces and control surfaces, the weights of components, the aerofoil of the surfaces, lift and drag coefficients, incidences, dihedral control movements, engine and propeller sizes, engine thrust lines, and so on. Similar parameters for gas turbine powered models and helicopters are also available.

In addition to a great variety of aircraft types, it is also possible to select alternative flying sites and backgrounds, wind velocities, including thermal activity, and even the roughness of the take-off and landing surface. Viewing positions can be varied between a fixed viewing state, similar to a normal model flying pilot location, to a cockpit mode and a 'tail chase' viewpoint of following the aircraft. A two-player mode is available, allowing such activities as glider towing, combat and pylon racing, but the flight practice performing basic and aerobatic manoeuvres are not overlooked. There is a minimum computer requirement to run these systems.

Minimum system requirements:
- 100 per cent Intel Pentium II compatible processor with at least 450MHz
- open GL ICD compatible graphic card with at least 16MB
- 64MB RAM
- 160MB of free hard-disk space
- CD-ROM drive
- a free link at the serial interface (COMPORT) to connect the interface cable
- a transmitter with pupil socket. The enclosed interface cable has an adapter for all usual types of remote controls, for example Futaba, JR, Graupner, Multiplex, Hitec, Sanwa and Airtronics
- Windows 98/ME/2000/XP with Direct X version 8.0a or higher.

Recommended system requirements:
- 100 per cent Intel Pentium II compatible processor with at least 700MHz
- 100 per cent AMD Athlon compatible processor with at least 700MHz

- open GL ICD compatible graphic card with at least 32MB
- 128MB RAM.

There are more basic simulators on the market, with lower minimum system specifications, and the realism of these flying aids is constantly being improved. In addition to being an aid to training, they are entertaining in their own right and great enjoyment can be had pretending to be the pilot of a WWI biplane, a modern jet or a helicopter, as well as flying these aircraft in exotic locations.

How good are they at actually teaching you to fly? They certainly help in the initial phases in learning orientation of the model, the effects of the controls and the handling of the transmitter to the stage of being able to operate all of the controls without having to look down at the transmitter; this action could be disastrous if you were actually flying the model. They are good confidence boosters and are certainly recommended for practice before attempting to fly a model for the first time. They cannot, however, simulate the immediacy, the adrenaline rush or the commitment involved in the real flying of a model aircraft. When it comes to this stage you will need strong nerves and, even more importantly, an experienced flyer by your side.

When it comes to more advanced flying simulation, or just fun operation, a contest menu, where the competitors are flying against the clock, may include balloon bursting, pylon racing, spot landing and 3D competitions. On the more serious side the parameters of a model design, such as wingspan, weight, centre of gravity, moment arms, tail areas, aerofoils, incidences and dihedral can be varied on a program and it is even possible to introduce an airframe strength factor, which, if exceeded in flight, will cause a structural failure. Gas turbine engines and helicopters are also catered for with variable parameters.

In some respects, the upmarket simulators are ahead of the game. One of the expansion packs includes a program on the Harrier Jump Jet, complete with rotating nozzle control. At the time of writing, a miniature, fully controlled Harrier has yet to be flown. Perhaps the impetus provided by flying a simulated Harrier, together with the advances of gas turbine engines, will ensure that this goal will be achieved in the very near future.

CHAPTER 14

There to Help You

Where will you buy your equipment from? Will it be from a model shop retailer, by mail order, through the Internet or from one of the trade show/model meetings proliferating around the country? It is a sad fact that there are fewer and fewer 'genuine' model shops about now. There are toy shops which may sell a few model kits, engines and radios, but they are unlikely to have the salesperson expertise to answer your questions on radio-controlled model aircraft subjects. If you don't have a model retailer near you, you will probably make your purchases through mail order specialists, via the advertisements in the modelling magazines, or, increasingly, through the Internet. Good as these ways may be, and the services offered are often exceptionally good and rapid, they do have the disadvantage that you cannot see, or handle, the goods before you purchase them. If you don't like what you have purchased you can return it to the supplier and they may give you a credit for the return, but it's all a bit of a bother. However, you are probably going to have the largest selection of products and prices through these means. Model meetings, where there is a reasonable trade representation, do give you the chance to view modelling products at first hand and to talk to sellers with knowledge of their subject, but the stallholder will only be able to take a percentage of his stock with him and will probably concentrate on the fast-selling items.

What about buying second-hand? There seem to be plenty of bargains in the free ads at the back of magazines and at the swap-meets. Buying any radio equipment second-hand must have a certain risk factor, as how do we know that it has not been damaged, or that there may not be an intermittent fault? You can quickly lose the money saved from buying second-hand by crashing a couple of models. New equipment has

guarantees and faults are unlikely with modern sets; if you buy second-hand, will you be able to purchase spares for it, or get it serviced? My advice would be to have with you an experienced flier if you are contemplating buying second-hand radio gear, to advise you on the equipment to buy and even then only to purchase with an agreement that it is on a test basis for a period of a month, on a money back if not satisfied arrangement. To a lesser extent, the same conditions might apply for buying engines and airframes, but you can usually tell if an engine has been damaged by closely inspecting it. Turning the engine over by hand should also indicate whether all the parts are moving smoothly and whether it has had a lot of running. There will usually be fellow club members with equipment and engines to sell and providing they are not actually giving up the hobby, at least they will still be there to question if a purchase turns out to be faulty.

Completed airframes are in a slightly different category, as careful modellers may have flown a particular model until they want a change and the airframe may be in perfectly good condition. Some modellers actually prefer building to flying and will want to sell the model before it has flown. There are some undoubted bargains to be had with finished models, where they can be purchased, well built, for less than the price of the kit and the covering. Again, though, I would stress the importance of having an experienced modeller's opinion so that you avoid buying a poorly constructed model, the wrong type, or one with warps and misalignments.

FLYING TRAINING

Personalized flying training is offered by a number of commercial establishments, either on a one to one basis, or with small groups. Advertisements for these radio-control flying schools can be found in the magazines. The schools can also usually offer accommodation packages and simulator experience. Models can be supplied for training, which includes helicopters, or you can take your own models along.

The MAA (Model Aviators Association) has activity holidays at Filey, Yorkshire, in May and Exmouth, Devon, in September/October each year. At these one-week events it is possible to have tuition on fixed-wing and helicopter models, and slope-soaring gliders feature strongly at the meetings. Accommodation, at caravan parks, is in chalets or caravans, and this is the only charge, apart from a small charge for the Filey flying site; all the flying, tuition and fuel for the trainers is free. Sharing a hobby with like-minded people is usually good fun and having these theme holidays by the sea allows the less aerominded members of the family also to enjoy themselves. There are plenty of other family activities at the caravan parks and interesting places nearby to visit.

Fancy going further afield for your modelling holiday? The RC Hotel in Corfu is rapidly gaining in popularity and reports from modellers who have visited Spiro's establishment are most encouraging. Adjacent to the hotel is the flying field, complete with clubhouse and hard runway. There is a wide variety of fixed-wing models to fly, ranging from trainers to 3D models, and helicopter training is also a speciality. Nor are the ladies left out – with a Majestic Major model on the books, the transmitter is handed around to them to try their hands at controlling the vintage aeroplane. The only worry, from their male partners, is that they might get too good at it or become totally hooked! What is agreed upon, by the visitors to RC Hotel, is the very friendly atmosphere and camaraderie to be found there. Corfu town is also a delightful place to visit, with beaches nearby for the sun worshipper.

MAGAZINES APLENTY

The UK has never been short of specialist magazines on the subject of aeromodelling, both those published in the country and imported publications. In addition to the general aeromodelling titles, covering subjects other than just radio control, there are radio-control only magazines and then the specialist subjects of scale, helicopters, electric and glider flight. These titles will keep you up to date with the hobby, provide reviews of commercial introductions, have how-to-do-it articles and let you know what events are forthcoming.

GOVERNING BODY

The governing body of aeromodelling in the UK is the British Model Flying Association (BMFA), which is responsible for the general regulation of the sport and the FA1 records and competitions. Most clubs are affiliated to the BMFA and membership includes insurance and a quarterly publication, *The BMFA News*. The address for the BMFA is:

British Model Flying Association
Chacksfield House
31 St Andrews Road
Leicester
LE2 8RE
Tel: 0116 2440028
Fax: 0116 2440645
Web site: www.bmfa.org
E-mail: admin@bmfa.org

The following list is not intended to be comprehensive and the addresses and contacts may change from time to time. Where contact cannot be made it is suggested that you consult the model magazines or the BMFA.

BMFA Recognized Specialist Bodies

**The Aerobatic Helicopter Association inc.
BRCHA (AHA inc. BRCHA)**
71 Laughton Road
Northolt
Middlesex UB5 5LN
Secretaries: Dave and Julie Fisher
Tel: 0208 841 6781

British Association of Radio-Controlled Soarers (BARCS)
186 Brickley Lane
Devizes
Wiltshire SN10 3DA
Secretary: Mark Easey
Tel: 01380 730506

British Electric Flight Association (BEFA)
37 Church Street
Horsley
Derbyshire DE21 5BQ
Secretary: J. Peter Turner
Tel: 01332 881265

British Miniature Pylon Racers Association (BMPRA)
394 Livingstone Road
Bolton Villas Estate
Bradford
West Yorks BD2 1QD
Secretary: Ralph Darnborough
Tel: 01274 583466

British Space Modelling Alliance
25 Huntingdon Drive
Castle Donington
Derby DE74 2SR
Secretary: Stuart Lodge
Tel: 01332 391690

British Waterplane Association (BWA)
36 Stirling Avenue
Leamington Spa
Warwickshire CV32 7HR
Secretary: G. N. Harrison
Tel: 01926 423756

Combat Flyers Association – Control Line (CFA)
40 Upthorpe
Cam
Dursley GL11 5HR
Secretary: Mick Lewis
Tel: 01453 542367

Control Line Aerobatics Pilots Association (CLAPA)
41 Broadwood Avenue
Ruislip
Middlesex HA4 7XS
Secretary: John Benzing
Tel: 01895 634428

Control Line Speed (SpeedCom)
Langley House
21 Polegate

Luton
Bedfordshire LU2 8AJ
Secretary: Jo Halman
Tel: 01582 424398

F3J UK Association
6 Dungarvan Avenue
Putney
London SW15 5QU
Secretary: Nick Evans
Tel: 0208 876 3008

Gas Turbine Builders Association
Christmas House
5 Stoneham Street
Coggeshall
Essex CO6 1TT
Secretary: John Wright
Tel: 01376 562478

Great Britain RC Aerobatic Association (GBR-CAA)
84 Hollymoor Road
Hollymoorside
Chesterfield S42 7DX
Secretary: Stuart Mellor
Tel: 01246 568043

International Miniature Aerobatic Club (IMAC)
31 Basnett Street
Burnley
Lancashire BB10 3EQ
Secretary: Philip Goddard
Tel: 01282 433837

Jet Modellers Association (JMA)
Upperfield Cottage
Upperfield
Midhurst
West Sussex GU29 9AE
Secretary: Chris Gregory
Tel: 01730 813540

United Kingdom Rocketry Association (UKRA)
26 Old Road
Farsley LS28 6BQ
Secretary: Darren Longhorn
Tel: 0113 2298189

Vintage Team Race Special Interest Group (VTR-SIG)
20 Saggars Close
Madely
Telford
Shropshire TF7 5TR
Secretary: Dennis Ward
Tel: 01952 586451

Independent Associations and Organizations

Model Aviators Association
(Modelling Holidays)
c/o Grimsby Model Centre
22 Lord Street
Grimsby
North East Lincolnshire DN21 2LU
Tel: 01472 322874

Club 2000 and Sport 40 (Pylon racing)
108 Mantilla Drive
Coventry CV3 6LJ
Secretary: Graham Clarke
Tel: 024 7641 1142
E-mail: ukpylon@lineone.net

Large Model Association (LMA)
Orchard Cottage
The Street
Acol, Birchington
Kent CT7 0JA
Secretary: Dave Hayfield
Tel: 01843 841691

Power Scale Soaring Association (PSSA)
52 Mountway
Waverton
Chester CH3 7QF
Secretary: Alan Hulme

SAM Zero (Association of Vintage Aeromodellers)
21 Burns Lane
Warsop
Mansfield
Notts NG20 0PA
Secretary: Keith J Harris
Tel/Fax: 01623 842167

SAM 35 (Vintage)
39 Mount Pleasant Avenue
Exmouth
Devon EX8 4QW
Secretary: Rose-Mae Duffy
Tel: 01395 223769

SAM 1066 (Vintage)
24 Pine Trees
Weston Favell
Northants NN3 3ET
Secretary: David Baker
Tel: 01604 406822

½th Scale Combat
(WWII style streamer combat)
Secretary: Dave Dempster
Tel: 01582 866119
E-mail: dempster@excite.com

Old or new, large or small, it is possible to model any prototype aircraft and – with experience and a little luck – get it flying.

APPENDIX I

Glossary of Aeromodelling Terms

Aerobatics Advanced manoeuvres performed by an aircraft.

Airscrew Alternative name for a propeller.

Aliphatic resin Water-based adhesive that dries crisply and is used for basic wood joints.

Amphibian Aeroplane capable of operating from both land and water.

ARF and **ARTF** Almost ready to fly model, supplied in kit form for quick assembly.

ARTC Almost ready to cover kit.

Autogyro Aircraft with freely rotating rotors and conventional engine and propeller providing thrust.

Balloons Lightweight filler in the form of micro glass spheres; it is mixed with epoxy.

Balsawood Hardwood species that grows very rapidly and produces very lightweight, light-coloured wood. Extensively used in aeromodelling.

Bearer Hardwood (beech or mahogany) rail used for mounting IC engines.

Bellcrank Used for changing direction of linkage through 90 degrees by means of a pivoting plate.

Biplane Aeroplane having two wings, one above the other; when the lower wing is less than 50 per cent area of the top wing it is known as a sesquiplane.

Blind nut (Anchor nut) Secured nut which, when fixed to wood, will allow a bolt to be screwed in and out without need to access the nut.

Bulkhead Front fuselage former, also known as the firewall.

Bungee Cotton-covered rubber used for catapult-launching gliders and for springing undercarriage axles.

Camber Curved centre line of an aerofoil section.

Cap strip Balsa strip applied to the top and lower surfaces of wing ribs.

Carbon fibre Extra strong material used for reinforcing structures and nylon mouldings.

Centre section Centre area of wing adjacent to fuselage, usually flat.

Chamfer Angled cut on material.

Charger Electronic unit for charging cells, e.g. nickel cadmium, nickel metal hydride and 'wet' and 'gel' cells.

Clevis (Snap link) For connecting pushrods to control horns and servo arms and to give adjustment of length. Also available in ball link form with ball and socket joint.

Closed-loop control Pair of cables connected to each side of the servo output and control horns to act in a pull–pull movement of the control surface.

Clunk tank Fuel tank with weighted fuel pick-up on a flexible tube for feeding in all aircraft positions.

CNC Computer numerically controlled machine parts are very accurate and repeatable.

Collet For retaining wheels to undercarriage legs.

Combat Competition flying where the aim is to cut the streamer attached to your opponent's model.

Compression ignition engine More commonly known as the diesel engine.

Cowling Enclosure around the engine, normally removable.

Cyanoacrylate (CA) Rapidly acting adhesive, also known as instant and miracle glue. Available in various viscosities.

Dope Generic name for nitrate and buytrate cellulose finishes. Shrinking dope is used for tautening tissue, silk and nylon, non-tautening dope for filling the weave.

Doubler Second layer of balsa or plywood to reinforce a structural area.

Dremel Manufactured series of motorized tools.

Dural Aluminium alloy used for undercarriages, etc.

Endgrain When balsawood is cut across the grain instead of along the grain. Crossgrain refers to balsa sheet when the grain traverses the fuselage top and lower surfaces and is not fixed with the grain going lengthways of the fuselage.

EP Electric power.

Epoxy Two-part adhesive with setting times from four minutes to twenty-four hours. Good for wood, metal and plastics.

EPS Expanded polystyrene. Available in various densities and used for veneered wing cores, etc.

Firewall Front bulkhead to which the engine bearers or mount are fitted.

Flight box Portable box containing all the tools, accessories, fuel and starting equipment required at the flying site.

Floats For flying models off water and replacing the normal undercarriage and wheels.

Flying boat Aeroplane utilizing a boat-type hull to allow the taking off and alighting on water.

Flying wing Aeroplane with no tail surfaces.

Glass fibre (GRP) Glass woven cloth or mat, layered with epoxy resin to form mouldings or skinning of veneers.

Glider Unpowered aircraft.

Glow engine Internal combustion engine using a glow plug for igniting the fuel/air mixture.

Glow plug Platinum wire coil in the ignition plug is initially heated with a battery, but continues to glow, when the engine is running, by compression.

Heat-shrink covering Commercially available plastic film and fabric covering materials in a wide range of colours. Applied with a hot iron to activate the adhesive, they are tautened by a further application of heat.

Helicopter Aircraft deriving lift from powered rotors.

Horn Control horn for fitting to elevators, rudder and ailerons to which the pushrod linkage is connected.

IC Internal combustion, i.e. glow, diesel and spark ignition engine.

Jet Gas turbine engine or an aircraft powered by a gas turbine engine.

Jig Adjustable building aid to hold components in place during construction.

Keel (Spine) Centre outline backbone on which half fuselage formers are fixed.

Keeper Moulded accessory for retaining wire pushrod ends to control horns and servos.

Laminate Multi-layers of material glued together to give increased strength, as in laminated tail-surface outlines.

Landing gear Alternative name for undercarriage.

Leading edge Front area of a lifting surface.

Linkage Mechanical connection between the servos and control surfaces and other controls.

Liteply Lightweight form of plywood.

Longeron Longitudinal spars in the fuselage.

Mylar Plastic material used to form control-surface hinges.

Ornithopter Aircraft creating flight by flapping its wings, as with a bird.

Parachute Apparatus to allow a load to descend slowly to earth, or to retard a landing aircraft in the form of an airbrake.

Permagrit Commercial range of abrasive tools.

Piano wire, music wire High-tensile steel wire used to form undercarriages, etc.

Planform Aircraft viewed from directly above.

Planking Sheeted areas formed with narrow strips of wood.

Polyhedral Wing, or other flying surface, having three or more dihedral breaks.

Polypropylene Flexible plastic used for moulded control-surface hinges.

Prototype Original design, which can be used to describe the full-sized aircraft from which the model is based.

Pterodactyl Swept-wing tailless model, influenced by the flying birdlike reptile.

PTFE tube Polyterafluoroethylene, a light-weight smooth-walled plastic tubing used for control linkages.

Pusher Aeroplane with the engine located in front of the propeller.

Pushrod Linkage between the servo and the control horn, normally in rigid form.

PVA (Polyvinyl acetate) White glue, moderately slow drying, suitable for all wood to wood joints. Also available in 'waterproof' quality.

PVC (Polyvinyl chloride) Clear plastic sheet used for moulding cockpit canopies, etc.

Pylon racing Competitive racing around a triangular course.

Razor plane Miniature wood plane using a razor blade as the cutting element.

Razor saw Very fine-toothed small saw for cutting thicker balsa strip and sheet.

Receiver (Rx) Electronic unit located in the aircraft for receiving signals from the transmitter.

Retracts Retractable undercarriage mechanism.

Root Innermost rib of a lifting surface to the fuselage or centre.

Safety nut Domed propeller retaining nut, rounded for safety reasons.

Scale model Miniature flying replica of a full-size aircraft.

Seaplane Model capable of taking off and landing from water.

Servo Electro-mechanical actuator taking the signals from the receiver and translating them into movements of the control linkages.

Servo deadband Where no movement occurs around the neutral setting when a control signal is given. Virtually non-existent with quality servos.

Sheeting Thin balsawood, or other woods, covering an open framework.

Side view The aircraft viewed exactly from the side.

Silicone Tubing used for connecting the fuel tank and the engine and in semi-liquid form as a filler and waterproofing sealant.

Slope soarer Glider relying on obtaining lift through the air rising from sloping ground.

Snake Common name used for a control linkage constructed from a flexible rod, or small tube, inside a larger diameter outer tube. Where stranded steel cable is used for the inner it is known as a Bowden cable.

Spar Spanwise structural member to which the wing ribs are attached.

Split frequencies The wave bands allocated for use by radio-control model enthusiasts are divided, usually at 10kcs spacing, and accurately controlled by transmitter and receiver crystals, or PCM electronically synthesized systems.

Sponson Stub wings attached to the hull of a flying boat.

Step Location of the vertical break on the lower surface of the floats or hull.

Sweep back Angle of the wings, rearward, relative to the lateral datum.

Tailless Aeroplane without any tail surfaces.

Tailplane Fixed portion of the horizontal tail surface to which the elevators are hinged.

Template Metal or wood pattern used to form similar parts in a variety of materials.

Test stand Instrument for holding a model engine firm and when test running.

Thermal Column of rising air resulting from a temperature differential to the surrounding air.

Thermal soarers Glider reliant on warm air currents to stay in the air.

Torque rod Rod, supported in a tube, which imparts movement from one end to the opposite end.

Tow hook Attachment on the fuselage of a glider for locating the tow line.

Tow line Launching line by which the glider is towed into the air.

Tractor Propeller in front of the engine, pulling the aeroplane.

Transmitter (Tx) Hand-held radio-control emitter of radio signals to the receiver.

Trim Minor control movements operated by adjustments of the trim controls on the transmitter, adjacent to the main control sticks.

Triplane Aeroplane with three wings.

V-tail Tail surface configuration where the rudder and elevator controls are operated in the diagonal 'V' formation.

Webbing Sheet, normally with the grain vertical, glued between the top and lower spars of a flying surface.

Winch Hand- or power-operated drum for winding in the glider tow line.

Wing ribs Aerofoil section components to support the wing covering.

3D Name given to models capable of performing extreme manoeuvres.

Glossary of Aerodynamic Terms

Aerofoil (Airfoil) Cross section of a lifting service such as an aircraft wing.

Aileron Movable control surface on the wing to control roll.

Angle of attack Angle at which a lifting body is presented to the air in flight.

Angle of incidence Angle of the wing and other surfaces relative to a datum line shown on the plan drawings.

Aspect ratio Ratio of the span to the area.

Balance point Point at which the model will balance, normally in the horizontal plane.

Ballast Weight added to a model to adjust the balance point, or increase the wing loading.

Bank Lateral angle of the model in a turn.

Centre of gravity (C of G) Point at which the model will balance in both the horizontal and vertical planes. Often incorrectly used for the horizontal balance point only. Usually denoted thus: ◗

Centre of pressure Point on the wing at which the centre of lift acts.

Chord Width of the aerofoil.

Control surface Movable area of the aerofoil to vary the lift and cause a change of direction.

Datum line Construction reference line from which all measurements and angles are made.

Dihedral Upward angle, towards the tips, of a lifting surface.

Down thrust Downward angle of the thrust line (motor) relative to the datum.

Drag Combined resistance of the airframe to movement through the air.

Elevator Control surface, attached to the tailplane, to control pitch movements.

Elevons Combined elevator and aileron functions, as used on canards and deltas.

Fin Fixed portion of the vertical stabilizing surface.

Flaperons Combined flap and aileron functions.

'G' forces Increased load on the aircraft due to centrifugal forces (as in looping manoeuvres).

Lift Force acting at right angles to the flight direction, overcoming gravity.

Pitch Rise and fall of the aircraft nose relative to the line of travel. Also a term to describe the theoretical distance travelled by the tip of a propeller in one revolution.

Roll Movement of the aircraft around the longitudinal axis.

Rudder Movable control surface attached to the fin.

Span Dimension from tip to tip of a lifting surface.

Stability Ability of the aircraft to stabilize to a flight attitude as dictated by the control inputs.

Stall Loss of lift resulting from an excessive angle of attack.

Thrust Force provided by the propeller, jet or rocket, or as a function of gravity.

Torque effect Reactive force produced by a rotating propeller, normally counteracted by the use of engine side thrust or rudder offset.

Some aircraft types will never be seen flying again in their original form, but it is possible to recreate them in radio-controlled model form. This Me 262 replica, powered by two miniature gas-turbine engines has been demonstrated at many publically attended model meetings and never fails to impress the spectators.

Upthrust Upward angle of the engine propeller shaft respective to the model datum.

Wash-in Downward twist in the wing trailing edge towards the tip.

Wash-out Upward twist in the wing trailing edge towards the tip.

Wing loading Relationship of the wing area to the total weight of the aircraft.

Yaw Rotation of the aircraft around the vertical, initiated by the movement of the rudder.

APPENDIX III

UK Frequencies for Model Aircraft

Ch. No.	Frequency	Ch. No.	Frequency	Ch. No.	Frequency
Ch 55	34.950	Ch 73	35.130	Grey/Brown	26.975
Ch 56	34.960	Ch 74	35.140	Brown	26.995
Ch 57	34.970	Ch 75	35.150	Brown/Red	27.025
Ch 58	34.980	Ch 76	35.160	Red	27.045
Ch 59	34.990	Ch 77	35.170	Red/Orange	27.075
Ch 60	35.000	Ch 78	35.180	Orange	27.095
Ch 61	35.010	Ch 79	35.190	Orange/Yellow	27.125
Ch 62	35.020	Ch 80	35.200	Yellow	27.145
Ch 63	35.030	Ch 81	35.210	Yellow/Green	27.175
Ch 64	35.040	Ch 82	35.220	Green	27.195
Ch 65	35.050	Ch 83	35.230	Green/Blue	27.225
Ch 66	35.060	Ch 84	35.240	Blue	27.255
Ch 67	35.070	Ch 85	35.250		
Ch 68	35.080	Ch 86	35.260		
Ch 69	35.090	Ch 87	35.270		
Ch 70	35.100	Ch 88	35.280		
Ch 71	35.110	Ch 89	35.290		
Ch 72	35.120	Ch 90	35.300		

27mHz band – also used for surface vehicles. Pennants as for the colour description.

35 mHz band. Pennants on transmitter. Orange background with channel numbers in white.

Index